Great Britain's
ROYAL TOMBS

A Guide to the Lives and Burial Places of British Monarchs

*Michael
Thomas Barry*

Schiffer
Publishing Ltd

4880 Lower Valley Road • Atglen, PA 19310

Type set in Acadian/Century Schoolbook/Avenir

ISBN: 978-0-7643-4129-8
Printed in China

Schiffer Books are available at special discounts for bulk purchases for sales promotions or premiums. Special editions, including personalized covers, corporate imprints, and excerpts can be created in large quantities for special needs. For more information contact the publisher:

Published by Schiffer Publishing, Ltd.
4880 Lower Valley Road
Atglen, PA 19310
Phone: (610) 593-1777; Fax: (610) 593-2002
E-mail: Info@schifferbooks.com

For the largest selection of fine reference books on this and related subjects, please visit our website at **www.schifferbooks.com**

We are always looking for people to write books on new and related subjects. If you have an idea for a book, please contact us at **proposals@schifferbooks.com**

This book may be purchased from the publisher.
Please try your bookstore first.
You may write for a free catalog.

In Europe, Schiffer books are distributed by
Bushwood Books
6 Marksbury Ave.
Kew Gardens
Surrey TW9 4JF England
Phone: 44 (0) 20 8392 8585; Fax: 44 (0) 20 8392 9876
E-mail: info@bushwoodbooks.co.uk
Website: www.bushwoodbooks.co.uk

Dedication

This book is lovingly dedicated to my mother, Dolores Barry. Whose thoughtful sacrifices, kindheartedness, and uncompromising devotion have helped me become the man and author I am today.

Contents

Introduction

On April 29, 2011, more than two billion people watched the royal wedding of Prince William and Kate Middleton on television or on-line. Why is the world so fascinated with the British Monarchy and what fuels this obsession? They did nothing to earn it such interest but were simply born into it, which of course only makes celebrity even more potent. The royals are the supreme curiosity, famous because they are famous. This one, moreover, wasn't just any royal wedding. It also offered "closure" of a kind to a royal drama matched in modern times only by the abdication crisis of 1936 (when Edward VIII gave up the throne to marry, Wallis Simpson). When modern society thinks of royalty, many still think of Diana. Whose own marriage in 1981, and its tumultuous aftermath and then her tragic death, transfixed us all. Now the first-born son who looks so like his mother is marrying. Diana was never to be Queen; but in William the future King her destiny is to be fulfilled.

This interest with royalty and other celebrity veneration stems from what has recently been called the "cult of celebrity." People across the globe and especially in the United States have become obsessed with every aspect of the lives of the royals, present and past. The large-scale public reactions that followed the death of Diana, Princess of Wales, on August 31, 1997, and that of Queen Elizabeth the Queen Mother on March 30, 2002, illustrate the long-standing tendency of prominent British royal deaths to stir an emotional response from millions who had never personally been acquainted with the deceased. Royal deaths have also evoked important forms of ritual and symbolic commemoration that are significant both in the context of the evolution of British civil religion and national identity, and in shaping and representing wider social and cultural responses to death. Despite occasional subversive undertones, the expression of such collective grief usually provided a potent legitimatization of the institution of the monarchy and the existing social and political order.

There are few descriptions of the deaths and burials of the early Anglo-Saxon monarchs. The evidence must be pieced together from casual textual references, monastic records, and archaeological remains. This indicates that the bodies and memories of early English kings were systematically evoked by living royalty. This at a time when regular hereditary succession was rare, new and aspiring rulers advanced their political ambitions by forging connections with their dead predecessors. The king's body was regarded as a repository of dynastic memory and used as political propaganda during the period of time between the end of one reign and the beginning of the next. The high-status burial was used to enhance the legitimacy of reigning monarchs and proclaim dynastic continuity. Royal crypts were increasingly modeled on saint's shrines, identifying kings with Christian elites and distinguishing them in death from ordinary laymen. The king's corpse often became integral to the transfer of royal power and early Anglo-Saxon monarchs were crowned beside their predecessor's tomb. In these examples, royal corpses and tombs functioned as symbols of royal authority, advertising the unique status of the monarchy and the legitimacy of new rulers. With conquest and usurpation, royal burial practices changed to include desecrated or concealment of their rivals bodies to suppress the royal claims of competing dynasties (such as during the Wars of the Roses). Foreign conquerors such as the Danes and Normans diverted attention from the bodies and tombs of deposed native rulers in order to de-emphasize the change in regime. These deviations from normal burial indicate that royal memory and dynastic legitimacy were linked to the treatment of the ruler's remains, and that modes of honorable and dishonorable burial were systematically used to construct signifying narratives about royal continuity, legitimacy, and authority.

In the late eleventh and early twelfth centuries English royal burials were relatively unceremonial, low-key affairs, a contrast with the rites of other contemporary rulers such as the Holy Roman Emperors. This might have been caused by reforming ecclesiastics and the importance attached by the monarchs to obtaining personalized intercession from ascetic monks. By the early fourteenth century, however, English sovereigns were commemorated after death in magnificent ceremonies and monuments. In the intervening centuries, those kings and their followers had shown a growing interest in the creation and promotion of royal saint-cults; in the honoring of royal remains; in public and splendid funeral ceremonies and lavish tombs; and in the creation and development of imposing burial-churches at Westminster. During this time there was an increasing emphasis upon the image and ceremonial display of the monarchy which was rooted to a large extent in the personal and political rivalry of the rulers and the splendors of royal burials can be seen as one important part of those developments.

The deaths of Tudor monarchs, such as Henry VIII in 1547 and Elizabeth I in 1603, were followed by elaborate ceremonies, combining religious and secular elements, and reflected genuine depth of public affection. During the reign of James I these rituals were developed further into a "theatre of death" through which the new Stuart dynasty sought to assert its prestige, but in so doing it began to exceed popular sentiment. At this point royal funeral ceremonies, like those of all members of the elite, were controlled by precise regulations. These were designed to ensure that public appearance was sustained and stabilized. This was done to ensure that political order would not be disrupted because of the monarch's death.

A low point in the fortunes of the British monarchy came in January 1649, when, following its victory over Charles I in the English Civil War, Parliament sentenced the king to death "by the severing of his head from his body." When, however, the king was publicly executed on the balcony of Whitehall Palace, one observer recorded that the fall of the axe was greeted with "such a groan by the thousands then present as I never heard before." Charles, who conducted himself at the last moments with great dignity, claimed that he died a martyr, and subsequent religious veneration for his memory and the restoration of the monarchy in 1660 indicated that his enemies had indeed overreached themselves by committing regicide.

From the seventeenth until the early nineteenth century, royal funerals took place at night. This custom was intended to lessen the burden of precise heraldic regulation, which was already beginning to seem antiquated. It had the effect of giving enhanced drama to the occasions, lit by torchlight, but reduced the scope for public participation. In the meantime, few royal deaths inspired strong public emotions. Notable exceptions were the untimely death of Queen Mary II in 1694, and the death of Princess Charlotte in 1817, who was the daughter of George IV and second in line to the throne. In 1821 the funeral procession of George IV's estranged wife, Caroline of Brunswick was accompanied by demonstrations against the king and the government, who were blamed for disrespectful treatment of the deceased. In general, the Stuart and Hanoverian royal houses inspired dutiful observance rather than intense feeling. In an era that in its overall response to death, tended to emphasize ritual rather than emotion.

There was a gradual change in attitudes during the long reign of Queen Victoria (1837–1901). The funeral of Prince Albert in 1861 was a private affair, but it was accompanied by strong expressions of collective public grief. In the decades that followed, Victoria made mourning a way of life. Increasingly, the royal family came to be viewed as national symbols of joy and sorrow. There was a growing tendency for the public to view its royal bereavements in a quasi-personal way. This phenomenon was strikingly illustrated by sentiment following the early death of the queen's grandson, Prince Albert Victor in 1892, and on Victoria's own demise in 1901. Meanwhile precedents for a more grandiose form of public mourning were set by two major non-royal funerals, those of war heroes, Admiral Horatio Nelson in 1806 and the Duke of Wellington in 1852. These trends continued with large-scale funerals for Queen Victoria and Edward VII.

Since World War I there have only been two deaths of reigning monarchs, George V in 1936 and George VI in 1952. Both gave rise to strong public emotion, which was focused by repetition of essentially the same forms of ritual used in 1910 during Edward VII's funeral. Until the end of the twentieth century, responses to the deaths of other members of the royal family were relatively low-key. In 1997, things changed with the tragic and untimely death of the young and vivacious Princess Diana. Her funeral was televised worldwide and evoked shock and sadness. By contrast, the death of the Queen Mother in 2002 (at the age of 101) was hardly unexpected, but it evoked a mood of sadness and celebration. Her funeral followed a broadly similar pattern to that of her husband King George VI. Even here, though, there were innovations that reflected the social changes of the intervening half century, including the presence of the Princess Royal among the male mourners following the coffin, and the conveyance of the body to its final resting place at Windsor by road rather than railway.

Overall responsibility for the funerals of sovereigns rests with the Earl Marshal, an office of state held on a hereditary basis by the Dukes of Norfolk, who are assisted by the heralds of the College of Arms. The funerals of other members of the royal family are organized by Lord Chamberlain's office, which is part of the permanent royal secretariat. Numerous other agencies are involved in more complex and large-scale rituals. These have included the Office of Works (for temporary additions to buildings), the church, the armed services, the police, and the railways. Until the beginning of the nineteenth century royal funerals were usually held in London with burials at Westminster Abbey. George III, however, moved the royal burial place to St. George's Chapel in Windsor Castle, thus focusing ceremonially on what was then a relatively small country town, several hours journey from the capital in pre-railway days. Scope for public participation was therefore limited. Only following the death of

Queen Victoria was there a decisive move back to a more public and large-scale ceremonial event. Her funeral, which included a spectacular naval review and a military procession through central London, represented a return to a "theatre of death" on a scale not seen since the early seventeenth century. The trend was confirmed upon the death of her son Edward VII when a further ritual of a public lying-in-state in Westminster Hall was added and proved enormously popular.

Major royal funerals, especially those of sovereigns, were made up of a series of ceremonies extending over several days, public and private, religious and secular, and presenting different aspects of the deceased. For example, Edward VII's body initially lay privately in his bedroom at Buckingham Palace, before being moved ceremonially to the Throne Room, and then in a street procession to Westminster Hall. After the three days of the public lying-in-state, there was a further street procession to Paddington Station, a train journey to Windsor, a procession from the station to the Castle, and a culminating religious service in St. George's Chapel.

The apparent seamlessness of such events conceals a reality of extensive improvisation and last-minute decision making. Royal funerals unlike coronations, jubilees, and weddings need to be arranged in a time scale measured in days rather than months. Although Queen Victoria was eighty-one at the time of her death, no developed plans for her funeral were in place and the ten days between her death and funeral were marked by confusion. Although some discreet advance planning can be made, the exact circumstances of a death are unforeseeable and, in particular, the unexpected death of a relatively young person, as in the case of Princess Diana, is likely to catch the authorities almost wholly unprepared.

During the nineteenth and early twentieth century's the days of royal funerals were increasingly marked by parallel processions and church services in provincial towns and cities. By this means many people remote from London or Windsor were able to achieve a sense of participation in a national ritual. Solidarity in grief was expressed by the wearing of mourning clothes and emblems such as black armbands. In this period instructions for the general wearing of mourning for periods of several weeks drew general compliance, giving a somber atmosphere to the streets. From the mid–twentieth century onward, the advent of radio and, eventually, television intensified this sense of involvement while shifting it from the communal public religiosity of streets and places of worship to the individualistic and domestic environment of people's homes. Film and television have increased consciousness of royal funerals as mass spectacles, as manifested in the unprecedented size of the worldwide television audience that watched Princess Diana's funeral.

As in the aftermath of death in private life, responses to royal deaths have been shaped by contingent circumstances and emotions, which were often fluid and fast moving. Explicit social, cultural, and political agendas were seldom articulated. Nevertheless, a number of strong implicit functions; Princess Diana's funeral, with novel elements such as the Elton John song "Goodbye England's Rose/Candle in the Wind," showed the way in which long-standing tradition is continually being reshaped by the British community just as Diana reshaped the traditions of royalty while alive.

First, there was the need to reaffirm the social and political hierarchy that had been disrupted by the death. This function was especially strong in the early modern era of close heraldic regulation, but persisted in the nineteenth and twentieth century's, with processions and other rituals being designed to display order and stability. At the same time, from the early twentieth century onward, public lyings-in-state, and large crowds whether present in person or participating at a distance through radio and television constituted a democratic element. Conversely, however, on some occasions responses to royal deaths have had a subversive dimension. Public reactions to the deaths of Princess Charlotte in 1817 and Queen Caroline in 1821 were colored by hostility to the Tory government of the day and to the Prince Regent, who succeeded to the throne as George IV in 1820. Such a tendency to question rather than sustain the existing order recurred in the hostility expressed toward the surviving royal family following Princess Diana's death.

Second, the aftermath of royal deaths has provided an opportunity for affirming or reshaping the image of the deceased. In life Prince Albert was liable to be seen as a meddling foreigner exercising an inappropriate influence over the government, but in death he became a symbol of ideal English manhood. Queen Victoria was celebrated as an ideal of motherhood, but the reality of her relationships with her children and grandchildren was much more ambivalent. Princess Diana, perceived in life as sometimes wayward and manipulative, became a quasi-saint in death.

Third, collective mourning for royalty has been a focus for common identity within the multinational United Kingdom state and, in the past, the diverse and scattered territories of the British Empire. Royalty are perceived to transcend social and political divisions to a degree that has only been matched by exceptional non-royal figures (i.e., Sir Winston Churchill, who died in 1965). The psychological constraints imposed by a sense of decency in the face of death made open dissent very rare, even in countries such as India and Ireland where British rule was otherwise strongly contested.

Fourth, royal deaths have served as a communal representation of private fears and grief. Thus Princess Charlotte was identified with the numerous early-nineteenth-century young women who died in childbirth, just as Princess Diana's car crash painfully reminded the public of this characteristic form of death for late-twentieth-century young women. Prince Albert's early death was a focus for the personal bereavements of other widows and young children, while in responding to the deaths of Queen Victoria and subsequent monarchs, members of the public showed themselves to be recalling or anticipating losses of their own parents and grandparents.

Finally, royal deaths have marked the passage of time. Many people recall their own exact circumstances when they heard of the death of Princess Diana, or among an older generation, George VI. Monarchs who reigned for a long period, such as George III (1760–1820), seemed to symbolize a whole era, and their passing therefore stirred a sense of discontinuity and new beginnings. This phenomenon was especially pronounced in the case of Queen Victoria, whose death coincided closely with the beginning of the twentieth century, and has recurred in relation to Queen Elizabeth the Queen Mother, whose long life spanned the whole of that same century.

Overall, responses to British royal deaths can be set within a broadly theoretical perspective. In other words they serve as a ritual expression of social solidarities and a means for regenerating and sustaining the fabric of national life. They are also a significant component of a British form of civil religion, being an occasion for the affirmation both in rituals and in speeches and sermons of the perceived fundamental spiritual values focused upon the institution of the monarchy. For example, at the lying-in-state of Edward VII, the Archbishop of Canterbury spoke of a renewing of a sense of national mission. Upon the death of George VI the sentiments evoked by the death and accession of monarchs have a quality that it is no impiety to call religious. By the time of Princess Diana's death the explicitly Christian content of such excessive sentimentality had become significantly narrower, but the sense of a spiritual dimension to national grief remained.

The British experience invites comparison with other countries that have remained monarchies in the contemporary era. The deaths of King Olaf V of Norway in 1991 and of King Baudouin of Belgium in 1993 were followed by widespread public grief, which gave occasion for significant reaffirmations of national unity and identity. Further afield the elaborate rituals that follow the deaths of Thai monarchs constitute politically significant affirmations of continuity and royal prestige, while the assassination of King Birendra of Nepal in 2001 evoked intense and emotionally charged reactions. Monarchs, in contrast to most presidents and prime ministers, normally hold office for life, and accordingly become for their generation seemingly permanent carriers and symbols of national identity. Their deaths, inevitable as they are in the course of nature, are therefore particularly psychologically disorienting for their people. A study of the ways in which nations react to this disruption of the fabric of seeming normality both adds to understanding of attitudes to death itself, and illuminates wider historical and social processes.

My intention in writing this volume is to celebrate the history and culture of the British monarchy from Egbert (AD 801) to George VI (1953). Chronicling over 1500 years of English history into a concise volume such as this was a daunting task, and I must emphasize that it is not just about death, dying, and cemeteries. Its main function is to celebrate the lives of these extra-ordinary people and does not set out to venerate death. Why then are the lives, deaths and gravesites of these crowned heads so fascinating to us? Is it that their joys, loves, triumphs, defeats, and last moments all encompass a life we do not have? In other words, are these people more than the granite, the marble, and the ornate edifices that mark their tombs? I think the answer is simply; yes, they are more. In the end, I believe it is very simple: the reasons we search out these final resting places is because we all wish to be remembered. I have attempted to find and photograph as many of the royal gravesites as possible, but the sheer number has unfortunately led me to make some drastic cuts, and I apologize for not including them all. The stories of the Kings and Queens of England have been told and retold over the past 1,500 years within countless volumes. It is not my intention to delve into comprehensive accounts of their lives, deaths, and final resting places, but to capsulate, as brief a format as possible, the important aspects of their stories.

The cult of celebrity, in which many people propel themselves today, has become a new form of religion. The searching out and visitation of the graves of royalty, the famous, or infamous, has become a growing past time for a large number of fans. Whatever the reason for visiting the graves of the rich, famous, infamous, and noteworthy, the main enjoyment is being as close to our heroes and history as possible. Our presence in these cemeteries, mausoleums, churches and cathedrals announces that there is an unbroken chain that stretches back to the roots of western civilization and this by extension links us to the future. How a society remembers its dead is a direct reflection of the morals and ethics upon which a society is to be judged by future generations.

—Michael Thomas Barry, Orange, California

Reign	King's & Queens of Britain
802-839	**EGBERT** m. Redburga (d. 795) c. Ethelwulf
839-858	**ETHELWULF** m. Osburga (d. 856) c. Ethelbald, Ethelbert, Ethelred I, Alfred the Great
858-860	**ETHELBALD**
860-865	**ETHELBERT**
865-871	**ETHELRED I**
871-899	**ALFRED THE GREAT** m. Ealhswith of Merica (d. 968) c. Edward the Elder
899-924	**EDWARD THE ELDER** m. Ecgwynn (d. date unknown) c. Aethelstan, Edmund I m. Edgiva of Kent (2nd wife d. 968) c. Eadred
924-939	**AETHELSTAN**
939-946	**EDMUND I** m. Elfgifu of Shaftesbury (d. 944) c. Eadwig, Edgar I
946-955	**EADRED**
955-959	**EADWIG**
959-975	**EDGAR I** m. Ethelflaed (d. date unknown) c. Edward the Martyr m. 2nd wife Elfrida (d. 975) c. Ethelred the Unready
975-987	**EDWARD THE MARTYR**

Reign	King's & Queens of Britain
987-1013	**ETHEL THE UNREADY** m. Emma of Normandy (d.975) c. Edward the Confessor m. 2nd wife Elfgifu of York (d. date unknown) c. Edmund Ironside
1013-1014	**SWEYN FORKBEARD** m. Sigrid the Haughty (d. date unknown) c. Cnut
1014-1016	**ETHEL THE UNREADY**
1016	**EDMUND IRONSIDE** m. Ealdgyth (d. 1016) c. Edmund (d. 1016), Edward the Exile
1016-1035	**CNUT** m. Emma of Normandy (d. 975) c. Harthacnut m. Elfgifu of Northhampton (d. 1040) c. Harold Harefoot
1035-1040	**HAROLD HAREFOOT**
1040-1042	**HARTHACNUT**
	Godwin of Wessex (Earl to Cnut) m. Gytha (d.1053) c. Edith of Wessex, Harold Godwinson
1042-1066	**EDWARD THE CONFESSOR** m. Edith of Wessex (d. 1075)
	Edward the Exile (d. 1057) m. Agatha (d.1093) c. Edgar the Etheling
1066	**HAROLD GODWINSON**
1066	**EDGAR THE ETHELING**

Reign	King's & Queens of Britain

1066-1087 **WILLIAM the CONQUEROR**
m. Matilda (d. 1083)
c. Robert Curthose (d. 1134), William Rufus, Henry I, Adela

1087-1100 **WILLIAM RUFUS**

1100-1135 **HENRY I**
m. Matilda of Scotland (d. 1118)
c. William (d. 1120), Richard (d.1120), Matilda

Adela (daughter of William the Conqueror) (d. 1137)
m. Stephen of Blois (d. 1102)
c. Stephen

Henry V, Holy Roman Emperor (d.1125)
m. Matilda Lady of the English (daughter of Henry I)

1st 1135-Apr. 1141 **STEPHEN**
2nd Nov. 1141-1154 m. Matilda of Boulogne (d. 1152)
c. William (d. 1120), Richard (d.1120), Matilda

Apr.-Nov. 1141 **MATILDA LADY of the ENGLISH**
m. Henry V, Holy Roman Emperor (d.1125)

m. *2nd husband* Geoffrey Plantagenet (d. 1151)
c. Henry II

Reign	King's & Queens of Britain	Reign	King's & Queens of Britain

HENRY II (1154-1189)
m. Eleanor of Aquitaine (d. 1204)
c. Henry (d. 1183), Richard I, Geoffrey (d. 1186), John

RICHARD I (1189-1199)

JOHN (1199-1216)
m. Isabella of Angouleme (d. 1246)
c. Henry III

HENRY III (1216-1272)
m. Eleanor of Provence (d. 1291)
c. Edward I

EDWARD I (1272-1307)
m. Eleanor of Castile (d. 1290)
c. Edward II

m. Margaret of France (d. 1318)

EDWARD II (1307-1327)
m. Isabella of France (d. 1358)
c. Edward III

EDWARD III (1327-1377)
m. Philippa of Hainault (d. 1369)
c. Edward the Black Prince, Lionel of Antwerp, John of Gaunt, Edmund of York (d.1402)

Edward the Black Prince (d. 1376)
m. Joan of Kent (d.1385)
c. Richard II

Lionel of Antwerp (d.1368)
m. Elizabeth de Burgh (d.1363)
c. Philippa (d.1382)

John of Gaunt (d.1399)
m. Blanche of Lancaster (d.1368)
c. Henry IV

Edmund of York (d.1402)
m. Isabella of Castille (d. 1392)
c. Richard of Cambridge, Edward of York (d. 1415)

RICHARD II (1377-1399)
m. Anne of Bohemia (d. 1394)

m. Isabelle of Valois (d.1409)

Pilippa (d.1382)
(daughter of Lionel of Antwerp)
m. Edmund Mortimer (d. 1381)
c. Roger Mortimer

HENRY IV (1399-1413) *(son of John of Gnaut)*
m. Mary de Bohun (d. 1394)
c. Henry V

Roger Mortimer (d.1398)
m. Eleanor jof Holland (d. 1405)
c. Edmund (d.1425), Anne Mortimer

HENRY V (1413-1422)
m. Catherine of Valois (d. 1437)
c. Henry VI

Richard of Cambridge (d.1415)
(son of Edmund of York)
m. Anne Mortimer (d. 1411)

Catherine of Valois (d.1415)
(1st wife of Henry V)
m. Owen Tudor (d.1461)
c. Edmund Tudor (d 1456)

Reign | King's & Queens of Britain

1422-1461 — **HENRY VI**
m. Margaret of Anjou (d. 1482)
c. Edward of Westminster (d.1471)

Richard of York (d.1460)
m. Cecily Neville (d. 1495)
c. Edward IV, Richard III, George of Clarence

1st Mar. 1461-Oct. 1470 — **EDWARD IV**
2nd Apr. 1471-1483 — m. Elizabeth Woodville (d.1492)
c. Edward V, Richard, Elizabeth

1483 — **EDWARD V**

1483-1485 — **RICHARD III**
m. Anne Neville (d.1485)
c. Henry VII (Tudor), Edward Prince of Wales (d. 1484)

Reign	King's & Queens of Britain
1485-1509	**HENRY VII** m. Elizabeth of York (d. 1503) c. Mary Tudor, Arthur, Henry VIII, Margaret Tudor
	Mary Tudor (d. 1456) m. Charles Brandon (d. 1545) c. Francis Grey, Henry Brandon
	Arthur (d. 1502) m. Catherine of Aragon
1509-1547	**HENRY VIII** m. Catherine of Aragon, 1509 (d. 1536) c. Mary I
	m. Anne Boleyn, 1533 (d. 1536) c. Elizabeth I
	m. Jane Seymour, 1536 (d. 1537) c. Edward VI
	m. Anne of Cleves, 1540
	m. Catherine Howard, 1540 (d. 1542)
	m. Catherine Parr, 1543

Reign	King's & Queens of Britain
1547-1553	**EDWARD VI**
1553	**LADY JANE GREY**
1553-1558	**MARY I** m. Philip II of Spain (d. 1598)
1558-1603	**ELIZABETH I**
	Mary Queen of Scots (d.1587) m. Henry Stuart (d.1567) c. James I

Reign	King's & Queens of Britain

1603-1625 · **JAMES I**
m. Anne of Denmark (d. 1619)
c. Henry (d. 1612), Elizabeth, Charles I

Elizabeth (d.1662)
m. Frederick V (d.1632)

1625-1649 · **CHARLES I**
m. Henrietta Maria of France (d. 1669)
c. Charles II, Mary, James II, Elizabeth, Anne,
    Henry, Henrietta

Sophia (d.1714)
m. Ernest Augustus of Hanover (d.1698)
c. George I

1649-1660 · **ENGLISH COMMONWEALTH
(OLIVER CROMWELL)**

1660-1685 · **CHARLES II**
m. Catherine of Braganza

1685-1688 · **JAMES II**
m. Anne Hyde (d. 1671)
c. Mary II, Anne

m. Mary of Modena (d.1718)
c. James Francis Edward Stuart

1688-1702 · **WILLIAM III & MARY II**
Mary II's reign lasted till 1694

Reign	King's & Queens of Britain

1702-1714 · **ANNE**
m. George of Denmark (d. 1708)

1714-1727 · **GEORGE I**
(son of Sophia and Ernest Augustus of Hanover)

James Francis Edward Stuart (d.1766)
(Old Pretender)

Charles Edward Stuart (d.1788)
(Bonni Prince Charlie, Young Pretender)

Charlotte of Albany (d.1789)

Charles Edward Stuart Count of Roehenstart
(d.1854)

Reign	King's & Queens of Britain	Reign	King's & Queens of Britain

1714-1727 — **GEORGE I**
m. Sophia Dorothea of Celle (d.1726)
c. George II

1727-1760 — **GEORGE II**
m. Caroline of Ansbach (d.1737)
c. Frederick Prince of Wales

Frederick Prince of Wales (d. 1751)
m. Princess Augusta of Saxe-Gotha (d.1772)
c. George III

1760-1820 — **GEORGE III**
m. Charlotte of Mecklenburg-Strelitz (d.1818)
c. George IV, Frederick of York (d. 1827),
William IV, Edward of Kent, Ernest
Augustus of Hanover (d. 1851), Adolphus of
Cambridge (d. 1850)

1820-1830 — **GEORGE IV**
m. Caroline of Brunswick (d.1821)

1830-1837 — **WILLIAM IV**
m. Adelaide of Saxe-Meiningen (d.1849)

Edward of Kent (d.1851)
m. Victoria of Saxe-Coburg (d.1861)
c. Victoria

1837-1901 — **VICTORIA IV**
m. Albert of Saxe-Coburg & Gotha (d.1861)
c. Edward VII, Alice, Alfred, Helena, Louise,
Arthur, Leopold, Beatrice

1901-1910 — **EDWARD VII**
m. Alexandra of Denmark (d.1925)
c. Albert, George V, Louise, Victoria, Maud,
Alexander

1910-1936 — **GEORGE V**
m. Mary of Teck (d.1953)
c. Edward VIII, George VI, Mary, Henry,
George, John

1936 — **EDWARD VIII**
m. Wallis Simpson (d.1986)

1936-1952 — **GEORGE VI**
m. Elizabeth Bowes-Lyon (d.2002)
c. Elizabeth II, Margaret

1952-Present — **ELIZABETH II**
m. Philip of Edinburgh
c. Charles, Anne, Andrew, Edward

Chapter One

The Bastions of Royal Burials

Winchester Cathedral

Winchester Cathedral is one of the largest cathedrals in England, with the longest nave and overall length of any gothic cathedral in Europe. It was founded in 642 on an immediately adjoining site to the north of the present day cathedral. This building was known as the Old Minster, which became

The Nave of Winchester Cathedral

part of a monastic settlement in 971. Saint Swithun was originally buried near the Old Minster and then inside, before being moved to the New Norman cathedral. The Old Minster was demolished in 1093 and its outline on the north side of the cathedral is outlined in red brick, King Alfred the Great and his son Edward the Elder were first buried here before being moved to Hyde Abbey.

Six Royal Mortuary chests adorn the choir section of the cathedral and within these boxes rest the remains of some of the early Anglo-Saxon monarchs and include; Cnegils (1st Christian king of Wessex), Cenwalh, Egbert (1st over lord of all Saxon kingdoms), Ethelwulf (father of Alfred the Great), Edred, Cnut, and Emma (wife of Ethelred the Unready and Cnut). Unfortunately, no one knows exactly who lies in which chest. In 1642, Oliver Cromwell's Parliamentarian soldiers broke open the chests and threw the bones on the cathedral floor. The remains were later gathered together and redistributed into the current chests and locations.

On April 8, 1093, in the presence of nearly all the bishops and abbots of England, the monks moved from the Saxon church of the Old Minster to the new one. After Henry VIII seized control of the Catholic Church in England and declared himself head of the Church of England, the Benedictine foundation, and the Priory of Saint Swithun were dissolved (1539), and the cloister and chapter house were demolished, but the cathedral was left standing. Some of the famous events that took place in the Old Minster and Cathedral were the funerals of King Harthacnut (1042) and William Rufus (1100), the coronation of Henry the Young King and Margaret of France (1172), the second coronation of Richard I (1194), the marriages of King Henry IV and Joan of Navarre (1403), and Queen Mary I and Philip II of Spain (1554).

OLD MINSTER

THE REMAINS OF THE "OLD MINSTER" are made clearly visible by the outline of brickwork that was laid out in the 1960s and is adjacent to present day Winchester Cathedral. This was the original burial locations for numerous Kings and Queens of Wessex, as well as St. Swithun.

GRAVE MARKERS OF KING ALFRED THE GREAT, EDWARD THE ELDER, AND QUEEN EALHSWITH at Hyde Abbey Gardens in Winchester.

OTHER FAMOUS INTERMENTS INCLUDE:

HENRY OF BLOIS (1101-1171): Bishop of Winchester, was the brother of King Stephen, grandson of William the Conqueror and presided over the trial of Thomas Becket during the reign of Henry II.

WILLIAM EDINGTON (D.1346): Bishop of Winchester and Lord High Treasurer during the reign of Edward III.

WILLIAM WYKEHAM (1324-1404): Bishop of Winchester and Chancellor of England during the reigns of Edward III and Richard II.

HENRY BEAUFORT (1374-1447): Bishop of Winchester, grandson of Edward III and member of the Regency Council that over saw the trial and execution of Joan of Arc in 1431.

STEPHEN GARDINER (1497-1555): Bishop of Winchester and Lord Chancellor during the reign of Mary I.

JANE AUSTEN (1775-1817): Literary great.

KING WILLIAM II (RUFUS) AND RICHARD, DUKE OF BERNAY: Sons of William the Conqueror.

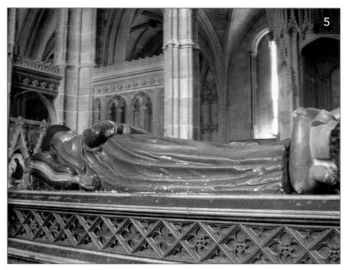

1. THE CHOIR of Winchester Cathedral.

2. ROYAL MORTUARY CHEST, which reportedly contains the remains of King Egbert.

3. ROYAL MORTUARY CHEST of King Eadred.

4. CHANTRY TOMB of BISHOP HENRY BEAUFORT at Winchester Cathedral.

5. CLOSE-UP VIEW OF THE TOMB EFFIGY of Henry Beaufort.

Westminster Abbey illuminated.'

The Collegiate Church of St. Peter at Westminster, popularly known as Westminster Abbey, is a large Gothic church located in the city of Westminster. It is the traditional place of coronation and burial site for English monarchs. According to a tradition the abbey was first founded around AD 624 but proven origins state that, around 960, Saint Dunstan installed a community of Benedictine monks there. Between 1042 and 1052, Edward the Confessor began rebuilding St. Peter's Abbey in order to provide himself with a royal burial church. It was the first church in England built in the Norman Romanesque style. It was consecrated on December 28, 1065; a week later, on January 5, 1066, Edward the Confessor died and was buried within the abbey. During his life Edward acquired a reputation for holiness, and after his death stories of miracles he had worked began to circulate. The monks of the abbey promoted the cult and emphasized his saintly character. In 1161, Edward was canonized and his body was moved to a shrine in front of the altar.

Harold Godwinson was probably crowned at the abbey, but the first documented coronation was William the Conqueror's on December 25, 1066. The Abbey became the coronation site of Norman kings, but no monarchs were interred there until Henry III. In 1245, during the reign of Henry III, construction of the present building was begun. No English king had a greater devotion to Edward the Confessor than Henry III, who came to the throne in 1216. Henry conceived the idea of building an entirely new Anglo-French Gothic style church, which would have a magnificent shrine for Edward the Confessor at its heart.

Between 1245 and 1517, the abbey was enlarged and remodeled numerous times but largely finished by the architect Henry Yevele in the reign of Richard II. In 1503, Henry VII began work on a new Lady Chapel to house the tomb of his wife Elizabeth of York, which was completed in 1509. In 1540, Henry VIII was resolved to close all of the monasteries, and Westminster was no exception. Its role as coronation church and royal burial mausoleum probably protected it from destruction. Soon after its dissolution, Henry VIII established the abbey as a cathedral church. Under Mary I the monastery was restored but was quickly dissolved during the reign of Elizabeth I and then designated a "Royal Peculiar."

Within every nook and niche of its hallowed halls is entombed a pantheon of British history, from kings and queens, to statesmen, scientists, and poets. In 1670, George II was the last British monarch to be buried within the abbey.

THE SHRINE OF ST. EDWARD THE CONFESSOR, which is located behind the high altar at Westminster Abbey, with the tomb of Henry V in the background.

A church has stood within Windsor Castle for centuries; Henry III dedicated one to Edward the Confessor on the site of what is now the Albert Memorial Chapel. In 1348, King Edward III founded two new religious colleges: St. Stephen's at Westminster and St. George's at Windsor. The new college at Windsor was attached to the Chapel of St. Edward the Confessor which had been constructed by Henry III in the early thirteenth century. The chapel was then rededicated to Virgin Mary, St. Edward the Confessor, and St. George the Martyr. The chapel became the Mother Church of the Order of the Garter, and a special service is still held there every June and is attended by the members of the order. Their heraldic banners hang above the upper stalls of the choir where they have a seat for life.

The period 1475-1528 saw a radical redevelopment of St. George's Chapel, set in motion by Edward IV and continued by Henry VII and Henry VIII. The thirteenth century Chapel of St. Edward the Confessor was expanded into a huge, new, Cathedral-like chapel under the supervision of Richard Beauchamp, Bishop of Salisbury, and the direction of the master mason Henry Janyns. The chapel was a popular destination for pilgrims during the late medieval period, which was purported to contain several important relics: the bodies of Sir John Schorne and Henry VI, as well as fragment of the "True Cross," held in a shrine called the Cross of Gneth.

The chapel suffered a great deal of destruction during the English Civil War. Parliamentary forces broke into and plundered the chapel and treasury in 1642. Further pillaging occurred in 1643 when the fifteenth century chapter house was destroyed, lead was stripped off the chapel roofs, and elements of Henry VIII's unfinished funeral monument were destroyed or stolen. Following his execution in 1649, Charles I was buried in a small vault in the center of the choir in the chapel, which also contained the coffins of Henry VIII and Jane Seymour. A program of repair was undertaken at the chapel following the restoration of the monarchy. In the early 19th century, King George III ordered construction and excavation of a royal burial crypt, beneath what is now known as the Albert Memorial Chapel. The reign of Queen Victoria saw further changes: The east end of the choir was reworked in devotion to Prince Albert; the Lady Chapel, which had been abandoned by Henry VII was completed (renamed the Albert Memorial Chapel); and a set of steps were built at the west end of the chapel to create a ceremonial entrance to the building.

This chapel is among the most important medieval chantry foundations to have survived in England. The college, itself a medieval chantry, also contains a number of independent chantries in the form of altars and small chapels dedicated to various members of the English monarchy and also to a number of prominent courtiers, deans, and canons. Henry VIII had intended a chantry to be built in the chapel, despite the fact that he instituted the religious changes which brought about the Reformation in England and the eventual suppression of chantries. The status of the college as a royal foundation saved it from dissolution during the Reformation. As a result, many of the smaller chantries within the chapel were preserved and are among the last of their kind in England. The chapel has been the site of many royal weddings and funerals, such as the marriage Prince Charles and Camilla Parker Bowles in 2005. The chapel is also the final resting place of Edward IV, Henry VI, Edward VII, Henry VIII, Charles I, George III, George IV, William IV, George V, and George VI, along with an assortment of other royal and noteworthy people.

Chapter Two

The House of Normandy (1066-1154)

The history of Anglo-Saxon England broadly covers early medieval England from the end of Roman rule and the establishment of Anglo-Saxon kingdoms in the 5th century until the Conquest by the Normans in 1066. The term Anglo-Saxon is a term used by historians to designate the Germanic tribes who invaded the south and east of Great Britain beginning in the early 5th century AD. The term is also used for the language now called Old English, spoken and written by the Anglo-Saxons and their descendants in much of what is now England and some of southeastern Scotland between at least the mid-5th century and the mid-12th century.

The *Pax Britannica*, the relative peace that Britain enjoyed under Roman rule was unsteady even before the last legions left in AD 407. Major raids in the northern and south-east by barbarian forces had already begun by AD 367, without support from Rome, Britain struggled to defend its borders from the Picts and Caledonians in the north and Germanic tribes (including the Angles, Saxons, and Jutes) in the east. As the Saxons migrated in ever greater numbers, they established territories led by tribal warlords who styled themselves as rulers, known as a Bretwalda. The first of these was Aelle, King of the South Saxons from AD 477. By the end of the 6th century the Germanic invaders held large amounts of territory: the Saxons settled in the south and west, the Jutes on the Isle of Wight and the Angles in the east and north. The different tribes shared a common language and customs and came to known as one people, the Anglo-Saxons. Seven of these sub-kingdoms formed a loosely based confederacy known as the Heptarchy, which all jostled for supremacy; which included Wessex, Kent, East Anglia, Mercia, Essex, Sussex, and Northumbria.

Eventually Wessex became the dominant kingdom and its rulers evolved into the supreme sovereigns of all England. The Royal House of Wessex began in the 6th century under King Cedric and continued to gain strength over the next two hundred years. In the late 8th century, the first Viking incursions into Britain began, when an isolated party landed on the south coast of Portland and killed the king's chief magistrate at Dorchester. The Viking raiders most often targeted monasteries, carrying off priceless artifacts and valuables, and murdering or enslaving their occupants, striking at the core of Christian Britain, which was its cultural and political power base. They sacked and desecrated these wealthy enclaves, time and time again. They were not an organized force and these raids were almost always isolated incidents, with marauding bands of Vikings taking opportunities where they presented themselves. Where these Vikings encountered resistance, they were ruthless.

In 831, Ethelwulf of Wessex defeated the Danes at the Battle of Acleah, but increasingly the Anglo-Saxon's answer was to bribe the Danes. In 865 a huge Viking force known as the Great Army arrived and Northumbria, which was already weakened by internal strife, fell, then East Anglia and Mercia were conquered. Wessex, under the leadership of King Alfred the Great was the only Saxon kingdom to retain its independence. Under Alfred's son Edward the Elder, Wessex military strength increased and East Anglia was recaptured.

At the end of the 10th century, there were renewed Danish invasions led by Harold Bluetooth and his son, Sweyn Forkbeard. This time, there was no Alfred the Great to repel the onslaught. Instead, Ethelred the Unready's inability to defend his kingdom led to England's subjugation to the Scandinavian empire under King Cnut. In September 1066, William of Normandy landed with the largest fighting force since Roman times (this would be the last foreign invasion of England until 1688). William defeated Anglo-Saxon King Harold Godwinson at the Battle of Hastings (October 14, 1066) and by December the Norman was enthroned at Westminster Abbey. Native Anglo-Saxon attempts to restore rule under Edgar the Etheling (grandson of Edmund Ironside) were unsuccessful. By the end of William's reign, Anglo-Saxon England had been irretrievably altered. Instead of Burghs, built by the Saxons to protect the people, castles had been erected to intimidate. Monumental churches were built, French and Latin became languages of the land, and the Anglo-Saxon nobility were replaced with a ruling class of haughty foreign aristocrats. Despite William's policy of ruthlessness and brutality, he was well respected as a leader, and is remembered as the most potent of all English monarchs. Through the political marriage of Matilda of Scotland (Edmond Ironside's Great Granddaughter and Edward the Confessor's great-grandniece) and Henry I (William the Conqueror's son), the royal houses of Wessex and Normandy were linked. The ensuing rivalry between Henry I's daughter Empress Matilda and his nephew Stephen destabilized the realm and eventually led to the end of the House of Normandy.

William the Conqueror

(December 25, 1066 - September 9, 1087)

BORN: 1027 at Falaise, Normandy

PARENTS: Robert, Duke of Normandy and Herleva of Falaise

CROWNED: December 25, 1066, Westminster Abbey

CONSORT: Matilda of Flanders

DIED: September 9, 1087, at Rouen, Normandy

BURIAL: Abbaye-aux-Hommes

In September 1066, upon landing in England, William stepped off his boat and slipped and fell into the mud. Picking himself up and aware that such an occurrence would be seen as a bad omen, he clenched the soil in his hands and said "See I grasp England in my hand."

-William the Conqueror

William was the illegitimate son of Robert, Duke of Normandy and Herleva of Falaise. He was born circa 1028 at the Chateau de Falaise in Normandy. When Duke Robert died in 1035, his young son, William (aged 7) inherited the Dukedom of Normandy and his uncle Gilbert of Brionne (Robert's half-brother) was appointed guardian. In 1040, an unsuccessful assassination attempt on the life of William only succeeded in killing Gilbert of Brionne, after which, he was forced to accept Ralph of Wacy (the alleged ringleader of the assassination plot) as his guardian. By the mid-1040s, William had reached adulthood and began to assert his own authority. He began a campaign to relentless warring and expansion of his lands. In 1053, William married Matilda of Flanders, the daughter of Count Baldwin of Flanders. The marriage was a political union but over time they grew quite fond of one another and had nine children.

Legend states that around 1064 Harold Godwinson of Wessex was shipwrecked off the French coast, near Ponthieu, and imprisoned by Count Guy of Ponthieu in lieu of ransom. When Duke William heard of this, he demanded that Harold be released into his custody, and, conditional upon his release, Harold swore fealty and allegiance to William's claim to the English throne upon Edward the Confessor's death. William contended that Edward the Confessor had promised him the throne and when the English king died on January 5, 1066, Harold, contrary to his promise, declared himself king. When William was informed of this, he was enraged by Harold's betrayal and immediately began preparations for an invasion of England to take what he believed was his by right.

William undertook a huge risk by invading England, for Harold was a capable military leader and was defending his own territory. Duke William was fortunate to land his invasion force uncontested, because Harold was busy fighting Tostig Godwinson and Harald of Norway in the north. After victory in the north, Harold marched his tired army over 200 miles to fend off William in the south. On the morning of October 14, 1066, William and Harold's armies clashed in the epic Battle of Hastings. The ensuing engagement lasted all day and, although the numbers of combatants were equal on both sides, William had a slight advantage having cavalry, infantry, and archers, while Harold had only infantry. At first, William's forces sustained heavy casualties and were driven back in confusion,

but the English, ill advised, left their entrenched position and pursued the retreating Normans. This allowed William's cavalry and archers to enter the battle, decimating the English in open terrain. Near dusk, the English made their last stand. A final charge by the Norman cavalry resulted in victory and the death of Harold. The remaining English fled the field of battle in great haste. It must be noted that medieval era battles rarely lasted more than two hours; that Hastings lasted nine hours indicates the determination of both William and Harold's armies. Battles almost always ended at sundown, regardless of who was winning and Harold was killed shortly before sunset. Had Harold survived the final Norman cavalry charge, his army would have been reinforced and the next day's battle would most assuredly have been a victory for the English.

An early account of the battle states that Harold was killed by four soldiers (one of which probably included Duke William), and his body was brutally dismembered. Another account written thirty years after the battle reports that Harold was shot in the eye with an arrow. Later accounts reflect one or both of these two versions. A figure in the panel of the Bayeux Tapestry with the inscription "Harold Rex Interfectus Est" (Harold the King is killed) is depicted gripping an arrow that has struck his eye, but some historians have questioned whether this man is intended to be Harold, or if Harold is the figure to the right beneath a horse. The account of the contemporary chronicler William of Poitiers states that the body of Harold was given to William Malet for burial, was stripped of all badges of honor, and could only be identified by certain marks on his body. The corpse was brought to William's camp, and given to Malet, but not to Harold's mother, who had offered to pay a large sum for her beloved son's remains. William thought it unseemly to receive money for such merchandise, and considered it wrong that Harold should be buried as his mother wished, since so many men lay unburied because of his greediness. Another source states that Harold's widow, Edith the Fair, was called to the battlefield to identify the body, which she did by some private mark known only to herself.

Following the battle, William waited for a formal surrender of the English, but the Witan proclaimed Edgar the Etheling (grandson of Edmund Ironside) king. Unfortunately,

1. CHATEAU DE FALAISE, Normandy, the birth place of William the Conqueror.

2. QUEEN MATILDA OF FLANDERS making a tapestry, from Pictures of English History by George Routledge & Sons (1868).

3. A PLAQUE MARKS THE SPOT at Battle Abbey where Harold Godwinson was killed during the Battle of Hastings.

1. Alleged grave of Harold Godwinson at Waltham Abbey in Essex.

2. Abbeye-aux-Dames in Caen, Normandy, which contains the tomb of Matilda of Flanders.

3. Tomb of Matilda of Flanders at the Abbey-aux-Dames.

4. The Tower of London was built in 1066 by William the Conqueror and has been used as various times as a royal residence, prison, treasury, armory, and menagerie. The peak period of use came in the 16th and 17th centuries.

(TOP) ABBEY-AUX-HOMMES IN CAEN, Normandy, where William the Conqueror is buried.

(BOTTOM) THE TOMB OF WILLIAM THE CONQUEROR at Abbeye-aux-Hommes.

Edgar was unable to muster enough support and was forced to submit to William. On Christmas Day 1066 at Westminster Abbey, near the tomb of Edward the Confessor, William of Normandy was proclaimed King of England. His wife, Matilda was crowned queen in May 1068. She died fifteen years later on November 2, 1083, in Normandy. Her final resting place is at the Abbaye-aux-Dames in Normandy.

During William's reign, he initiated many reforms. He also faced stiff resistance and rebellion, all of which were defeated. He restructured the shires and commissioned the "Domesday Book," which was a survey of England's productive capacity, a precursor to the modern census. William also built numerous castles, chief among them, the Tower of London, which would shore up the national defense of the realm. In 1087, while besieging the town of Mantes, France, William fell from his horse and suffered fatal abdominal injuries. On his deathbed, he divided his possessions and named his second son, William Rufus as heir to the throne of England. His eldest son Robert Curthose, received the Duchy of Normandy, and his youngest son Henry was granted a large sum of money, which was earmarked to buy land. William died from his injuries on September 9, 1087, at the Convent of St. Gervaise in Rouen. His death was followed by a macabre scene, in which the servants began to plunder the kings bedchamber. They took everything and left William's lifeless body naked on the floor. When order was restored, the king's body was taken to the abbey of St. Stephen and eventually to the Abbaye-aux-Hommes for burial.

In a most un-regal postmortem, it was found that William's body would not fit in its sarcophagus. The remains had bloated because of warm weather and an attempt was made to close the coffin. Members of the clergy applied pressure to the lid of the coffin and this caused the abdominal wall to burst, releasing horrible smelling gases throughout the church. William's original tombstone of black marble, the same as Queen Matilda's at the Abbaye-aux-Dames, was destroyed by the Calvinists in the 16th century. The grave was defiled again during the French Revolution, and the remains were scattered. Today, only William's left femur, some skin particles, and bone dust remain in the tomb. The current marker, which dates from the early 19th century is inscribed in Latin and translated reads; Here was buried, invincible, William the Conqueror, Duke of the Normans and King of the English, he was the founder of this church and died in 1087.

William II

(September 9, 1087 - August 2, 1100)

WILLIAM RUFUS, King of England, from a 1800s engraving.

BORN: Circa 1056 in Normandy

PARENTS: William the Conqueror and Matilda of Flanders

CROWNED: September 26, 1087, at Westminster Abbey

CONSORT: Unmarried

DIED: August 2, 1100, in the New Forest

BURIAL: Winchester Cathedral

William II was the second son of William the Conqueror and Matilda of Flanders; he was born around 1056 in Normandy. He gained the nickname "Rufus" from his red hair and ruddy complexion. He inherited the throne after the death of his father in 1087, this in spite of expectations that his older brother Robert Curthose would ascend to the throne. As a result, a great rivalry erupted between the siblings, which lasted for years and threatened not only William's reign, but the stability of the realm after his death. He was an unpopular king, particularly with the church, but like his father was a great warrior and continued to consolidate Norman rule in England.

William Rufus was crowned king of England on September 26, 1087, by Lanfranc (the Archbishop of Canterbury) at Westminster Abbey. During his reign there were several unsuccessful attempts to place his brother Robert on the throne. William was an unpopular ruler and imposed numerous taxes on the nobility. He was also disliked by the Church and unlike his father, was not a committed Christian. Over his twelve year reign, William Rufus was involved in numerous military campaigns in Wales, Scotland, and Normandy.

On August 2, 1100, William organized a hunting party in the New Forest. Those present were Walter Tyrell (or Tirel), Henry (the king's younger brother) and numerous other nobles. The hunting party spread out as they chased their prey. At some point, a wayward arrow, perhaps grazing a deer, lodged in the chest of William. Without uttering a word, the king fell from his horse and died. Those in attendance were stunned and quickly left the scene. Henry hastened to Winchester to secure the royal treasury. In the nine centuries following William's tragic death, there have developed numerous conspiracy theories.

THE DEATH OF WILLIAM RUFUS of England, from Ridpath's Universal History (1895).

According to contemporary chroniclers, rightly or not, William's death was judged to have been an accident and not murder. It was noted that those present at the scene had tried to help the stricken king, but nothing could be done and fearing they would all be charged with murder, panicked and fled the scene. The unwise decision to leave hastily allowed conspiracies of assassination to develop. It was also noted that Walter Tyrell was an expert archer and was considered unlikely to have fired such a reckless shot. Moreover, Henry, an heir to the throne benefited directly from William's death. William Rufus never married and had no children. Modern scholars have reopened the question of possible assassination but it has not been universally accepted. Following his death, local farmers conveyed the body to Winchester, where on August 3, 1100, it was hastily buried at Winchester Cathedral. There was little fanfare and few people were in attendance. In 1968, William's crypt was opened and inside was found many bones, along with the shaft of an arrow, possibly that which had killed the king.

WILLIAM RUFUS'S CRYPT at Winchester Cathedral.

THE RUFUS STONE was erected in 1745 and marks the spot where William Rufus was killed by an arrow shot by Sir Walter Tyrell, on August 2, 1100.

Henry I
(August 2, 1100 - December 1, 1135)

King Henry I of England, published in London by Thomas Kelly (1830).

BORN: **September 1068 in Shelby, Yorkshire**

PARENTS: **William the Conqueror and Matilda of Flanders**

CROWNED: **August 6, 1100, at Westminster Abbey**

CONSORT: **Matilda of Scotland and Adeliza of Louvain**

DIED: **December 1, 1135, at Saint Denis-en-Lyons Castle in Rouen, France**

BURIAL: **Reading Abbey (presumed lost)**

Henry I was the youngest son of William the Conqueror and Matilda of Flanders. He was born in September 1068, probably at Selby in Yorkshire. He was named Henry after his mother's maternal uncle, King Henry I of France. On the death of William the Conqueror, Normandy was bequeathed to Robert Curthose, England was left to William Rufus, and Henry received a large sum of silver. Henry was groomed to enter the priesthood and well educated, and was the only Norman king to be literate. Because of this education, he was given the nickname "Beauclerc" meaning good writer. Although he was studious, he was also ambitious, and when his brother William Rufus was killed, either by design or accident, Henry seized the throne. His reign proved to be long and successful. He could be harsh to the point of savagery, but he inspired loyalty among his followers and was capable, clever, and adept at diplomacy. During his reign England was at peace and its territories were expanded.

He was crowned at Westminster Abbey on August 6, 1100, and promised to reform the abuses of his brother's reign. Henry cemented his popularity, particularly among the native Anglo-Saxons, by marrying Matilda of Scotland (sometimes referred to as Edith or Maud); she was the daughter of Malcolm III, King of the Scots and Saint Margaret (the sister of Edgar Etheling and great-grand niece of Edward the Confessor). She proved to be a good and respected queen and followed the example of her saintly mother. Though Henry was unfaithful to Matilda, their union was generally considered a good marriage by royal standards and helped to unite the rival claims of the Norman and Wessex Houses. Like so many rulers before and after him, Henry proved to be a serial adulterer and spawned more illegitimate chil-

QUEEN MATILDA OF SCOTLAND, from *Biographical Sketches of the Queens of England* by Mary Howlitt (1866).

dren (25) than any other English king in history. Henry had only two legitimate children, a daughter Matilda (who later was married to Henry V, Holy Roman Emperor) and William Adelin (who drowned in the wreck of the White Ship, November 25, 1120).

In 1101, Robert Curthose (Henry's older brother) invaded England in another attempt to cease the throne, but a negotiated peace was settled before any bloodshed. In return for a large sum of money, Robert renounced his claim to the English crown and returned to Normandy. Five years later, Henry led an English army into Normandy and defeated Robert at the Battle of Tinchebray (September 1106). Robert was imprisoned for the rest of his life and died on February 3, 1134 at Cardiff Castle in Wales. He was buried in the abbey church of St. Peter in Gloucester (renamed Gloucester Cathedral). The exact location of his burial is difficult to establish, legend states that he requested to be buried before the High Altar, but the tomb effigy visible to the public is empty.

Queen Matilda died on May 1, 1118, at Westminster Palace and the death of her only son in the White Ship tragedy of November 1120 most certainly contributed to her early demise. She was remembered by her subjects as "Matilda the Good Queen" and for a time was considered for sainthood. She was buried at Westminster Abbey and her unmarked tomb is located to the right of the original shrine to Edward the Confessor. Following Queen Matilda's death, Henry married the young and beautiful Adelizia of Louvain, but the marriage produced no children.

In May 1125, after the death of her husband, Holy Roman Emperor Henry V, Matilda (Henry I's daughter) returned to England and was named heir to the throne. The proud and haughty Matilda was then ordered to marry Geoffrey Plantagenet, the son of Fulk V, Count of Anjou. She reluctantly agreed to the union, but personally loathed her new husband, which was fully reciprocated. When the reluctant and quarrelsome pair was finally ordered to do their duty and produce an heir to the throne, a son, the future Henry II of England was born.

In 1135, Henry travelled to Normandy to visit his grandchildren and he quarreled with the overbearing Matilda and her husband. Henry was now elderly and these fights affected him profoundly. He died on December 1, 1135, at Saint Denis-en-Lyons castle, most likely from food poisoning, due to over indulging on lampreys (which were probably infected with salmonella). His body was returned to England and was buried at Reading Abbey. His tomb was destroyed during the dissolution of the monasteries in the middle 16th Century. Today, Reading Abbey stands in ruins but a memorial plaque hangs near the spot where Henry was originally buried. After Henry's death, despite his oath of allegiance, the throne was seized by his nephew Stephen. Nineteen years of civil war were to follow as Stephen and Matilda became locked in a bitter struggle for possession of the crown.

(TOP) RUINS OF READING ABBEY, where Henry I was buried.

(BOTTOM) MEMORIAL PLAQUE which marks the location at Reading Abbey where Henry I was buried.

After Henry's death, Adeliza of Louvain married William d'Aubigny (1st Earl of Arundel), who had been one of Henry's chief advisors. Although her new husband was a staunch supporter of Stephen during the Anglo-Norman civil war, Adeliza championed Matilda's cause. Adeliza died on April 23, 1151, at the Abbey of Affligem and was buried at the abbey. During the French Revolution the abbey was destroyed and her grave was desecrated. Her remains were then reburied in the cloister of the rebuilt abbey.

AFFLIGEM ABBEY IN BRABANT, Belgium, where Adeliza of Louvain, second wife of King Henry I of England is buried.

31

Empress Matilda, Lady of the English

(April 7, 1141 - November 1, 1141)

BORN: February 7, 1102

PARENTS: Henry I of England and Matilda of Scotland

CROWNED: Uncrowned

CONSORT: Henry V, Holy Roman Emperor and Geoffrey Plantagenet, Count of Anjou

DIED: September 10, 1167, at Rouen, France

BURIAL: Originally at the Abbey of Bec-Hellouin, now at Rouen Cathedral

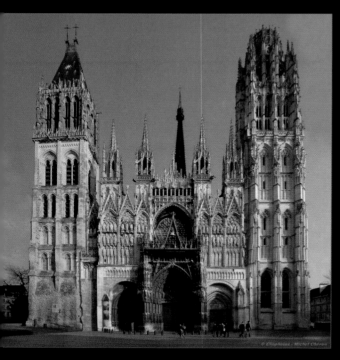

ROUEN CATHEDRAL, where Empress Matilda, Lady of the English, is buried.

Lady Matilda was born on February 7, 1102, and was the daughter and only surviving legitimate child of Henry I of England. Upon her brother's tragic death in the White Ship disaster of 1120, Matilda became the heir to the throne. As a child, she was betrothed to and later married Henry V, Holy Roman Emperor, acquiring the title of Empress. They had no known children. When the Emperor died in 1125, Matilda remained unwed for several years but in 1128, against her will she was married to Geoffrey, Count of Anjou, with whom she had three sons, the eldest of whom became Henry II of England.

ST. JULIEN'S CATHEDRAL in Le Mans, Normandy, where Geoffrey Plantagenet, Count of Anjou, the father of Henry II was buried.

Matilda was the first female ruler of England and the length of her effective reign was only for a few brief months. She was never crowned and failed to consolidate her power (legally or politically). For this reason, she is normally excluded from lists of English monarchs and her rival (and cousin) Stephen of Blois is listed as king for the period 1135-1154. Their rivalry for the throne led to years of civil war and was known as the "The Anarchy." Although the civil war was eventually decided in Stephen's favor, his reign was troubled. In 1153, Stephen's son Eustace IV of Boulogne died and with no surviving son's was forced to name Matilda's son, Henry, as heir to the throne.

During her later years, Empress Matilda retired to Rouen, where she maintained her own court. She often intervened in the quarrels between her sons and by 1141, gave up hope of ever being crowned queen. Her name always preceded that of her son Henry II, even after he became King of England. Geoffrey, Count of Anjou, died on September 7, 1151, and was buried at St. Julien's Cathedral in Le Mans, Normandy. His tomb was destroyed during the French Revolution. Empress Matilda died near Rouen, Normandy, on September 10, 1167, and was originally buried at the Abbey of Bec-Hellouin. The abbey was destroyed during the French Revolution, but her remains were left untouched. In 1847, her coffin was discovered and transferred to Rouen Cathedral, where her tomb epitaph reads: "Great by Birth, Greater by Marriage, Greatest in her Offspring: Here lies Matilda, the daughter, wife, and mother of Henry."

Stephen

KING STEPHEN of England, from an engraving published in *Barclay's Universal Dictionary (1830)*.

BORN: Circa 1097 in Blois, France

PARENTS: Stephen, Count of Blois and
Adela of Normandy

CROWNED: December 26, 1135, at Westminster Abbey
and December 25, 1141, at Canterbury Cathedral

CONSORT: Matilda of Boulogne

DIED: October 25, 1154, at Dover

BURIAL: Faversham Abbey

Henry I's choice of his daughter Matilda as his heir was unpopular among the Anglo-Norman nobles, so when Stephen, a favorite nephew of Henry I made a bid for the throne, he was successful in gaining support. Intelligent and well liked, Stephen was quite different from his ruthless Norman predecessors. But his reign was initially contested by the Empress Matilda, who helped plunged England into civil war. Stephen eventually gained the upper hand, but he proved to be the last of the Norman kings when Matilda's son, Henry, was accepted as his successor.

Stephen was born circa 1097 in Blois, France. He was the third son of Stephen, Count of Blois and Adela (daughter of William the Conqueror). He was raised by his uncle, Henry I of England, and received vast lands in England, Normandy, and the county of Boulogne. With a number of other nobles, he initially pledged to support Henry I's daughter, Matilda, as successor to the English throne. Nevertheless, many English aristocrats (including Stephen) were reluctant to accept a woman ruler. Consequently, after Henry I's death in December 1135, the leading lords and bishops welcomed Stephen when he crossed the English Channel to claim the crown. He was crowned king on December 24, 1135, at Westminster Abbey. He married Matilda of Boulogne in 1125; she was the daughter of Eustace III, Count of Boulogne, and Mary of Scotland. Together they would have four children. During the ensuing civil war she proved to be one of her husband's greatest assets.

Stephen's affable character was a welcome contrast to the harsh and sometimes brutal reign of his Norman predecessors, but his lack of ruthlessness was also a disadvantage, as it allowed his kingdom on both sides of the Channel, to fall into anarchy and chaos. The first real threat to his rule came from one of Henry I's illegitimate sons, Robert Fitzroy, Earl of Gloucester, who had switched allegiance from Stephen to Empress Matilda. In 1139, the Empress was imprisoned at Arundel Castle but was freed after a few weeks in captivity. She set up a rival court in the West Country, a threat that Stephen managed to contain until an uprising in East Anglia changed the circumstances. In the ensuing battle for Lincoln in February 2, 1141, Stephen was captured and Empress Matilda took control and moved to London. She was not liked and public support quickly dwindled. Stephen's wife, Queen Matilda of Boulogne rallied the people of London and Empress Matilda was driven out.

In Winchester, Stephen's brother, Henry, (the Bishop of Winchester), who had earlier defected to Empress Matilda's faction, changed sides again and with a small force laid siege to the royal castle at Winchester. On July 31, 1141, Empress Matilda's army swooped on Winchester and Bishop Henry fled with his men to Wolvesey Castle. While putting the castle under siege, Empress Matilda set up her headquarters in the royal castle, and Earl

Robert established his command at Winchester Cathedral.

Queen Matilda of Boulogne and other supporters of Stephen quickly assembled an army of relief and set up camp on the east side of Winchester. They proceeded to blockade Empress Matilda's forces in the city. Suffering from a lack of food and to weaken the blockade Earl Robert attempted to fortify the city, but was defeated with heavy losses. This convinced Earl Robert that he must quit Winchester and begin an orderly withdrawal. Earl Robert, commanding the rearguard, was surrounded and surrendered with his men. The Rout of Winchester was a major setback for Empress Matilda. She exchanged Robert of Gloucester for King Stephen. Although Stephen was restored to the throne, the civil war raged on for another six years, during which he exercised nominal control over most of the kingdom. On October 31, 1147, Robert of Gloucester died at Bristol Castle and Lady Matilda gave up the fight for the throne and returned to France, though she still harbored ambitions that her son Henry might one day ascend to the throne of England.

On May 3, 1152, Matilda of Boulogne died from fever at Hedingham Castle. She was buried at Faversham Abbey. Following his wife's death, Stephen's only real concern became the succession of his son, Eustace to the throne. On August 7, 1153, this changed when Eustace died. Stephen lost heart and signed the Treaty of Wallingford, which designated, Lady Matilda's son, Henry, as heir to the throne of England. On October 25, 1154, only fourteen months after signing the treaty of succession, Stephen fell ill with a stomach disorder (most likely appendicitis) and died at a local priory in Dover. His remains were interred next to his wife and son at Faversham Abbey. The abbey was demolished during the dissolution of the monasteries in the 16th century and their graves were lost. Although the abbey was dissolved, the nearby St. Mary of Charity Church remained untouched. It is alleged that Stephen and Matilda were secretly reburied somewhere on the grounds of this church, but the exact location is unknown. With Stephen's death and the succession of Henry of Anjou (as Henry II) to the throne of England, the reign of the Norman kings of England came to an end.

1. RUINS OF WOLVESEY CASTLE, where Empress Matilda was defeated in July of 1141.

2. THE RUINS OF FAVERSHAM ABBEY, from an engraving by Elisha Kirkall (1722).

3. ST. MARY OF CHARITY CHURCH in Faversham, Kent, where King Stephen was allegedly buried.

Chapter Three

The Plantagenets (1154-1399)

I n 1154, Norman rule gave way to the Angevin Dynasty (rulers from Anjou in France) with the mighty Henry II as its ruler. He was the first in a long line of fiery Plantagenet kings that would rule England for two hundred forty-five years. They were a remarkable family, providing England with fourteen of its monarchs. The surname Plantagenet, which was to become one of the most famous in England, is said to be derived from a nickname adopted by Geoffrey, Henry II's father, and refers to his habit of wearing a sprig of broom or planta genista in his helmet. Henry II's accomplishment in holding together the largest empire in Western Europe heralded a new reformation in Anglo-Norman culture. His reign over England was essentially French in culture and language and was regarded as little more than an efficient source of revenue for the French provinces. Two and a half centuries later, as Richard II abdicated in favor of his cousin Henry IV, a unique English nation was created. By then most of the French lands had been lost and the Anglo-French conflict known as the Hundred Years War had begun. Wales and Ireland had been subjugated and brought under English dominion. Governance and administration, which had proven astoundingly stable, had grown increasingly sophisticated. Above all, royal authority, which had been immeasurably strengthened by succession and medieval ethics, was nevertheless subject to the ideals of the Magna Carta and to a fledgling parliament that had begun to represent all levels of English society.

Popular legends surrounding the origin of the Angevin dynasty suggested that they were the progeny of the devil. While Gerald the chronicler of Wales is the key source for these stories, they often borrowed elements of the Melusine legend. For example, Gerald wrote of "a certain countess of Anjou" who rarely attended mass, and one day flew away, never to be seen again. A similar story was attached to Eleanor of Aquitaine in the thirteenth century. Gerald also presents a list of sins committed by Geoffrey Plantagenet and his son Henry II as further evidence of their "corrupt" origins. According to Gerald, these legends were not always discouraged by the Angevins. Richard I was said to have often remarked that his family "come of the devil, and to the devil they would go." A similar statement is attributed to St. Bernard regarding Henry II, whose sons reportedly defended their frequent infighting by saying "Do not deprive us of our heritage; we cannot help acting like devils." The legends surrounding the Angevin's spread into English folklore and led some historians to give them the epithet "The Devil's Brood."

Then came the highly aesthetic Henry III and his son, the determined Edward I, who conquered Wales and became known as the "Hammer of the Scots" for his military campaigns in Scotland, where he fought William Wallace and Robert the Bruce. Then Henry V conquered France and bequeathed both kingdoms to his pious and ineffectual son, Henry VI. After 1399, the Plantagenet self-destructed and subdivided into the Houses of Lancaster and York in the bloody dynastic struggles known as the Wars of the Roses. The Yorkist king Richard III was the last Plantagenet monarch; he was killed at the Battle on Bosworth Field in 1485 and Henry Tudor was proclaimed king. The legitimate male line of the House of Plantagenet became extinct with the execution Edward of Warwick in 1499.

Henry II

Henry II of England, from an engraving published by Thomas Kelly in 1830.

BORN: March 5, 1133, at Le Mans, France

PARENTS: Geoffrey Plantagenet and Matilda
Lady of the English

CROWNED: December 19, 1154, at Westminster Abbey

CONSORT: Eleanor of Aquitaine

DIED: July 6, 1189, at Chinon Castle in Anjou, France

BURIAL: Fontevraud Abbey

"What a parcel of fools and bastards I have nourished in my house, that not one of them will avenge me of this one upstart clerk"

-King Henry II of England

Henry was born on March 5, 1133, in Le Mans, France, and was the eldest son of Matilda and Geoffrey Plantagenet. When Henry I died in 1135, the succession to the throne of England was in dispute. Some members of the nobility threw their loyalty behind the legitimate heir, Empress Matilda, but numerous Anglo-Normans barons did not want a woman ruler and supported Stephen. For the next eighteen years there was civil war between the supporters of Matilda and Stephen. As neither side was strong enough to achieve an outright victory, the result was a long conflict that created a great deal of hardship for the people of England. Eventually, Stephen won out but without a surviving heir to the throne, he was forced to make Matilda's son Henry of Anjou, heir to the English throne.

The young Henry continued his mother's war against Stephen after she abandoned the conflict and returned to France in 1148. The next five years saw Henry and Stephen fight to a virtual stalemate but things changed in 1153, when Stephen's only son and heir died. The Treaty of Wallingford of 1153, ended the civil war, known as the "Anarchy" and named Henry of Anjou as Stephen's heir to the throne. When Stephen died the next year, Henry ascended to the throne unopposed.

In her own right, Eleanor of Aquitaine was one of the wealthiest and most powerful women in Western Europe during the High Middle Ages. As well as being Duchess of Aquitaine, she, was during her life time, both the Queens of France (1137–1152) and England (1154–1189). The only other to hold these titles was Margaret of Anjou whose status as Queen of France is disputed. Eleanor succeeded her father as Duchess of Aquitaine and Countess of Poitiers at the age of fifteen, and thus became the most eligible bride in Europe. Three months after her accession as Duchess, she married the future Louis VII, son of King Louis VI of France. As Queen of France, she participated with her husband in the unsuccessful Second Crusade of 1145-1149. Soon after, Louis VII and Eleanor agreed to dissolve their marriage, primarily upon Eleanor's own desire and the fact that she had only produced two daughters and no male heirs. The marriage was

Eleanor of Aquitaine, from *Biographical Sketches of the Queens of England* by Mary Howlitt (1866).

annulled on March 11, 1152, on the grounds of consanguinity within the fourth degree, but their daughters were declared legitimate and custody of them awarded to Louis. Eleanor's lands in Aquitaine and Poitiers were restored to her control. Upon arriving in Poitiers, she was engaged to Henry II of England (ironically, they were cousins within the third degree). On May 18, 1152, Eleanor and Henry were married and over the next thirteen years, she bore eight children. She and Henry's marriage became estranged and she was imprisoned between 1173 and 1189 for supporting her son, Henry (the Young King) in rebellion. Following Henry II's death, Eleanor acted as a regent for her son Richard I, while he was on the Third Crusade. Eleanor survived her son Richard and lived well into the reign of her youngest son King John. By the time of her own death on April 1, 1204, she had outlived all of her children except John and was buried at Fontevraud Abbey.

On December 19, 1154, Henry II was crowned king at Westminster Abbey. He was the first monarch to be proclaimed "King of England" as opposed to "King of the English." Henry was one of the most extraordinary and charismatic characters in the history of the English monarchy. At the height of his powers he had dominion over most of the British Isles and much of France, holding together his empire by sheer force of personality. For bringing order to England, which had been ravaged by years of civil war, Henry has been described by many historians as the greatest king that England has ever known. The only shadows on his reign were the grisly murder of his chancellor Thomas Becket and the rebellion and the treachery of his own family.

From an early age Henry had been groomed to be the next king of England. His mother, Lady Matilda had employed the best scholars in Europe to educate her son and Henry was a willing student and never lost his love of learning. One of his close friends said that Henry had a tremendous memory and rarely forgot anything he was told and would spend hours studying Roman history. He was particularly interested in Emperor Augustus. Henry realized that, like Augustus, his first task must be to eliminate those that had the power to remove him. This meant that Henry had to control the nobility, and deport all foreign mercenaries. He then took action to unite all the people of England, allowing several of Stephen's officials to keep their government posts. Another strategy used by Henry was to arrange marriages between rival families.

When Henry became king he appointed Thomas Becket as his chancellor. Becket's job was important as it involved the distribution of royal charters, writs, and letters. The king and Becket soon became close friends. When Theobald, Archbishop of Canterbury, died in 1162, Henry chose Becket as his replacement. This angered many top leaders in the church, who saw Beckett as being non-religiously trained and a pawn of the king. Nonetheless, he was appointed Archbishop of Canterbury in June of 1162.

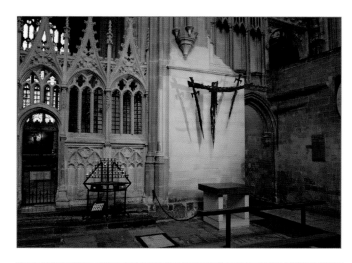

(TOP) THOMAS BECKET's tomb at Canterbury Cathedral.

(BOTTOM) THE CHAPEL OF FONTEVRAUD ABBEY.

A great deal of Henry's reign was spent at war protecting his French provinces. He excelled at this and even added new territory, making him the most powerful monarch in Western Europe. When he was not working on government business he loved hunting and, unlike his predecessors, cared little for appearance and preferred hunting clothes to royal robes. He detested the pomp and ceremony of being king and believed people had to earn respect. He was quick to lose his temper and often upset important people by shouting at them. Yet, when dealing with the poor or a defeated enemy, he had a reputation for being polite and kind. An extremely intelligent man with tremendous energy, Henry made several important legal reforms and is considered to be the founder of English common law, but his attempts to reform the courts controlled by the church led to conflict with his friend Thomas Becket.

In 1163 after being away for an extended period, Henry arrived back in England and was told of the dramatic increase in crime throughout the kingdom. He was told that as many as one hundred murderers had escaped proper punishment because they had claimed their right to be tried in church courts. Those that had sought the privilege of a trial in these courts were not exclusively clergymen. These courts would not impose punishments that included execution or mutilation and this was seen advantageous. Henry decided that clergymen found guilty of serious crimes should be handed over to the royal courts for punishment. At first, Thomas Becket agreed with Henry but after consulting other church leaders changed his mind. Henry was furious and believed he had been betrayed by his friend.

In 1164, Becket was involved in yet another dispute, this time over land and stolen finances. Henry ordered him to answer the allegations and when Becket refused to appear, all his property was confiscated. To avoid further controversy, Beckett offered to repay any alleged stolen funds. Henry refused the offer and insisted that the Archbishop be tried. When Henry mentioned that other charges, such as treason might be added to the offenses, Becket fled to France but eventually agreed to return to England. However, as soon as he arrived on English soil, Becket caused further controversy by excommunicating the Archbishop of York and other leading churchmen who were supporters of Henry. The king was in Normandy at the time, and became enraged when he heard the news and supposedly shouted out: "Will no one rid me of this turbulent priest?" Four of Henry's knights, heard his comments and travelled to England to visit Becket. When they arrived at Canterbury Cathedral on December 29, 1170, they demanded that Becket pardon those he had excommunicated, when he refused, they hacked him to death with their swords. The Christian world was shocked by Becket's murder. The pope immediately canonized Becket, who became a symbol of Christian resistance to the power of the English monarchy. His shrine at Canterbury Cathedral became one of the most important sacred pilgrimage sites in the country. Although Henry admitted that his comments had led to the death of Becket; he argued that he had neither commanded nor wished the man's death. In 1172, Pope Alexander III accepted these arguments and absolved Henry from Becket's murder.

Tomb effigies of Henry II and Eleanor of Aquintaine at Fontevraud Abbey.

Keeping close control of his empire was one of Henry's greatest strengths, but his wife and sons grew increasingly impatient with his reluctance to relinquish any real authority. This dissatisfaction was exacerbated by the fact that the marriage between Henry and Eleanor had become estranged. The queen had become increasingly resentful of Henry's promiscuity, specifically his public liaison with Rosamund Clifford. Eleanor retired to her own court at Poitiers and began to plot her husband's downfall and the advancement of her favorite son, Richard. When, in 1173, Henry (the Young King), Richard, and Geoffrey rebelled against their father, Queen Eleanor actively encouraged them. It was also supported by the kings of France, Scotland, and numerous barons who had been appalled by Thomas Becket's murder. Henry quickly crushed the rebellion, forced Scotland to submit, and placed Eleanor under house arrest. During this period, John had remained Henry's only loyal son.

In June 1183, Henry "the Young King" died and, in 1185, Geoffrey was killed in a tournament. Henry's empire would now be divided between Richard and John but the dynastic rivalry continued unabated. In 1189, Richard joined forced with Philip of Spain to challenge Henry yet again. Henry was forced to negotiate a humiliating peace agreement and discovered that his favorite and perceived loyal son, John had fought alongside his enemies. He had suffered from manic depression all his life and the stresses caused by family struggles might have hastened his death. On July 6, 1189, suffering from pneumonia and deserted by all but an illegitimate son, Geoffrey, Archbishop of York, Henry II died at Chinon, France. He was buried at Fontevraud Abbey. However, there is no remaining physical presence of Henry on the site. The tombs of Henry II, Eleanor, and Richard I are empty. Their remains were possibly destroyed during the French Revolution. It is generally believed that the location of their bones is known, but the French government will not grant permission to excavate, because finding the bodies are not where they are thought to be may result in a decrease in tourism.

Richard I
(July 6, 1189 - April 6, 1199)

BORN: September 8, 1157, at Beaumont Palace, Oxford

PARENTS: Henry II of England and Eleanor of Aquitaine

CROWNED: September 2, 1189, at Westminster Abbey and April 10, 1194, at Winchester Cathedral

CONSORT: Berengaria of Navarre

DIED: April 6, 1199, at Chalus, France

BURIAL: Fontevraud Abbey

"From the Devil we sprang and to the Devil we shall go."
-Richard I of England

Richard I, also known as "Lionheart," was born at Beaumont Palace, Oxford, on September 9, 1157, the third son of Henry II and Eleanor of Aquitaine. He was his mother's favorite. After the birth of their youngest child, John, Richard's parents drifted into open hostility. The neglected Eleanor returned to her native France and there established her own court. She took Richard with her and designated him heir. Richard was known to be fond of music and was nurtured in the troubadour culture of his mother's homeland. From the outset, Richard exhibited the volatile disposition and energy inherent in the Plantagenet family. In 1172, when he was fourteen years old, Richard was invested with his mother's inheritance of Aquitaine and Poitou. He joined his discontented elder brother Henry (the Young King) in open rebellion against their father Henry II. The untimely death of young Henry in June 1183 made Richard the heir to the entire Angevin Empire. Despite his father's request that he pass Aquitaine to his brother John, the family feuding continued.

When Henry II died in 1189, Richard was again in open rebellion against his father. Upon succeeding to the throne, he acted in an uncharacteristically generous way to all who had remained loyal to his father and one of his first actions as king was to order the release of his mother, Queen Eleanor from captivity. His coronation took place in Westminster Abbey on September 23, 1189 (he was crowned for a second time on April 10, 1194 at Winchester Cathedral after his return from the Crusades). Richard spent nearly all of his reign, either on Crusade or in France, but despite this he is remembered as a national hero in Britain. He was a brilliant intellect, highly successful warrior, extremely arrogant, and often ruthless and brutal. His attention was not centered on government but on leaving for the Third Crusade, whose aim was to recapture Jerusalem from the Saracens. Impatient to leave, he stayed in England just long enough to raise money for his travels and to bribe his younger brother John, to stay out of his kingdom. In the summer of 1190, Richard and his ally Philip II of France set off to do battle with the Kurdish warrior Saladin.

En route, Philip and Richard quarreled over the latter's procrastination over marrying Philip's sister Alice (he had been engaged to her for 20 years). Eleanor of Aquitaine was instead arranging for

BERENGARIA OF NAVARRE, from *Biographical Sketches of the Queens of England* by Mary Howlitt (1866).

41

Richard to marry Berengaria of Navarre, the daughter of Sancho VI of Navarre. Richard and Berengaria had met only once prior to their betrothal, at a tournament at Pamplona. They were married on May 12, 1191, at the Chapel of St. George in Limassol, Cyprus. This prompted Philip to return early from the Crusade and invade Normandy. The English contingent of the Third Crusade arrived at Acre in the Holy Land in the summer of 1191. Richard's reputation seems to have arrived before him and on July 11th, the Moslem defenders surrendered the city. On September 7, 1191, at Arsuf, Richard's army defeated Saladin. Richard then marched on Jaffa, and began to strengthen it as a garrison for Jerusalem. His army arrived at the foothills of the Holy City on January 3, 1192, and a truce was negotiated with the Moslems.

While Richard was a great military commander, he was a poor politician. Under the Treaty of Ramla of 1192, Richard agreed that Jerusalem would remain in Muslim hands but stay open to Christian pilgrims. Nonetheless, Richard's crusading exploits became the tales of a hero and bolstered his reputation. On his way home in 1192, he was captured by Leopold of Austria and sold to the Holy Roman Emperor who demanded a huge ransom for his release. John saw his opportunity and reneged on his agreement with Richard and, with the support of disaffected nobles and the ultimate aim of seizing Richard's throne, returned to England to set up his own court. With the help of Hubert Walter (Chief Justiciar), and Queen Eleanor, John was kept in check. The money for the king's ransom was raised, which amounted to the equivalent of three times the annual revenue of the Crown. Richard was freed and came to England in March 1194 for what would be his last visit. He stayed just two months and returned to France to recover the territories forfeited during his captivity.

In the spring of 1199, a horde of Roman treasure was discovered by a peasant tending a field in Chalus, France. Richard, as overlord, claimed the find as his own and when it was not handed over besieged the castle of Chalus-Chabrol. On the evening of March 26, 1199, while Richard was surveying the siege, an archer fired a crossbow arrow, which embedded itself in the kings left shoulder. Richard attempted to pull the arrow out but the shaft broke, leaving the arrow head in his flesh. Although later attempts were successful in removing the entire arrow, the wound became infected.

Richard asked to have the crossbowman brought before him but the man turned out to be a boy. The boy claimed that Richard had killed his father and two brothers in battle, and that he shot the king in revenge. The boy expected to be executed but Richard, in an uncharacteristic moment of compassion, and as a last act of mercy, forgave the boy of his crime, saying, "Live on, and by my bounty behold the light of day," then ordered the boy freed. Richard then set his affairs in order and named his brother John as heir to the throne. In 1190, Richard had designated his nephew, Arthur of Brittany as his heir apparent, but because of his youth (being only 12 years of age) Richard believed he was not ready to

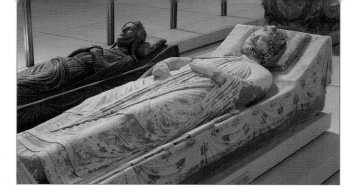

govern. In April of 1203, Arthur vanished mysteriously and his puzzling disappearance has given rise to various legends, one of which is that King John (in order to suppress rival claims to the throne) personally murdered him and had the body dumped into the Seine. None of these allegations have ever been substantiated. The reign of Richard's successor, John, would see the end of Henry II's great Angevin Empire.

Richard died on April 6, 1199, in the arms of his mother, Eleanor of Aquitaine. During his reign he had spent less than six months in England. According to one chronicler, Richard's last act of chivalry proved fruitless; in an orgy of medieval brutality, the boy archer was brutally tortured and killed soon after the king's death. Richard's heart was buried at Rouen Cathedral in Normandy; his entrails were buried in the Chapel of the Castle de Chalus-Chabrol (where he died) and the rest of his remains were interred at Fontevraud Abbey.

Richard and Berengaria of Navarre had no children. She never visited England during Richard's lifetime, although there is evidence that she may have visited England following his death. The traditional description of her as the only English queen never to set foot in England would still be literally true, as she did not visit England during the time she was Richard's consort. She certainly sent envoys to England several times, mainly to inquire about the pension she was due as dowager queen, which King John failed to pay. Although Eleanor of Aquitaine intervened and Pope Innocent III threatened John with an interdict if he did not pay Berengaria, John still refused to pay. Her pension was only reinstated during

ABBEY OF L'EPAU IN LE MANS, where Berengaria of Navarre, Queen consort of Richard I, died on December 23, 1230 and was buried.

the reign of Henry III. Eventually, she settled in Le Mans, one of her inherited properties, and became a benefactress of the Abbey of L'Epau in Le Mans. She never remarried and entered into a quiet life at the abbey. Berengaria died there on December 23, 1230, and was buried within the abbey. Her grave was thought to be lost, but during a restoration of the abbey in 1960, a skeleton thought to be hers was discovered. These remains are now preserved beneath a stone effigy of the queen, which is located in the chapter house of the abbey.

(TOP) TOMB EFFIGY OF RICHARD I at Fontevraud Abbey.

(BOTTOM) TOMB EFFIGY OF BERENGARIA OF NAVARRE in the chapter house of the Abbey of L'Epau.

John
(April 6, 1199 - October 19, 1216)

BORN: December 24, 1167, at Beaumont Palace in Oxford

PARENTS: Henry II of England and Eleanor of Aquitaine

CROWNED: May 27, 1199, at Westminster Abbey

CONSORT: Isabel of Gloucester and Isabella of Angouleme

DIED: October 18, 1216, at Newark Castle in Nottinghamshire

BURIAL: Worcester Cathedral

John was power hungry, spoiled, cruel and narcissistic and as such has been given the reputation as one of the worst monarchs in English history. His reign oversaw the loss of most of the English held territory in France, which his brother and father had fought so dearly to defend. There was such immense fiscal pressure on the kingdom that his barons were brought to the point of open rebellion. In 1215, they forced him to sign the Magna Carta, which imposed limits on the king's power. When he died in 1216, the country was in the midst of civil war. The last of the English Angevin line of Plantagenet monarchs, John was born on December 24, 1167, at Beaumont Palace in Oxford. He was the younger brother of King Richard I and the youngest son of Henry II and Eleanor of Aquitaine. As a child, John tended to be overshadowed by his older brother Richard. Like his father, John developed a reputation for violent rages. Upon King Henry II's death in 1189, John was left no land and because of this was given the nick-name "Lackland" meaning no land.

After his father's death, John attempted to seize the throne from his brother. Although unsuccessful, John finally acceded legitimately when, on his death bed, Richard forgave him and named him his heir. Richard died on April 6, 1199, and John was made King of England. He was crowned on May 27, 1199, at Westminster Abbey. On August 29, 1189, he married Isabel of Gloucester at Marlborough Castle. She and John were second cousins and both were great grandchildren of Henry I of England. The marriage was put under prohibition because of its illicit degrees of relationship, but was lifted by Pope Clement III, who granted

a dispensation to marry but forbade the couple from having sexual relations. With John now on the throne and the issue of succession being a major concern, an annulment was quickly arranged, which Isabel did not contest. She later married Geoffrey de Mandville, Earl of Essex. On October 14, 1217, she died at Keynsham Abbey and was buried at Canterbury Cathedral.

One year after the annulment John married Isabella of Angouleme. She was the daughter of Aymer Count of Angouleme and Alice of Courtenay. Their marriage took place on August 24, 1200, in Bordeaux and together they had ten children (one of which was the future King Henry III). King John was thrown into conflict with Phillip II of France over this marriage, because Isabella had originally been betrothed to another man. As a result, Philip confiscated all English territory in France, which led to war.

During his disastrous campaign to reclaim lost French territory, John damaged his reputation even further by killing his nephew, Arthur of Brittany, who was a perceived threat to the throne.

John's personal life had a heavy impact on his reign and contemporary chroniclers wrote that he was sinfully lustful and lacking in piety. It was common for kings and nobles of the period to keep mistresses, but many complained that John's mistresses were married noblewoman, which was considered unacceptable at the time. For the next eight years, John attended to domestic matters and feuded openly with the clergy. As a result of his open refusal to appoint Stephen Langton as Archbishop of Canterbury, a papal injunction was placed on the kingdom and John was excommunicated. In 1212, the pope declared John no longer the legal King of England, which was disastrous because he needed papal support to keep royal authority. John then agreed to hold his lands in fiefdom of the papacy and an enormous sum of money was extorted from the English barons to fund previously unsuccessful military campaigns in France. When another military campaign was launched in 1213 to regain lost French territories, the stakes were high. The English defeat at Bouvines in 1214 was disastrous for John. The English barons broke out in open rebellion and on June 15, 1215, in the meadow of Runnymede, near Windsor Castle, King John was forced to sign the Magna Carta, which limited the powers of the monarchy. When John later reneged on the agreement the English barons retaliated by welcoming Philip II of France's son Louis into England. This plunged England into civil war. Louis gained control of the south east and captured the Tower of London in May 1216.

In September 1216, John renewed his attempt to put down the rebellion, marched from the Cotwolds, and attacked eastwards towards London. At King's Lynn, John contracted dysentery, which would ultimately prove fatal. The king travelled west and was said to have lost a significant part of his baggage train along the way, which included the crown jewels, which were swept away as they crossed a tidal estuary. By October 1216, John faced a stalemate and his illness grew worse. As he reached Newark Castle, he was unable to travel any further; he died on the night of October 18, 1216, and was buried at Worcester Cathedral at the foot of the altar of Saint Wulfstan. When the tomb was opened during renovations in 1797, John's remains were found to be shrouded in a monks cowl (possibly worn as a disguise for his passage through purgatory), also present was a sword and scabbard. It was said that the exposure rapidly turned the remains to dust.

When King John died in October 1216, Queen Isabella's first act was to arrange the speedy coronation of her nine-year-old son Henry at Gloucester Cathedral. The following July, less than a year after his ascension to the throne, Isabella left Henry in the care of William Marshal, 1st Earl of Pembroke, and returned to France to assume control of her inheritance of Angouleme. She has been described as being vain, capricious, and troublesome, and could not reconcile herself to the necessary loss in rank that resulted after the death of her husband. She resented having to give precedence to women who were now of higher rank than she, a mere Dowager Queen and Countess of Angouleme. During the French invasion of England during the First Baron's War in May 1216, she actively conspire against King Louis of France, along with other disgruntled nobles who sought to create an English-backed confederacy that would unite the provinces of the south and west against the French king. In 1244, after the confederacy had failed and peace was made with King Louis, an assassination attempt was foiled. Under questioning the assailants confessed to having been in Isabella's pay. Alerted to the arrests, Isabella fled to Fontevraud Abbey and claimed sanctuary. She died there on May 31, 1246, and was first buried in the abbey's churchyard (as an act of repentance for her many misdeeds). Years later on a visit to Fontevraud Abbey, her son Henry III was shocked to find his mother buried outside of the abbey and ordered her remains moved inside and placed next those of Richard I.

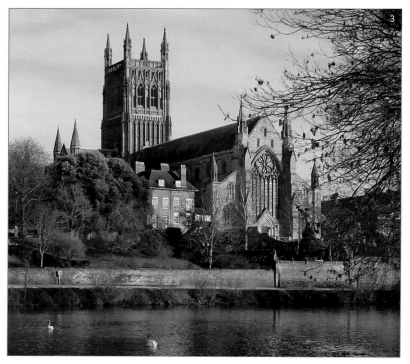

1. JOHN SIGNS THE MAGNA CARTA, from Cassel's History of England (1902).

2. NEWARK CASTLE, where King John died on October 18, 1216.

3. WORCESTER CATHEDRAL, where the remains of King John are interred.

4. TOMB OF KING JOHN at Worcester Cathedral.

5. Tomb effigy of Isabella of Angouleme (second wife of King John) at Fontevraud Abbey.

46

Henry III
(October 18, 1216 - November 16, 1272)

KING HENRY III, from an engraving by Thomas Kelly (1830).

BORN: November 13, 1207, at Winchester Palace

PARENTS: John and Isabella of Angouleme

CROWNED: October 28, 1216, at Gloucester Cathedral
and May 17, 1220, at Westminster Abbey

CONSORT: Eleanor of Provence

DIED: November 16, 1272, at Westminster Palace

BURIAL: Westminster Abbey

*"Qui non dat quod habet non accipit ille quod optat
(He who does not give what he has, does not receive what he wants).*
-Royal Motto of Henry III of England

Henry III was the eldest son of King John and Isabella of Angouleme. He was born on October 1, 1207, at Winchester Palace and ascended to the throne following the death of his unpopular father at the age of nine. The kingdom he inherited was in a state of anarchy and the young Henry was described as being a "pretty little knight" when crowned at Gloucester Cathedral on October 28, 1216. The highly capable William Marshall and Hubert de Burgh were appointed his guardian and co-regent. At the time of John's death, London and most of the channel ports were held by the French. In a popular move, Marshall announced his intention to rule by the terms of the Magna Carta. The French invaders were driven out and peace restored in England by 1217. In May 1219, William Marshall died, having served four generations of Plantagenet monarchs with great ability and the sole regency of England was left in the hands of Hubert de Burgh. Henry III was crowned for a second time in May 17, 1220, at Westminster Abbey.

Henry III could not have been less like his father in character, nor was he built in the usual Plantagenet mold. He was cultivated, aesthetic, petulant, and kind natured, but was weak and ineffectual.

In 1227, he reached adulthood and took over the reins of government. Hugh de Burgh was retained as his chief advisor. A contemporary stated of Henry III that "his mind seemed not to stand on a firm basis, for every sudden accident put him into passion." He was of middle height and like his father, inclined to be plump and had a drooping left eyelid that covered half of the eye, which rendered him a rather sinister appearance. On January 14, 1236, Henry married Eleanor of Provence at Canterbury Cathedral. She was the daughter of Raymond Berenger of Provence and Beatrice of Savoy. Like her mother, grandmother, and sisters, Eleanor was renowned for her beauty and strong will. She was not well liked by the people, but was completely devoted to her husband, and staunchly defended him. Together, she and Henry would have five children, including the future Edward I of England.

Eleanor of Provence, from *Biographical Sketches of the Queens of England* by Mary Howlitt (1866).

Henry reigned for more than half a century. Yet he had few of the attributes required of a medieval king. He lacked military prowess, was regarded as high handed and ineffectual, and he favored foreigners. By 1254, disaffection was rife among the nobles and Henry foolishly showered honors on his Queen's family, which increased their grievances. These unwise appointments coupled with Henry's pathological indecisiveness in government matters, produced political unrest. Because of this instability the nobles were forced to rebel. Henry relented and agreed to the Provisions of Oxford (1258); which provided that a council of fifteen would be appointed to help govern the country. It established a yearly parliament to monitor progress and basically abolished absolute monarchy. Henry's brother-in-law, the French-born Simon de Montfort (who was married to Henry's sister Eleanor) was elected to lead the council. Henry resented the intrusion of royal authority and ignored the Provision, reasserting his absolute power in 1261. The nobles again rebelled and, on May 14, 1264, at the hands of Simon de Montfort, Henry suffered a humiliating defeat and was captured at the Battle of Lewes. De Montfort and other magnates forced the king to acknowledge their demands. In August 1265, royal authority was reinstated, thanks to the military skill of Henry's son, Prince Edward at the Battle of Evesham. During the battle De Montfort was killed.

After Evensham, Prince Edward took an increasingly active role in government, leaving his father Henry III free to spend the remainder of his reign pursuing his interest in building and artistic patronage. His zeal and passion for the arts and architecture resulted in a vibrant cultural revival. Henry ordered many buildings to be reworked or newly constructed in the Gothic style. He personally oversaw the rebuilding of Westminster Abbey and a splendid new shrine for the saintly Edward the Confessor (whom Henry venerated). In 1269, the new abbey was re-consecrated, and the Confessor's body was reburied in a magnificent shrine.

Henry became ill at Bury St. Edmunds, where he suffered a stroke, and returned to Westminster Palace. On November 12, 1272, he died. Henry III was the first of the Plantagenet monarchs to be buried within Westminster Abbey. His body was temporarily laid to rest within the tomb of Edward the Confessor, while his own was being constructed (which lies to the left of the shrine). If nothing else, Henry III left an important architectural legacy to the country. Queen Eleanor remained in England after the death of her husband and helped raise her grandchildren. She died on June 24, 1291, at the convent of Amesbury, where a tomb was erected in her honor.

1. During the reign of Henry III, Westminster Abbey was rebuilt to house the Shrine of Edward the Confessor.

2. THE HOUSES OF PARLIAMENT were originally the Palace of Westminster, built in the 11th century. It was the primary residence of the kings of England until the 16th century. In 1834 a fire destroyed most of the original old palace and it was rebuilt. Henry III was born there in 1207 and died there in 1272.

3. TOMB OF HENRY III at Westminster Abbey.

4. AMESBURY ABBEY, the burial place of Eleanor of Provence.

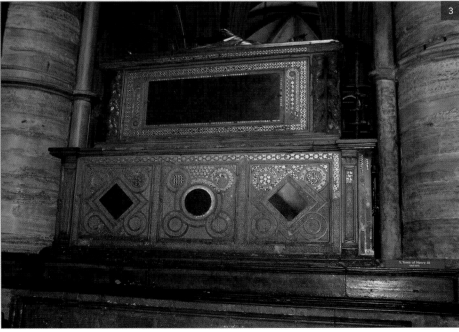

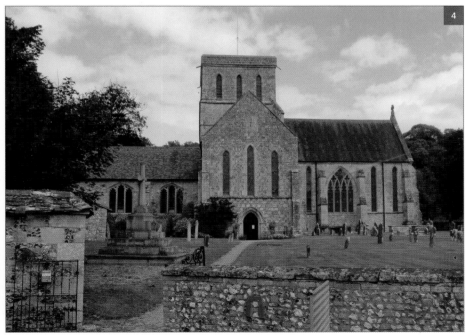

Edward I

(November 16, 1272 - July 7, 1307)

EDWARD I of England, from an engraving by Thomas Kelly (1830).

BORN: June 17, 1239, at Westminster Palace

PARENTS: Henry III and Eleanor of Provence

CROWNED: August 19, 1274, at Westminster Abbey

CONSORT: Eleanor of Castile and Margaret of France

DIED: July 7, 1307, at Burgh by Sands, Cumberland, England

BURIAL: Westminster Abbey

Often considered the greatest of the Plantagenet monarchs, Edward I was born on June 17, 1239, at the Royal Palace of Westminster. He was the eldest child of Henry III and Eleanor of Provence. He was named in honor of the Saxon King Edward the Confessor and gained the nickname "long shanks" because of his height. As a child, Edward was quite frail, and suffered from numerous life- threatening illnesses. On November 1, 1254, at the monastery of Las Huelas, Burgos, Spain, Edward (at the age of 15) married his second cousin once removed, the thirteen year old Eleanor of Castile. The union was a political move to settle a dispute over rights to Gascony. Eleanor was the beautiful dark-haired daughter of Ferdinand III of Castile and his second wife, Joan of Ponthieu, and the great- great granddaughter of Henry II and Eleanor of Aquitaine. Although their marriage was a political pact, Edward and Eleanor became deeply devoted to one another and she bore sixteen children, one of who was the future Edward II.

ELEANOR OF CASTILE, from a *Biographical Sketches of the Queens of England* by Mary Howlitt (1866).

As a young man, Edward joined the Eighth Crusade, taking his young wife Eleanor with him. He was in the Holy Land when he heard of his father's death, which affected him deeply. Edward returned to England and was crowned on August 19, 1274, at Westminster Abbey. Edward was far more suited to kingship than his father or grandfather and, thanks to him, the rebellion by Simon De Montfort was subdued. Edward's skill as a warrior and politician, and his strength of character and self-confidence, secured his position. In November 1290, Eleanor was accompanying Edward on a journey to Lincoln, when she developed a fever. Her condition worsened as they entered the village of Harby in Nottinghamshire. The royal entourage was forced to abandon the journey. The gravely ill queen was lodged in the house of Richard de Weston, where she died on the evening of the November 28, 1290. The normally stoic Edward was deeply affected by her death and he had memorial crosses (known as Eleanor's Crosses) erected at every spot where her body was halted during its journey back to London for burial. Today, only three of the original twelve crosses survive (Geddington, Northampton, and Waltham).

Eleanor's internal organs were buried in Lincoln Cathedral in a duplicate of the tomb at Westminster Abbey. The Lincoln tomb's original stone chest survives; its effigy was destroyed in the 17th century and replaced with a 19th-century copy. The queen's heart was taken with the body to London and was buried at the priory at Blackfriars. Eleanor's funeral took place at Westminster Abbey on December 17, 1290, and her remains were placed in a tomb near the high altar that had originally contained the body of Edward the Confessor and, more recently, that of Henry III, who was recently interred in a new tomb. Eleanor's body remained there until the completion of her own tomb (located to the right of Henry V's Chantry), which is adorned with a bronze effigy of the queen by William Torel. Nine years later, Edward married, seventeen year-old Margaret of France, daughter of Phillip III of France and Maria of Brabant. They were married at Canterbury Cathedral on September 8, 1299, and despite their sixty-year age difference, grew to be quite fond of one another.

Edward now turned his attention north to Scotland, where Alexander III of Scotland had recently died, leaving his young granddaughter, Margaret, known as the Maid of Norway, as heir to the Scottish throne. Edward proposed a marriage alliance between his son and Margaret by which he hoped to gain control of Scotland. However, Margaret died on her way to England, leaving the Scottish succession in dispute. Edward was asked by the Scottish nobles to arbitrate the claims of John de Balliol and Robert the Bruce. He chose Balliol, who was perceived as weak and could be manipulated.

By 1294, Edward faced problems on three fronts, Gascony, Wales, and Scotland. Once again Edward proved his strong leadership qualities when he quelled the Welsh in the spring of 1295, then returned to England and summoned the first Model Parliament to get agreement to campaign in Scotland and France. Infuriated by Scotland's alliance with France the previous year, Edward now wanted to conquer rather than just control the country. In March 1296, Edward led an army north to Berwick, where he stormed the inadequately defended border town and slaughtered its inhabitants. He then overran all of Scotland, and imprisoned John Balliol. The Stone of Scone, a venerated relic on which Scottish Kings had been crowned on since the Dark Ages, was taken to Westminster and was incorporated into the English coronation chair (it has only recently been returned to Scotland).

1. ELEANOR'S CROSS AT GEDDINGTON. Twelve crosses were erected by Edward I after the death of Eleanor to memorialize the locations where her body rested on its journey back to London. The Geddington Cross is one of only three such monuments to survive and is the best preserved.

2. TOMB OF ELEANOR OF CASTILE AT LINCOLN CATHEDRAL, which is purported to contain the queen's entrails.

3. MARGARET OF FRANCE, from *Biographical Sketches of the Queens of England* by Mary Howlitt (1866).

4. STIRLING BRIDGE with William Wallace monument in the background. Near here on September 11, 1297, Wallace defeated the forces of Edward I at the Battle of Stirling Bridge.

Edward then appointed three regents to rule Scotland: the Bishop of St. Andrews, Robert the Bruce, and John Comyn. Immediately the banner of Scottish resistance was taken up by William Wallace, who was both brave and a resourceful opponent. He routed the superior forces of Edward at Stirling Bridge September 11, 1297, and continued a guerilla war in the name of John Balliol that gained the support of the Scottish clans, but not the nobles. Wallace was defeated by Edward at the Battle of Falkirk on April 1, 1298. The spirited Wallace, unbroken, was later betrayed and captured. He was handed over to the English, tried for treason, and executed.

After Wallace's death, Robert the Bruce (following the murder of a rival claimant John Comyn) was crowned King of Scots. Abandoning conventional methods, Bruce tried to starve the English army out and made efforts to capture the English strongholds. Edward made his way north again to deal with the Scots and, in May 1307, was defeated at the Battle of Loudon Hill. Edward fell ill with a severe case of dysentery (most likely caused by cancer of the rectum) and died at Burgh on Sands in Cumberland on July 7, 1307. Apprehensive of his son's ability to continue his campaign in Scotland, he allegedly asked that his flesh be boiled from his bones, so that they could be carried with the army on every military campaign. He was instead buried his body at Westminster Abbey in a robe of imperial purple. Edward I's tomb at Westminster Abbey lies to the left of Edward the Confessor's Shrine and is topped with a bronze effigy. His marker reads "Here lies Edward I, the Hammer of the Scots."

Following Edward I's death, Robert the Bruce and the Scottish army soundly defeated the English led by Edward II at Bannockburn on June 23-24, 1314. This victory was but a first step in a ten year odyssey that finally led to full Scottish independence. Edward I's twenty-six year old widow, Margaret of France, never remarried and died on February 14, 1318, at Marlborough Castle. Nothing remains of the castle today, but legend states that it is the final resting place of Merlin from the King Arthur legend. Margaret was buried at Greyfriars Church in Newgate. The church was destroyed in the Great London Fire of 1666, was rebuilt, only to be destroyed again during the Blitz of 1940. Today, the ruins are a garden and the location of Margaret's grave is unknown and presumed destroyed.

1. MONUMENT AT BURGH BY SANDS, that marks the location where Edward I died in 1307.

2. TOMB OF EDWARD I at Westminster Abbey.

3. RUINS OF GREYFRIARS CHURCH in Newgate, where the remains of Margaret of France, Isabella of France, and Joan of Scotland were interred.

Edward II
(July 7, 1307 - January 25, 1327)

BORN: April 25, 1284, at Caernarfon Castle in Wales

PARENTS: Edward I and Eleanor of Castile

CROWNED: February 25, 1308, at Westminster Abbey

CONSORT: Isabella of France

DIED: September 21, 1327, at Berkeley Castle in Gloucester

BURIAL: Gloucester Cathedral

"Seldom did a son contrast so strangely with his father as did Edward of Carnarvon with Edward the Hammer of the Scots. The mighty warrior and statesman begot a shiftless, thriftless craven."

-Charles William Chadwick Oman
from his book, A History of England, 1895.

Edward II was like his father only in as much as he was tall and good looking. He had none of Edward I's leadership qualities and he preferred artistic and aesthetic pursuits to military campaigns and detail of government. Having inherited a stable and prosperous kingdom, he allowed it to descend into near anarchy. He showed open contempt for the wishes of his barons and heaped unwarranted riches on unsuitable favorites. Edward II was incompetent both militarily and administratively. His kingship would be defined by anarchy, betrayal, abdication, and finally by gruesome death.

Edward II was born on April 25, 1284, at Caernarfon Castle in Wales, the son of Edward I and Eleanor of Castile. He lacked the royal dignity of his father and failed miserably as king. On his deathbed, Edward I wished his son to continue his campaign against the Scots, who made one halfhearted foray before retreating to London. He was crowned at Westminster Abbey on February 25, 1308. Immediately he raised the resentment of the nobility by lavishing money and honors upon his unpopular male favorites. These and other unwise decisions would one day cost him his throne and life. Edward I's dream of a unified Britain quickly disintegrated under his weak son's rule. Rebellion among the English nobility opened the way for Robert the Bruce to re-conquer much of Scotland. In 1314, Bruce defeated English forces at the Battle of Bannockburn, which ensured Scottish independence.

Edward married Isabella of France on January 25, 1303, at Boulogne-Sur-Mer. She was the daughter of Philip IV of France and Joan I of Navarre. At the time of her marriage, Isabella was only twelve years old. She was described by contemporary chroniclers as being "the beauty of all beauties," which led to her nickname as Isabella the Fair. Throughout her life, she was noted as being both charming and diplomatic. She was particularly good at convincing people to follow her courses of action. Edward's preference for surrounding himself with unsuitable cronies and outsiders harkened back to the troubled reign of Henry III. The most infamous of his favorites was Piers Gaveston, a young man who was exiled by Edward I for his undue influence over the Prince of Wales and, most likely, Edward II's homosexual lover. The arrogant and immoral Gaveston was recalled from exile by Edward II and exerted undue influence over the new king. This alienated many leading nobles, who rallied in opposition behind the king's cousin, Thomas of Lancaster and Roger

(TOP) CAERNARFON CASTLE in Wales was the birthplace of Edward II.

(BOTTOM) ISABELLA OF FRANCE, from *Biographical Sketches of the Queens of England* by Mary Howlitt (1866).

de Mortimer. The Parliaments of 1310 and 1311 imposed restrictions on Edward's power and exiled Gaveston. A year later, Gaveston was back and led a revolt to restore Edward's powers. The rebellion was defeated and Gaveston was executed. Edward II was forced to accept the previous restriction on his rule as well as additional limitations. Although the Earl of Lancaster shared the responsibilities of governing with Edward, the king came under the influence of yet another contemptible favorite, Hugh Despenser, and his son. In 1322, Edward showed a rare display of resolve and gathered an army to meet Lancaster at the Battle of Boroughbridge in Yorkshire. Edward prevailed, Lancaster was executed, and Roger Mortimer was imprisoned at the Tower of London. Edward II and the Despensers were now back in power.

In late 1324, Edward sent Queen Isabella to France to negotiate peace terms over disputed territory in Gascony. She arrived in France in March 1325. During this period Roger Mortimer escaped from the Tower of London and arrived in France. He and Isabella then pursued a very open romance.

Isabella also persuaded Edward to send their young son, the future Edward III to France. This proved a gross tactical error, and helped to bring about the ruin of both Edward II and the Despensers, as Isabella now had the heir to the throne with her and declared that she would not return to England unless the Despensers were removed from power.

Isabella and Mortimer then began to plot an invasion of England to removed Edward from power. They raised money for a mercenary army that landed in England in September 1326. Edward was not very impressed by this small army and underestimated their resolve. He attempted raise an army of his own, but found it hard to find anyone who would fight against Mortimer and the Queen. Henry of Lancaster, showed his loyalties by raising an army, seizing a cache of treasure from Leicester Abbey, and marching south to join Mortimer. The invasion soon had too much momentum to be stopped. As a result, the army of the king failed to emerge and both Edward and the Despensers were forced to abandon London. The king first took refuge in Gloucester and then fled to South Wales in order to make a defense in Despenser's homelands. However, Edward was unable to rally an army, and on October 31, 1326, was abandoned by most of his servants, leaving him with only Hugh Despenser the Younger and a handful of others. Meanwhile, Hugh Despenser the Elder was captured and summarily executed for encouraging the illegal government of Edward and enriching himself at the expense of the kingdom.

Henry of Lancaster was dispatched by Mortimer to Wales to capture both Edward and the young Despenser. On November 16, 1326, the king and his remaining entourage were captured in open country near Tonyrefail. Hugh Despenser, the Younger was sent to Isabella at Hereford, while Edward was taken to Kenilworth. Despenser (the Younger) was tried and executed. On November 24, 1326, a huge crowd witnessed his brutal death, where he was stripped naked, hung, castrated, disemboweled, and drawn and quartered.

With Edward now imprisoned, Mortimer and Isabella faced the problem of what to do with him. The simplest solution would be execution: his titles would then pass to her son, whom Isabella could control. Execution would require the king to be tried and convicted of treason: and while most nobles agreed that Edward had failed to show due attention to his country, several argued that, appointed by God, the king could not be legally executed. It was initially decided that Edward would be imprisoned for life. However, the fact remained that the legality of power still lay with the king. Isabella had been given the Great Seal and was using it to rule in the names of her son, nonetheless, these actions were illegal and could, at any moment, be challenged. In these circumstances, Parliament chose to act as an authority above the king. Representatives were summoned and debates began. The Archbishop of York and others declared themselves fearful of the London mob and loyal to Roger de Mortimer. Others wanted Edward to personally speak in Parliament and abdicate, rather than be deposed. Mortimer called a secret meeting of the most powerful nobles at which it was unanimously agreed to remove Edward. Parliament eventually agreed to remove the king but demanded that the king be given an opportunity to abdicate rather than be forcefully removed.

On January 20, 1327, Edward II was informed at Kenilworth Castle of the charges brought against him: gross incompetence; allowing others to influence his governance to the detriment of the kingdom; pursuing occupations unbecoming a monarch; losing territory in Scotland, Gascony, and Ireland through failure of effective control; damaging the Church and imprisoning its representatives; allowing nobles to be disinherited, imprisoned, and executed; failing to ensure fair justice; and fleeing in the company of

a notorious enemy of the realm, leaving without an effective government, and thereby losing the faith and trust of his people. He was shocked by this judgment and wept openly while it was read, he was offered a choice: abdicate in favor of his son or relinquish the throne to someone else, presumably, Roger Mortimer, Edward chose to abdicate in favor of his son. The king's abdication was announced on January 24, 1327, and the following day fourteen year old, Edward III was proclaimed king, with his mother Queen Isabella and Mortimer named as regents. Meanwhile, Edward II remained a prisoner.

The government of Isabella and Mortimer was so precarious that they dared not leave the deposed king in the hands of their political enemies. Edward was taken from Kenilworth Castle to Berkeley castle in Gloucester and on September 21, 1327, was murdered on the orders of Isabella and Mortimer. The popular story that the king was assassinated by having a hot poker thrust into his bowel (after starvation failed) has no basis in contemporary accounts. The closest chronicler to the scene stated that it was "popularly rumored" that Edward had been suffocated. Most chronicles did not offer a cause of death, but all agree that he was most likely murdered. A public funeral was held for the king, which was attended by Isabella, after which Edward's body was interred at Gloucester Cathedral. Many years later, an elaborate tomb was erected by his son, Edward III.

Following the public announcement of the king's death, the regency of Isabella and Mortimer did not last long. They made peace with the Scots in the Treaty of Northampton, but this move was highly unpopular. Consequently, when Edward III came of age in 1330, one of his first acts was to have Roger Mortimer arrested for treason and executed. His mother was spared and given a generous allowance, but required to retire from public life. As the years went by, Isabella doted on her grandchildren, including Edward, the Prince of Wales (known as Edward of Woodstock and later as the Black Prince), and became increasingly interested in religion. She remained, however, a prominent member of her son's court. On August 22, 1358, she died at Castle Rising in Norfolk. Her body was returned to London and buried at Greyfriars Church in Newgate. At her own request, she was buried wearing her wedding dress and with Edward II's heart. At the time, the church was already the burial spot of Margaret of France, and it was where Queen Joan of Scotland would eventually be buried, as would Edward III's daughter Isabella. The Dowager Queen's tomb would become a treasured burial and pilgrimage site for Plantagenet women. The church was destroyed during the Blitz of 1940 and all of the graves, including Isabella's, were lost. Although her reputation has been almost universally maligned, her reign was in many ways a success. She helped dispose of a dreadful king and replaced him with an exceptional one. She has been blamed for starting the Hundred Years War, but it was not her vanity that perpetuated it. Isabella was a strong willed and unbelievably immoral woman, but in the end was a rather magnificent and effective queen.

1. BERKELEY CASTLE, where Edward II was murdered in 1327.

2. GLOUCESTER CATHEDRAL.

3. TOMB OF EDWARD II at Gloucester Cathedral.

4. CASTLE RISING, Norfolk, where Isabella of France died on August 22, 1358.

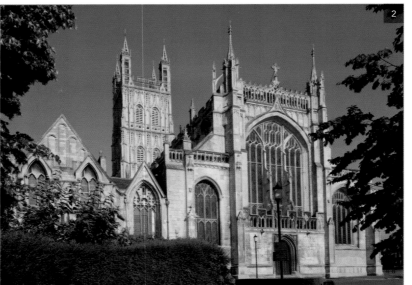

Edward III

(February 1, 1327 - June 21, 1377)

EDWARD III OF ENGLAND, from a 19th century engraving.

BORN: November 13, 1312, at Windsor Castle

PARENTS: Edward II of England and Isabella of France

CROWNED: February 1, 1327, at Westminster Abbey

CONSORT: Philippa of Hainault

DIED: June 21, 1377, at Sheen Palace in Surrey

BURIAL: Westminster Abbey

"Let the boy win his spurs." -Edward III of England

speaking of his son Edward the Black Prince's military victory over the French at the Battle of Crecy in 1346

The fifty-year reign of Edward III saw the restoration of good relations with the English barons, who flocked to the colorful and cultured court with renewed respect for the monarchy. Governmental reforms affirmed the power of the emerging middle class in Parliament while placing the power of the nobility into the hands a few. Chivalric code reached an apex in English society, but only masked the greed and ambition of Edward and his barons. Edward and his son Edward, Prince of Wales, expanded England's holdings in France to the extent that they nearly matched those of the great Angevin King Henry II. However, Edward outlived his successes and, by the time of his death, plague had ravaged his kingdom and most of his French territories were lost. The enormous cost of his campaigns made him unpopular and indebted. Nevertheless, Edward III is remembered as one of England's greatest warrior kings.

PHILIPPA OF HAINAULT, from *Biographical Sketches of the Queens of England* by Mary Howlitt (1866).

He was born on November 13, 1312, at Windsor Castle, the oldest child of Edward II and Isabella of France. The forced abdication of his father placed him on the throne of England at the age of fourteen. He was crowned on February 1, 1327, at Westminster Abbey and the first three years of his reign saw his mother and her lover, Roger de Mortimer, rule as regents. In 1330, eighteen year-old Edward instigated a palace revolt and assumed control of the government. He had Mortimer executed for treason and Isabella was exiled briefly from court. He was now free to rule as he pleased with the full support of the nobility. Among his many interests were war, culture, pageantry, women, and high living.

At the age of fourteen Edward had been betrothed to Philippa of Hainault, who was the daughter of William of Hainaut and Joan of Valois (a granddaughter of Philip II of France). Their marriage was a political ploy devised by Queen Isabella in exchange for assistance from the Count in her plan to overthrow Edward II. Because Edward and Philippa were second cousins, a Papal dispensation was required and eventually approved. They were married on January 24, 1328, at York, eleven months after Edward III had been crowned. Unlike many of her predecessors, Philippa did not alienate the English people by retaining her foreign entourage in court. She was crowned queen on March 4, 1330, at Westminster Abbey, and at the time was six months pregnant with her first child. She gave birth to a son, Prince Edward the following June just nine days before her sixteenth birthday. She and Edward III would have nine children.

War occupied the largest parts of Edward III's reign, first in Scotland and then in France, where his Gascony lands had been seized by the French throne. Through his mother, Isabella, Edward was a rival claimant for the French throne. In November 1337, Edward stated his intention to fight for his right to the French crown, and the ensuing conflict was known as the Hundred Years War. Early attempts to overcome the French were inconclusive, partly because Philip VI of France refused to fight. English fortunes changed in 1345 when they successfully regained territory in Gascony. Bolstered by this success, Edward launched a major invasion of Normandy in July 1346, and on August 26, 1346, Edward's outnumbered forces (estimated at 15,000) under the leadership of his son Prince Edward soundly defeated the superior forces of Philip VI (estimated at 100,000) at the Battle of Crecy. The outnumbered English used superior weaponry and tactics, such as the long bow to decimate the French troops. This battle is seen by many historians as the beginning of the end of classic chivalry.

During the onslaught of the Black Death in 1348-1350, military campaigning ceased. In 1356, active military excursions were resumed, and the Prince of Wales routed the French cavalry at Poitiers and captured the French king. In 1359, the Prince Edward laid siege to Paris and forced a negotiated peace, which culminated with the Treaty of Bretigny (1360). This treaty ceded large areas of northern and western France to the English. Despite Edward's early successes both at home and abroad, England's general prosperity remained muddled and the influence of the Church decreased, spearheaded by an ecclesiastical reform movement that challenged church exploitation by both the king and the pope. During 1348-1350, bubonic plague (the Black Death) ravaged the populations of Europe killing an estimated 100 million people and the English economy was struck hard by the ensuing rise in prices and wages. This, coupled with failed military excursions in France, caused excessive taxation and eroded Edward's popular support. On August 15, 1369, Philippa of Hainault died from kidney failure at Windsor Castle. She was given a state funeral and interred at Westminster Abbey. Her tomb was placed on the south side of the Chapel of Edward the Confessor. After her death, Edward took the deceitful Alice Perrers as his mistress. With Edward in his declining years and Prince Edward in poor health, Perrers and William Latimer (the chamberlain of the household) dominated the court with the support of John of Gaunt (Edward III's third son).

Edward, Prince of Wales and heir to the English throne died on June 8, 1376, from a long illness (historically suspected to be cancer). He was an exceptional military leader, his victories over the French at Crecy and Poitiers made him very popular during his life. Although Edward has in later years often been referred to as the Black Prince, there is no record of this name being used during his lifetime and instead was known as Edward of Woodstock, after his place of birth. His son Richard II would ascend to the throne of England following the death of his grandfather, Edward III. Prince Edward was buried at Canterbury Cathedral behind the choir section, near the shrine to Thomas Becket.

Edward III spent the last remaining years of his life grieving for his son and believed that his death was a punishment for usurping his father's (Edward II) crown. He died on June 21, 1377, at Sheen Palace (later known as Richmond Palace) from a stroke. He was buried next to Queen Philippa at Westminster Abbey, to the right of the Shrine of Edward the Confessor.

Tomb of the Black Prince at Canterbury Cathedral.

Tomb of Edward III at Westminster Abbey.

Richard II
(June 22, 1377 - September 30, 1399)

BORN: January 6, 1367, at the Abbey of
St. Andrew in Bordeaux

PARENTS: Edward, Prince of Wales (the Black Prince)
and Joan of Kent

CROWNED: July 16, 1377, at Westminster Abbey

CONSORT: Anne of Bohemia and Isabella of Valois

DIED: February 14, 1400, at Pontefract Castle

BURIED: Westminster Abbey

The reign of Richard II was a study in contradictions. He was a well educated, shrewd, and supremely cultured monarch, and a great patron of the arts, but he was also an extravagant, dogmatic, and tyrannical ruler who took little notice of his barons' interests and avoided Parliament. Richard's unshakable belief in absolute royal power and his inability to gain the loyalty of his most powerful barons inevitably led to rebellion. In 1399, Richard II was deposed, imprisoned, and then, eventually, starved to death. He was the last of the main line Plantagenet monarchs and was born on January 6, 1367, at the Abbey of St. Andrew in Bordeaux, France. He was the son of Edward the Black Prince, and Joan "the Fair Maid" of Kent. Richard was only ten years old when he ascended to the throne of England following the death of his grandfather Edward III. He was crowned on July 16, 1377, at Westminster Abbey. During the first years of his reign, England was led by a council under the control of his uncle, John of Gaunt. Many members of Parliament feared that John of Gaunt would usurp his nephew's crown and for this reason, the young king was quickly invested with the princedom of Wales and his father's other titles.

In 1382, at the age of fifteen, Richard married Anne of Bohemia, the daughter of Holy Roman Emperor, Charles IV, and Elizabeth of Pomerania. Their union was arranged to help elevate the Great Schism in the Papacy that had resulted in two rival popes. Pope Urban VI sanctioned the marriage between Richard and Anne, in an attempt to create an alliance against the French and their preferred pope, Clement VII. The marriage arrangement was unpopular with many members of the nobility and Parliament. Although Richard had been offered the betrothal of Caterina Visconti, the daughter of Bernabo Visconti of Milan (who had a large dowry), he chose Anne, who brought no financial benefit. Anne and Richard were married at Westminster Abbey on January 20, 1382, and this was the last such event to place there for the next 537 years.

Richard's rule over England came during a period of ever changing monarchial restrictions and economic hardships caused by the Black Death. In 1381, Wat Tyler led the Peasants' Revolt against the introduction of the oppressive poll tax. Tyler led a mixed group of peasants, craftsmen and tradesmen, in taking Canterbury, before advancing on London. He entered the city of London at the head of a group estimated at over 50,000. After crossing London Bridge without resistance, the rebels gained entry to the Tower of London and captured Simon Sudbury, the unpopular Archbishop of Canterbury, and several of his followers. The king then agreed to meet the rebel leaders and address their grievances. Richard and Tyler met at Smithfield, where the later decided to ride out alone and speak with the King. The unarmed Tyler was suddenly attacked without warning and killed by members of Richard's entourage. This threw the people into a panic and, not being organized as a military force, they fled for their lives, ending the Peasants' Revolt. The fact that Richard was only fourteen at the time enhanced his authority immensely and reinforced his conviction that he was God's representative on earth and that his right to rule was absolute.

This attitude infuriated the nobles, who were dismayed at the king's appointment of favorites, including Robert de Vere and others, as his closest advisors. Opposition to Richard's government reached its apex in 1386, when, without Parliaments consent, Robert de Vere was appointed Regent of Ireland. Five nobles including the king's uncle, Thomas of Gloucester, and his cousin, Henry Bolingbroke (the son of John of Gaunt), formed a council known as the Lords Appellants. They presided over the "Merciless Parliament" of 1368, and effectively seized control of England from Richard and his cronies. When Richard reached adulthood in 1389, he was able to assume direct rule and chose his own advisors.

On June 7, 1394, Anne of Bohemia died at Sheen Priory and her death from plague was a devastating blow to Richard. Although Anne was originally disliked by the chroniclers, there is some evidence that she became more popular with time. She was known to have been a very kind person and was well known for her tireless attempts to intercede on behalf of the people, procuring pardons for people in the Peasants' Revolt of 1381 and numerous other wrongdoers. She never fulfilled the traditional duties of queens; in particular, she did not bear children. This is emphasized in her epitaph, whereby she is mentioned as having been kind to "pregnant women." One chronicler said, "this queen, although she did not bear any children, was still held to have contributed to the glory and wealth of the realm, as far as she was able." Nevertheless, the fact that her popular legacy seems to have been that she was "Good Queen Anne" seems to suggest that this lack of children was unimportant to many contemporaries. Anne is buried at Westminster Abbey (to be joined there later by Richard II). Their joint tomb, now damaged, once showed them clasping hands. The inscription on her tomb describes her as "beauteous in body and her face was gentle and pretty." When her tomb was opened in 1871, it was discovered that many of her bones had been stolen via a hole in the side of the casket. On October 31, 1396, two years after Anne's death, Richard married Isabella of Valois. She was only six years old at the time and the daughter of Charles VI of France. Although the union was political, Richard and Isabella developed a mutually respectful relationship.

In the summer of 1397, the five former Lords Appellants were arrested and executed or exiled. One of those was Henry Bolingbroke, the future Henry IV. Free from restraint, Richard lost all vestiges of wisdom and became a paranoid, power-crazed despot. When John of Gaunt died on February 3, 1399, at Leicester Castle, Richard seized his lands. When Richard left for Ireland to quell a revolt, Henry Bolingbroke saw a chance to return to England, reclaim his lost lands and seize the throne. Allegiance to Richard almost entirely collapsed and, on August 19, 1399, at Flint Castle, Richard was forced to surrender to Bolingbroke and was then imprisoned at the Tower of London.

Bolingbroke was fully determined to take the throne, but presenting a justification for this action proved a dilemma. It was argued that Richard, through his tyranny and misgovernment, had rendered himself unworthy of being king. However, Henry was not next in the line to the throne; the heir presumptive was Edmund Mortimer, Earl of March, who descended from Edward II's second son, Lionel of Antwerp. The problem was solved by emphasizing Henry's descent in a direct male line, whereas Mortimer's was through his grandmother. The official account of events claims that Richard voluntarily agreed to abdicate his crown to Henry on September 29, 1399. Although this was most likely not the case, the parliament that convened the next day, accepted Richard's abdication and Henry was crowned king two weeks later.

The exact course of Richard's life after his abdication is unclear; he remained in the Tower of London until the later part of 1399, when he was taken to Pontefract Castle. Although Bolingbroke might have been willing to let him live, this all changed when it was revealed that the earls of Huntingdon, Kent, Somerset, and Rutland, and Thomas Despenser (all now demoted from the ranks they had been given by Richard) were planning to assassinate Henry and restore Richard to the throne, in what became known as the Epiphany Rising Revolt. Although averted, the plot highlighted the danger of allowing Richard to live and it is believed that the former king starved to death (either by choice or on purpose) on or around February 14, 1400. Richard's body was taken from Pontefract Castle and displayed at Old St. Paul's Cathedral to dispel any rumors that he might be alive and then buried at All Saints Church in Langley.

Even with these precautions, rumors that Richard was still alive persisted for decades after his death. In 1413, Henry V, in an effort both to atone for his father's act and to silence the rumors of Richard's survival, decided to have the body of Richard II removed from King's Langley Church to Westminster Abbey. There Richard was placed in a tomb next to his wife, Anne of Bohemia. The death of Richard II brought an end to the direct Plantagenet line and with the ascent of Henry IV to the throne, the Lancastrian branch began. After Richard's death, Queen Isabella was ordered by Henry IV to marry his son the future Henry V of England, but Isabella refused to have anything to do with the prince and ignored the demands. She returned to France and married her cousin Charles, Duke of Orleans. On September 13, 1409, she died while in childbirth. Isabella was buried at the Abbey of St. Laumer in Blois, France. In 1624, her tomb was opened and the body was found to be intact. The body had been wrapped in bands of linen plated with silver. Her remains were then transferred to the Church of the Celestines in Paris and subsequently destroyed during the French Revolution.

1. ISABELLA OF VALOIS, from *Biographical Sketches of the Queens of England* by Mary Howlitt (1866).

2. RUINS OF PONTEFRACT CASTLE, where Richard II died on February 14, 1400.

3. IN THE FOREGROUND, AT THE LEFT IS THE TOMB OF WILLIAM DE VALENCE, Earl of Pembroke (half-brother of Henry III), and at the right is the tomb of John of Ethan, Earl of Cornwall (second son of Edward II); In the background, at the left is the tomb of Richard II and Anne of Bohemia, in the center is the tomb of Edward III, and at the right is the tomb of Philippa of Hainault.

Chapter Four

The House of Lancaster and York (1399-1485)

he eighty-six years between the disposition of Richard II in 1399 and the death of Richard III in 1485 at Bosworth Field is one of the most chaotic periods in British history. Because Henry IV was also the claimant to the duchy of Lancaster, his son (Henry V) and grandson (Henry VI) are known as the monarchs of the House of Lancaster. In 1461, the House of Lancaster was deposed by Edward IV, son of Richard of York, whose dynasty is referred to as the House of York. The epic struggles between the Lancasters and Yorks, known as the Wars of the Roses, caused tremendous bitterness and bloodshed. In all likelihood, these events were no different than the civil wars of Stephen and Matilda and Henry II and his sons, but because there was no clear rule about succession, it became force rather than right that determined who would wear the crown.

Henry IV

(September 30, 1399 - March 20, 1413)

HENRY IV of England, from an engraving by Thomas Kelly (1830).

BORN: April 3, 1366, at Bolingbroke Castle
in Lincolnshire

PARENTS: John of Gaunt and Blanche of Lancaster

CROWNED: October 13, 1399, at Westminster Abbey

CONSORT: Mary de Bohun and Joan of Navarre

DIED: March 20, 1413, at Westminster Abbey

BURIAL: Canterbury Cathedral

The usurping of the throne by Henry Bolingbroke continued the Plantagenet rule, but began the Lancastrian branch. However, the questionable legitimacy of Henry's incumbency not only tarnished this able king's reign, but rocked the firmly established principal of inherited kingship, thereby undermining the stability that strict rules of succession had helped to ensure since the early 13th century. The consequences of this only became apparent when the madness of Bolingbroke's grandson, Henry VI, opened up a window of opportunity for the York Dynasty to stake a claim. So began the three decades of internecine fighting called the Wars of the Roses, which ended with the demise of the Plantagenet line and the succession of the House of Tudor.

Henry IV was born at Bolingbroke Castle on April 3, 1366, and was the oldest son of John of Gaunt and Blanche of Lancaster. Henry was intelligent, literate, cultured, politically astute, and a master warrior, and came to the throne by the simple expedient of seizing it from his first cousin Richard II. His claim to the throne was weak, but he was undoubtedly better equipped for kingship than his predecessor. In his youth Henry had all the vigor, charm, and accomplishments of the most successful of his Plantagenet ancestors. However, the incessant opposition to his rule, the extreme costs of the campaign to subdue his opponents, and his own remorse for his treatment of Richard II took their toll on Henry's health. He left his kingdom and the succession secure, but he died a wasted, broken man. On July 27, 1380 at Arundel Castle, Henry married Mary de Bohun, she was the daughter of Humphrey de Bohun, Earl of Hereford and Joan Fitzalan. They would have seven children (one of which was the future Henry V). Mary died on June 4, 1394, at Peterborough Castle, while giving birth to daughter Philippa and was buried at the Church of St. Mary de Castro in Leicester.

The very nature of Henry's usurpation of Richard dictated the circumstances of his reign and incessant rebellion became the order of the day. Henry was crowned on October 13, 1399, at Westminster Abbey and almost immediately, supporters of Richard revolted. In Wales, an uprising lasted until 1408; the Scots waged continual warfare throughout his reign; the powerful families of Percy and Mortimer (the latter possessing a stronger claim to the throne than Henry) rebelled from 1403 to 1408. Two political blunders in the latter years of Henry's reign diminished his support even further. First, his marriage to Joan of Navarre was highly unpopular. She was the daughter of King Charles II of Navarre and Joan of France. Joan became close friends with Henry while he resided at the Bretagne court during his banishment from England. They were married in 1403 and had no children, but she is recorded as having had a good relationship with Henry's children from his first marriage, often taking the side of the future Henry V in his quarrels with his

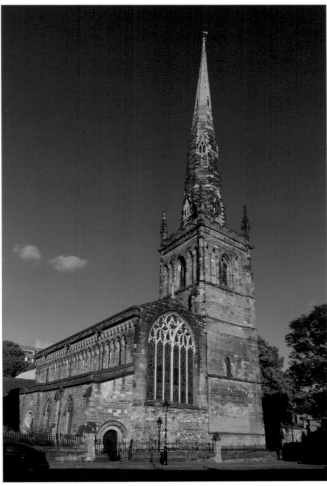

father. Nevertheless, during the reign of her stepson, Henry V, she was accused of using witchcraft to try to poison him and was imprisoned for several years in Pevensey Castle in Sussex, after which she lived quietly through Henry V's reign and into that of his son, Henry VI. She died on June 10, 1437, at Havering Palace in London and was buried at Canterbury Cathedral.

The second political blunder was the cost of putting down the countless rebellions that dogged his reign. Parliament used this opportunity to expand its powers in 1401, which secured recognition of freedom of debate and freedom from arrest for dissenting opinions. Another problem was that the Protestant movement founded by John Wycliffe (during the reign of Edward III) was gaining momentum and frightened both secular and clerical landowners, which led to the first anti-heresy statutes in 1401.

The later years of Henry's reign were marked by serious health problems, a guilty conscience, and the misery of living in the shadow of his more popular son, the future Henry V. He had a disfiguring skin disease and medical historians have long debated the nature of this affliction, which might have been leprosy or psoriasis. He also suffered from acute attacks of epilepsy and cardiovascular disease. Some chroniclers felt that he was struck with these illnesses as divine retribution for usurping the throne.

A prophecy foretold years prior stated that Henry would die in Jerusalem and the king took this to literally mean the Holy Land. He was taken ill at Westminster Abbey, while visiting the Shrine of Edward the Confessor in preparation for this journey to the Holy Land. On March 20, 1413, Henry IV died in the Jerusalem Chamber at Westminster Abbey. It was unusual in this period for a King of England not to be buried at Westminster Abbey, but Henry IV was instead interred at Canterbury Cathedral. His tomb and that of his second wife, Joan of Navarre are located on the north side of what is now the Trinity Chapel, near to the shrine of Thomas Becket. No other monarchs are buried in the cathedral, although his uncle, Edward, the Black Prince is buried on the opposite side of the chapel.

(TOP) RUINS OF BOLINGBROKE CASTLE, where Henry IV was born.

(BOTTOM) ST. MARY DE CASTRO CHURCH IN LEICESTER, where Mary of Bohun was buried.

1. JOAN OF NAVARRE, from *Biographical Sketches of the Queens of England by Mary Howlitt (1866)*.

2. CANTERBURY CATHEDRAL, where King Henry IV of England and Joan of Navarre are buried.

3. TOMB OF HENRY IV & JOAN OF NAVARRE.

4. TOMB EFFIGIES of Henry IV and Joan of Navarre at Canterbury Cathedral.

Henry V
(March 21, 1413 - August 31, 1422)

Born: September 16, 1387, at Monmouth Castle in Wales

Parents: Henry IV and Mary de Bohun

Crowned: April 6, 1413, at Westminster Abbey

Consort: Catherine of Valois

Died: August 31, 1422, at Chateau de Vincennes, France

Burial: Westminster Abbey

Henry of Monmouth, son of Henry IV was the last of the great warrior kings of the Middle Ages. In his short reign, he expanded England's territory in France, became the heir to the French throne, and led his army to victory in one of the most iconic victories in English history. He was a skillful military leader, matched only by his abilities as an administrator and politician. Despite requiring enormous sums for his military campaigns, he managed to hold the support of the barons and Parliament throughout his reign. Premature death robbed him of the chance to wear the crown of France, but he passed straight into legend as one of England's most heroic leaders.

Henry V was born on September 16, 1386, at Monmouth Castle, Wales, and was the eldest son of Henry IV and Mary de Bohun. Henry was an accomplished soldier and, at age fourteen, he fought and defeated the Welsh forces of Owen Glendower; at age sixteen, he commanded his father's forces at the Battle of Shrewsbury; and shortly after his accession to the throne put down a major uprising and an assassination plot by nobles still loyal to Richard II. Following the death of his father in March 1413, young Henry ascended to the throne. He was crowned on April 9, 1413, at Westminster Abbey.

Ruins of Monmouth Castle in Wales, where Henry V was born on September 16, 1386.

Catherine of Valois, from *Biographical Sketches of the Queens of England* by Mary Howlitt (1866).

In 1415, he proposed marriage between himself and Catherine of Valois, the daughter of Charles VI of France. As dowry he demanded the return of the old Plantagenet lands of Normandy and Anjou. Charles refused and Henry declared war, opening yet another chapter in the Hundred Years War. The French war served two purposes, first it was to gain lands lost in previous battles and second to focus attention away from any of his cousin's royal ambitions. Henry possessed a masterful military mind and defeated the French at the Battle of Agincourt on October 25, 1415. Despite being exhausted, outnumbered, and malnourished, Henry led his army to a decisive victory over the French. It is often argued that the French army was bogged down in the muddy battlefield, soaked from the previous night of heavy rain, and this hindered their advance, allowing them to be sitting targets for the flanking English and Welsh archers. Nevertheless, the victory is seen as Henry's greatest victory, ranking alongside Crecy and Poitiers as the greatest in English history.

Following the victory at Angincourt, Henry accelerated the war to a much larger scale. Lower Normandy was quickly conquered and Rouen was cut off from Paris. The siege of Rouen cast a dark shadow on Henry's reputation. The French commanders, knowing that they did not have the food provisions to sustain everyone, forced the woman and children out of the city. They unwisely believed that Henry would allow them to pass· through the battle lines unmolested, however, Henry refused to allow them to pass and they were left to starve in the ditches surrounding the town. In January 1419, Rouen fell and, by August, the English were outside the walls of Paris. After six months of negotiation, the Treaty of Troyes recognized Henry as the heir to the French throne. On June 2, 1420, he married Catherine of Valois. They would have only one child, the future Henry VI, who was born while his father was on campaign in France.

On June 10, 1421, Henry sailed back to France for what would be his last military campaign. Prematurely aged from many years of warfare, he became seriously ill and died on August 31, 1422, at the Chateau de Vincennes, near Paris. The cause of death was most likely dysentery, which he had contacted during the siege of Meaux. He died never having seen his young son and just prior to his death, named his brother John, Duke of Beford, as regent of France, and Humphrey, Duke of Gloucester, Lord Protector of England. The sickly Charles VI of France, to whom he had been named heir, survived Henry by only six weeks. Henry V's body was brought back to London with great pageantry for burial at Westminster Abbey, where he had directed a chantry chapel be built over his remains. It is located at the eastern end of Edward the Confessor's Chapel and was completed around 1431. The translated inscription on Henry's tomb reads; "Henry V, hammer of the Gauls, lies here. Henry was put in the grave 1422. Virtue conquers all."

Catherine of Valois was not quite twenty-one when Henry V died. Her father Charles VI of France died a couple of months later, making the young Henry VI, King of England and occupied northern France. However, Catherine was still young and deemed marriageable, which was point of concern for the Duke of Gloucester. Rumors swirled that Catherine planned to marry Edmund Beaufort, Count of Mortain. Gloucester was against the marriage, and the matter was brought before Parliament, which enacted a law which allowed the dowager queen to remarry only if granted permission from the new king and that this could only be granted once the monarch had reached adulthood. At the time the law was passed, Henry VI was only six years old. Thus any possibility of Catherine remarrying was nullified.

Catherine remained in the king's household, presumably to care for her young son, but most likely because Humphrey wanted to keep an eye on her. Despite this scrutiny, Catherine fell in love with a commoner named Owen Tudor. There are many tales, most unsupported, of how Catherine and Owen met. He was probably born around 1400, and may have gone to war in the service of Henry V. He was most likely appointed keeper of the queen's wardrobe and their relationship blossomed at Windsor Castle. Catherine became pregnant with Tudor's child in 1430 and it is unclear whether she and Owen were ever married. Moreover, even if they had been married, given the Parliamentary Act of 1428, the union was not lawful because the king had not given permission. From this relationship descended the future Tudor Dynasty. Over the centuries historians have asserted that Owen and Catherine must have been married, for this was a vital link in the argument for the legitimacy of the Tudor's right to the throne.

Catherine died at Bermondsey Abbey in London on January 3, 1437, shortly after giving birth, there were rumors she had cancer. Owen Tudor was arrested on unspecified charges shortly after her death, but later released. He lived until 1461, when he was executed by York forces following the Battle of Mortimer's Cross in Herefordshire. Their sons, Edmund and Jasper were given Earldoms by Catherine's other son, Henry VI. Edmund married Margaret Beaufort, a lady of royal descent, whose son became King Henry VII. Catherine was buried at Westminster Abbey next to Henry V. Her tomb originally boasted an alabaster memorial, which was deliberately destroyed during renovations to the abbey in the reign of her grandson, Henry VII. It has been suggested that Henry ordered her memorial to be removed to distance himself from his illegitimate ancestry. At this time, her tomb was accidently opened, revealing her corpse and for many years her tomb was a tourist attraction, where people paid to see her corpse.

This pedestal is erected to perpetuate the Memory of an obstinate, bloody, and decisive battle fought near this Spot in the civil Wars between the ambitious Houses of York and Lancaster, on the 2ᵈ Day of February 1461 between the Forces of *Edward Mortimer*, Earl of March, (afterwards *Edward* the *Fourth*) on the Side of York, and those of *Henry* the *Sixth*, on the Side of Lancaster.

The King's Troops were commanded by *Jasper* Earl of Pembroke. *Edward* commanded his own in Person, and was victorious. The Slaughter was great on both Sides Four Thousand being left dead on the Field and many Welsh Persons of the first distinction were taken Prisoners among whom was *Owen Tudor* (Great-Grandfather to *Henry* the *Eighth*, and a Descendent of the illustrious *Cadwallader*) who was afterwards beheaded at Hereford

This was the decisive Battle which fixed *Edward* the *Fourth* on the Throne of England who was proclaimed *King* in London on the Fifth of March following.

1. CHATEAU DE VINCENNES, where Henry V died on August 31, 1422.

2. ON FEBRUARY 2, 1461, near this monument, Yorkist forces defeated the Lancasters at the Battle of Mortimer's Cross. Owen Tudor was captured and executed.

3. RUINS OF BERMONDSEY ABBEY, London. Buried here was Catherine of Valois, wife of Henry V and lover of Owen Tudor.

Henry VI

(August 31, 1422 - March 4, 1461 and October 30, 1470 - April 11, 1471)

HENRY VI, from an engraving by Thomas Kelly (1830).

BORN: **December 6, 1421, at Windsor Castle**

PARENTS: **Henry V and Catherine of Valois**

CROWNED: **November 6, 1429, at Westminster Abbey**

CONSORT: **Margaret of Anjou**

DIED: **May 21, 1471, at the Tower of London**

BURIAL: **Originally at Chertsey Abbey, then St. George's Chapel**

Henry VI was less than a year old when he inherited the crowns of both France and England and almost immediately, his father's empire began to crumble. When he reached adulthood, Henry was overwhelmed by the demands of kingship, and his reign oversaw the loss of virtually all of England's territories in France. In 1453, he fell into his first bout of mental illness, which allowed the rival York's to stake a claim to the throne. Henry VI was the last monarch of the Lancastrian line of the Plantagenet dynasty. He was born on December 6, 1421, at Windsor Castle and was the son of Henry V and Catherine of Valois. He was barely nine months old when his father, Henry V, died while on a military campaign in France. Two months later he became King of France, when his grandfather, Charles VI died. During Henry's youth, the war in France had been executed loyally and ably by his uncle, John, Duke of Bedford, who struggled to retain his brother's conquests in France. While England was ruled by a council lead by Humphrey, Duke of Gloucester, youngest of Henry V's brothers. Henry VI was crowned King of England on November 6, 1429, at Westminster Abbey.

Henry was shy, pious, and averse to deceit and bloodshed. He did not appear to enjoy wearing the magnificent clothing expected of a sovereign and often dressed simply. He was uninterested in government and allowed his court to be dominated by a few favorites, most prominently William de la Pole, who, in 1444, negotiated a five year truce with France. According to the terms of a peace agreement between England and France, Henry was to marry Margaret of Anjou. She was the daughter of Rene of Anjou and Isabella of Lorraine. They were married on April 23, 1453, but the marriage was not popular.

That same year Henry began to exhibit signs of serious mental illness, by what was described as a "sudden fright," and entered frequent trance-

MARGARET OF ANJOU, from *Biographical Sketches of the Queens of England* by Mary Howlitt (1866).

70

like states, reacting to and recognizing no one. Catatonic schizophrenia or manic depression has been suggested as a likely diagnosis. This was probably an genetically inherited from his maternal grandfather, Charles VI of France, who himself suffered from bouts of schizophrenia. On October 13, 1453, Queen Margaret gave birth to a son, Edward, at the Palace of Westminster. Rumors swirled that the child was not the king's, but the result of an affair with Edward of Somerset. Queen Margaret was fiercely protective of her son and vigorously repudiated the false claims. Henry eventually recovered and when showed his son, declared himself pleased.

In 1454, after the king suffered another bout of mental incapacity, Richard of York was appointed Lord Protector, much to the disapproval of Queen Margaret, who strongly felt that she should govern England. An intense personal rivalry developed between Richard, Queen Margaret, and her favorite, Edmund of Somerset (who was descended from John of Gaunt and his mistress, Catherine Swynford). Richard of York had a strong claim to the throne in his own right, as his mother, Anne Mortimer was by the strict rules of primogeniture, the true heir of Richard II, as was her only son. Anne's claim derived from her descent from Edward III's second surviving son, Lionel, Duke of Clarence, while Henry VI's claim, although in the direct male line, was only through Edward's fourth son, John of Gaunt.

York and Somerset hated one another and enmity between the two eventually escalated into war. Attempts at discussion between Henry VI and Richard of York only evoked further anger. The first battle of the Wars of the Roses was fought at St. Albans on May 22, 1455. Here, Henry VI was defeated and captured and Somerset was killed. Richard of York was again appointed Lord Protector of England. Queen Margaret did not take the news well and assembled an army of her own, forcing Richard and his allies to flee London. York regrouped with the help of Richard Neville, Earl of Warwick, retook London and proclaimed himself king. The two sides eventually reached a deal, whereupon Henry was allowed to keep the throne for the remainder of his lifetime but upon his death, Richard and his heirs were to inherit the crown. No one thought Queen Margaret would accept the disinheriting of her son. On December 30, 1460, Queen Margaret's and Richard of York's armies met at the Battle of Wakefield. Richard's forces were defeated and he along with his second son, Edmund, were killed while leading a reckless charge. Their heads were impaled on spikes and placed on the city walls of York. What remained of their corpses was buried at Pontefract Castle, then in 1476 by royal decree both were reinterred at St. Mary and All Saints Church in Fotheringhay.

York's eldest son, Edward, Earl of March (the future Edward IV) was now leader of the Yorkist cause and his army defeated the Lancastrian army at the Battle of Mortimers Cross and Towton in the early spring of 1461. Queen Margaret and her son Edward of Westminster fled to Scotland and the hapless Henry VI was imprisoned at the Tower of London. Edward, Earl of March, was crowned king as Edward IV on June 28, 1461, at Westminster Abbey. Early in his reign he made a serious blunder and secretly married commoner Elizabeth Woodville. The old nobility, and in particular Richard Neville, Earl of Warwick, where alienated by the meteoric advancement of the new Queen's large and needy family. In 1470, Warwick, later referred to as the "kingmaker," seething with hatred of the upstart Woodville's, changed his allegiance to the House of Lancaster and was reunited with Queen Margaret.

Edward IV was now forced to flee the country before Warwick. Henry VI was briefly restored to the throne. A sad and pitiful figure, Henry was paraded through the streets of London and set up as a puppet king, through which the ambitious Warwick ruled. In early April 1471, Edward IV returned to England with an army and defeated Warwick at the Battles of Barnet and Tewkesbury. During the later battle, Henry's son and heir, Edward of Westminster was killed. Contemporary accounts are conflicting; some state that Edward was killed in battle, while others claim he was taken prisoner and executed. He was the only heir apparent to the English throne to ever to die in battle and was buried at Tewkesbury Abbey. Historians regard these battles as the most important clashes in

the Wars of the Roses, since it brought about a decisive turn in the fortunes of both kings. Edward's victories were followed by fourteen years of Yorkist rule over England.

Queen Margaret was taken prisoner and taken to the Tower of London, as was her son's widow, Anne Neville, the daughter of Richard of Warwick (she would later marry one of her husband's suspected killers, the future Richard III). She remained a prisoner until she was ransomed by Louis XI of France at the Treaty of Picquigny in 1475. The resentful ex-Queen retired to her native Anjou, where she took up residence at the Chateau of Dampierre, dying there on August, 25, 1482. She was buried at Saint Maurice de Angers Cathedral and during the French Revolution, her tomb was destroyed and the remains were lost.

Henry VI met his end at the Tower of London on the night of May 21, 1471. The death of his son had sealed his fate. While the prince lived, the removal of Henry was pointless. The Yorkist version of Henry VI's death states that he died of pure melancholy and displeasure upon hearing of his son's death. This story was not even accepted at the time and the majority of contemporary chroniclers believed Henry had been murdered as he knelt in silent prayer, most likely stabbed or clubbed to death by Edward's brother, Richard (the future Richard III). After the passage of over five hundred years this can never be properly ascertained, but Richard was known to be present at the Tower that night. Ultimately, the responsibility for Henry's murder can only be attributed to Edward IV, as he began to ruthlessly exterminate of all direct line male members of the House of Lancaster.

Henry VI was initially buried at Chertsey Abbey, where the cult of "Holy King Henry," although actively discouraged by Edward IV, grew after his death. During the reign of Richard III and to stop unwanted pilgrimages to his tomb, Henry's body was moved to St. George's Chapel at Windsor Castle. An unsuccessful attempt was made by Henry VII, to have his half-uncle canonized. Due to controversy over the manner of his death, George V gave permission to exhume the body in 1910 and the skeleton was found to have been dismembered before being placed in its coffin, not all the bones were present. The remains were recorded as being those of a strong man measuring five feet nine to five feet ten inches tall with light brown hair, found matted with blood on the skull. This confirmed that Henry had died as a result of blunt force trauma to the head. Today, Henry VI's tomb is located on the right side of the altar in the choir of St. George's Chapel.

(TOP) ST. MARY AND ALL SAINTS CHURCH, Fortheringhay, where Richard, Duke of York, and his son, Edmund, Duke of Rutland, are interred.

(BOTTOM) TEWKSBURY ABBEY, where Edward of Westminster, son of Henry VI, was buried.

1. Chateau de Dampierre, where Queen Margaret died in 1482.

2. Saint Maurice de Angers Cathedral, where Margaret of Anjou was interred.

3. The Wakefield Tower at the Tower of London, where Henry VI was murdered on the evening of May 21, 1471.

4. Floor plaque at the Tower of London, which marks the location of Henry VI's murder.

5. View of the choir area of St. George's Chapel. Henry VI is interred on the right side of the altar, Edward VII's tomb is immediately to the right and the marble tomb marker of Henry VIII, Charles I, and Jane Seymour is visible in the foreground center.

Edward IV

(March 4, 1461 - October 3, 1470 and April 11, 1471 - April 9, 1483)

Edward IV, from an engraving by Thomas Kelly (1830).

Born: April 28, 1442, at Rouen, France

Parents: Richard of York and Cecily Neville

Crowned: June 28, 1461, at Westminster Abbey

Consort: Elizabeth Woodville

Died: April 9, 1483, at Westminster

Burial: St. George's Chapel

Edward IV was the first king of the House of York and consolidated his claim to the throne by defeating the Lancastrians at the Battle of Towton in March 1461, the bloodiest battle in the Wars of the Roses. Henry VI was deposed and Edward crowned soon afterwards. With Henry's death in 1471, the drama of Edward's early years on the throne came to an end, and the king went on to enjoy a stable, peaceful reign. Under his careful administration the crown enjoyed its first period of solvency for several centuries and the kingdom's economy thrived. His unexpected death in 1483 left England in the control of his brother, Richard, the Duke of Gloucester.

Edward was born on April 28, 1442, in Rouen, France and was the eldest surviving son of Richard of York and Cecily Neville. Upon the death of his father at the Battle of Wakefield in 1460, Edward inherited his father's Yorkist claim to the English throne. He acquired the support of his powerful cousin, Richard Neville, Earl of Warwick, later to be known to history as Warwick the Kingmaker. Edward proved to be an able general, defeating the Lancastrians at Mortimers Cross in February 1461 and again at Towton March 29, 1461. The victorious Edward was crowned King of England three months later on June 28, 1461, at Westminster Abbey.

On becoming king (at the age of nineteen), Edward met and secretly married Elizabeth Woodville. She had come to petition him for the restoration of her son's estates. Initially, Edward wanted her to become his mistress, but she refused. Bewitched by her beauty, he finally proposed. His marriage to Woodville, the widow of Sir John Gorby, took place secretly and the exact date is not known. Tradition states that it took place on May 1, 1464, at the Woodville family estate in Northamptonshire. Elizabeth proved to be greedy and selfish, quickly persuading her infatuated spouse to arrange advantageous marriages among her large and needy family. She also successfully alienated Richard of Warwick, who switched allegiance to Henry VI.

Elizabeth Woodville, from *Biographical Sketches of the Queens of England* by Mary Howlitt (1866).

Edward IV tomb at St. George's Chapel.

Warwick's defection to the Lancastrian cause resulted in Edward's overthrow and a temporary resumption of the crown by Henry VI in October 1470. Edward fled to Burgundy with his younger brother Richard and regrouped. They invaded England in March 1471 and by May had defeated Warwick's forces at the Battles of Barnet and Tewkesbury. Warwick was killed at Barnet and his body was displayed at Old St. Paul's cathedral to quell any rumors of his survival. The Lancastrian cause reached its lowest point, when Henry VI, a prisoner in the Tower of London, was murdered on the night of May 21, 1471. In an attempt to consolidate power, Edward IV's two brothers, George and Richard were married to Isabella Neville and Anne Neville, the daughters of the now deceased Earl of Warwick. In 1478, George, Duke of Clarence was found guilty of plotting against Edward and executed on February 18, 1478, at the Tower of London.

An able ruler, Edward IV made an admirable attempt at reforming royal administration and the justice systems, and improving the kingdom's finances. But Edward's excesses finally got the best of him. His love for food was only matched by his insatiable appetite for woman. In March 1483 after a fishing trip on the River Thames near Windsor, Edward developed pneumonia. He died on April 9, 1483, at Westminster Palace and was succeeded to the throne by his twelve year-old son. Edward IV was buried at St. George's Chapel at Windsor Castle and his tomb is located to the left of the altar in the north choir aisle.

Elizabeth Woodville lived to see further reversals of Yorkist fortune, when her son Edward V was usurped by her brother-in-law, Richard of Gloucester (who had been appointed Lord High Protector). She saw her marriage to Edward IV declared invalid and her children declared bastards. Her two young sons, Edward V and Richard, Duke of York, (known to history as the Princes of the Tower) mysteriously disappeared. In an attempt to regain her lost influence, she changed allegiance to the Lancastrian, Henry Tudor, who was betrothed to her daughter, Elizabeth. After Tudor defeated Richard III at the Battle of Bosworth in 1485, Henry Tudor married Elizabeth of York. Elizabeth Woodville was restored to her position as Dowager Queen. For reasons that remain unclear, Woodville quarreled with her new son-in-law and was confined to a nunnery at Bermondsey in 1487. She died there on June 8, 1492, and was buried next to her husband, Edward IV at St. George's Chapel.

Edward V

(April 9 - June 26, 1483)

Edward V, from a 19th century engraving.

BORN: November 2, 1470, at Westminster Abbey

PARENTS: Edward IV and Elizabeth Woodville

CROWNED: Uncrowned

CONSORT: Unmarried

DIED: September 3, 1483, at the Tower of London

BURIAL: Originally at the Tower of London, now at Westminster Abbey

Edward V was the eldest son of Edward IV and Elizabeth Woodville. He was born on November 2, 1470, at Westminster Abbey, where his mother had taken sanctuary during the brief restoration of Henry VI to the throne. When Edward IV was reinstalled to the throne, Henry VI was again deposed. The young Prince Edward was sent to Ludlow Castle, near the border with Wales, for his education. On the death of his father (April 9, 1483), Edward journeyed to London with his maternal uncle, Anthony Woodville, who had been appointed his protector. Their progress was interrupted at Stony Stratford by his paternal uncle, Richard of Gloucester (the future Richard III). Woodville and other members of the young king's escort were sent to Gloucester, Edward, who seems to have been a promising and intelligent youth, objected, but was humiliatingly powerless. He was now in the protective custody of Gloucester, and together travelled on to London. When news of her son's capture reached Elizabeth, she fled to the sanctuary of Westminster Abbey with her remaining children.

While the grasping Woodville's had been unpopular, Edward IV had been much loved by the people, and therefore most were loyal to his son. Gloucester eased apprehension by explaining he was only countering a Woodville conspiracy and had taken Edward into his custody to protect him from harm. This explanation was generally accepted and the fears which had gripped the city were calmed. Young Edward was taken to the Tower of London to apparently await his pending coronation. There was nothing sinister detected at the time, for the Tower of London was a royal residence, as well as a prison.

The Duke of Gloucester convinced Queen Dowager Elizabeth that Edward needed the companionship of his younger brother Richard, who was removed from the safety of Westminster Abbey to the Tower. On June 13, 1483, a meeting of the high council was convened under the false pretext of discussing Edward V's coronation. Once convened, William (Lord Hastings) was arrested on charges of treason. While Hastings detested the Woodville's, he had been a close friend of Edward IV and would never have allowed the usurping of his son's throne; he was summarily executed.

Gloucester then began to outwardly protest the legitimacy of Edward IV, stating that he was not the true son of Richard Duke of York but the result of an illicit affair of his mother Cecily and a man named Blackburn. It was also argued that the Edward IV's marriage to Elizabeth Woodville was invalid, due to Edward's previous betrothal to Lady Eleanor Butler, rendering both Prince Edward and Richard of York bastards and ineligible to ascend the throne. The high council then called upon Richard of Gloucester to accept the crown as the true heir of York. After first feigning reluctance, Richard heartily accepted the offer and although many saw through this plot, no one dared to oppose him directly.

After Richard III's accession, the young princes were seen less and less within the Tower, and by the end of summer of 1483, they had completely disappeared. It is generally believed that they were murdered and the three principal suspects being Richard of Gloucester; Henry Stafford, Duke of Buckingham; and Richard's servant James Tyrrel. William Shakespeare depicted Tyrrel as the murderer (under King Richard's orders) in the play Richard III, using information from Thomas More, who wrote the Princes were smothered to death with their pillows and bedclothes. Bones were discovered in 1674 by workmen rebuilding a stairway in the Tower, and these remains were subsequently reinterred at Westminster Abbey. Today, the marble sarcophagus purported to contain the remains of the two Princes is located within the east wall of the north aisle of the Lady Chapel (near the tomb of Queen Elizabeth). However, it has never been proven that these bones were actually those of the young princes. In 1789, workmen carrying out repairs in St. George's Chapel at Windsor Castle accidentally broke into the vault of Edward IV and Elizabeth Woodville and adjoining their vault was found another previously unknown crypt, which contained two coffins of unidentified children. However no inspection or examination was conducted and the tomb was resealed.

(TOP) Bloody Tower at the Tower of London, where Edward V was held captive and murdered.

(BOTTOM) Murder of the two princes, the only sons of Edward IV of England, from an 19th century engraving by J. Rogers after a painting by Northcote and published by J. & F. Tallis.

Richard III

(June 26, 1483 - August 22, 1485)

RICHARD III of England, by G.N. Gardiner (1806).

BORN: October 2, 1452, at Fotheringhay Castle in Northamptonshire

PARENTS: Richard, Duke of York and Cecily Neville

CROWNED: July 6, 1483, at Westminster Abbey

CONSORT: Anne Neville

DIED: August 22, 1485, at Bosworth Field, Leicestershire

BURIAL: Originally at Greyfriars Church in Leicester, body was disinterred and is now lost

"Now is the winter of our discontent, made glorious summer by this sun of York."

- From William Shakespeare's play
Richard III, Act one, Scene one

Fairly or unfairly, Richard III is one of the most despised and often vilified characters in English history. He was the eleventh child of Richard, Duke of York, and Cecily Neville. He was born on October 2, 1452, at Fotheringhay Castle and was the last monarch of the Plantagenet Dynasty. He was the last English king to die in battle and his death is generally accepted as the delineation mark between the medieval and modern ages in English history. Richard has been implicated in the murders of Henry VI, Henry's son Edward of Westminster, George, Duke of Clarence, and his nephews Edward V and Richard, Duke of York.

Richard spent his childhood under the tutelage of his cousin Richard Neville, Earl of Warwick (later known as the "Kingmaker" because of his role in the Wars of the Roses). While Richard was at Warwick Castle, he developed a close friendship with Warwick's daughter, Anne, whom he would later marry. At the time of the death of his father and older brother at the Battle of Wakefield, Richard was only eight years old. He was sent into hiding in Burgundy, beyond the reach of Henry VI's vengeful Queen, Margaret of Anjou. He returned to England following the defeat of the Lancastrians at the Battle of Towton, and participated in the coronation of his elder brother Edward IV. Richard became embroiled in the rough politics of the Wars of the Roses at an early age, when Edward IV appointed him Commissioner of the Western Counties in 1464 (when he was 11) and by the age of 17, he had an independent military command.

In October 1470, Richard was again forced to seek refuge in the Low Countries of the Duchy of Burgundy. Richard along with his brother George and Edward IV fled to Burgundy after Richard of Warwick defected to the side of Margaret of Anjou. Richard played crucial roles in two battles, Barnet and Tewskbury, which resulted in Edward IV's restoration to the throne in spring of 1471. Following these decisive Yorkist victories, Richard married Anne Neville. She was the daughter of the now deceased Earl of Warwick and widow of Edward of Westminster, the son of Henry VI, who had been killed at the Battle of Tewksbury. Richard and Anne had one son, who died in infancy.

(top) Anne Neville, from *Biographical Sketches of the Queens of England* by Mary Howlitt (1866).

(BOTTOM) WARWICK CASTLE, where Anne Neville was born June 11, 1456.

During the reign of his brother Edward IV, Richard demonstrated his loyalty and skill as a military commander. He was rewarded with large estates and appointed as Governor of the North, becoming the richest and most powerful noble in England. Upon the death of Edward IV, on April 9, 1483, the late king's twelve-year-old son, Edward V, succeeded to the throne. Richard was named Lord Protector of England and quickly moved to keep the family of Elizabeth Woodville from exercising power. Elizabeth Woodville's brother and others were arrested and later executed under the accusation of having planned to assassinate Richard. He then took Edward and his younger brother, nine-year-old Richard, to the Tower of London. Shortly afterwards, during a meeting of the high council on June 13 at the Tower of London, Richard accused Lord Hastings and others of having conspired against him with the Woodville's, and Hastings was summarily executed.

Around that time, Robert Stillington (Bishop of Bath and Wells) informed Richard that Edward IV's marriage to Elizabeth Woodville had been invalid due to an earlier, just discovered, secret union between Edward and Eleanor Butler. This made any children by this marriage to Elizabeth Woodville illegitimate. Richard then assumed the throne and was crowned on July 6, 1483, at Westminster Abbey. The princes, still lodged at the Tower of London, gradually disappeared from sight. Although Richard III is generally accused of having Edward V and his brother killed, there is considerable debate about the actual fate of the princes of the Tower.

In 1483, a conspiracy arose among a number of disaffected nobles, many of whom were supporters of Edward IV. Led by Richard's former ally, Henry Stafford, Duke of Buckingham, they planned to depose Richard III and place Edward V back on the throne but when rumors swirled that Edward and his brother were dead, Buckingham changed plans and invited Henry Tudor to return from exile and accept the throne. Tudor gathered an army and made plans to invade England, but numerous delays stalled his arrival. Buckingham's army was greatly troubled by the same storm and deserted when Richard's forces came against them.

Anne Neville died of tuberculosis on March 16, 1485, at Westminster Palace and was buried at Westminster Abbey in an unmarked grave to the right of the High Altar. A bronze plaque was erected on a wall near her grave by the Richard III Society in 1960. At the time of his last stand against the Lancastrians, Richard was a widower without an heir. Henry Tudor and his newly assembled army successfully landed in England in the summer of 1485. The armies of Richard III and Henry Tudor met on August 22, 1485, at the Battle

of Bosworth Field. Initially, Richard's forces outnumbered those of Henry's, but things changed when Henry Percy, Earl of Northumberland, abandoned the king and defected to Tudor's side. This had a profound effect on the eventual outcome of the battle. The death of John Howard, Duke of Norfolk, Richard III's close companion, appears also to have had a demoralizing effect. Perhaps realizing that his chances at victory were slipping away, Richard led an impromptu cavalry charge deep into the enemy ranks in an attempt to end the battle quickly, by striking at Henry Tudor himself. Chroniclers of the period, note that Richard fought bravely and at one point unhorsed Sir John Cheney (a well-known jousting champion), killed Henry's standard bearer, Sir William Brandon, and came within a sword's length of Henry Tudor himself before being surrounded and killed. Tradition holds that his final words were "treason, treason, treason," when he found Northumberland had turned against him. Henry Tudor's official historian, would later record that Richard III, was killed while fighting in the thickest press of his enemies. Richard's crown was found under a hawthorn bush and placed upon Henry's head. Richard's body was unceremoniously stripped naked and flung over a horse and taken back to Greyfriars Church in Leicester, where it was displayed for two days then buried in an unmarked grave.

Legend states that on the eve of the Battle of Bosworth, Richard consulted a seer in the town of Leicester, who foretold that "where your spur should strike on the ride into battle, your head shall be broken on the return." On the ride into battle his spur struck the

bridge stone of the Bow Bridge; legend has it that, as his corpse was being carried from the battle, his head struck the same stone. Henry Tudor succeeded Richard to become Henry VII, thus ending the rule of the Plantagenet dynasty. It decisively finished the Wars of the Roses and began the Tudor Dynasty. Henry VII sought to cement his claim to the throne by marrying, Elizabeth of York, who was Edward IV's daughter. In 1495, Henry VII had a tomb built for Richard and according to one tradition, during the dissolution of the monasteries both the church and tomb were destroyed, the body was removed and thrown into the nearby River Soar. There is a memorial plaque on the site of the former church and the alleged bridge where his remains were thrown into the river.

1. RICHARD III and the Earl of Richmond at the Battle of Bosworth in 1485, from a 19th century engraving by J. Rogers after a painting by A. Cooper, and published by J. & F. Tallis.

2. BATTLE OF BOSWORTH FIELD memorial, where Richard III was killed.

3. RUINS OF GREYFRIARS ABBEY, where Richard III was originally buried after the Battle of Bosworth Field.

4. MEMORIAL MARKER for Richard III at Leicester Cathedral.

Chapter Five

The Tudors (1485-1603)

 fter Richard III's death, England was ruled by five sovereigns who are among the most well-known figures in English history. The Tudors were Welsh land owners in Northern Wales, who rose to prominence in the 15th century through Owen Tudor's romantic love affair with Henry V's French widow. The first Tudor monarch, Henry VII succeeded in ending the Wars of the Roses between the houses of Lancaster and York. A distant link with the House of Lancaster put them on the throne for 119 years, 49 of which were the reigns of two queens. During this period, England developed into one of the leading European colonial powers, with men such as Sir Walter Raleigh taking part in the conquest of the New World. Culturally and socially, the Tudor period saw many changes. The Tudor court played a prominent part in the cultural Renaissance taking place in Europe, nurturing cultural greats such as Shakespeare, Spenser, Marlowe, and Sidney. Three of the five Tudor monarchs were among the most effective ever to wear the English crown. Henry VII settled the Wars of the Roses, Henry VIII broke with Rome and declared himself head of the Church of England, closed down the monasteries, and, notoriously, beheaded two and divorced two more of his six wives. The turbulent changes of official religion resulted in the martyrdom of many innocent believers. The fear of Roman Catholicism induced by the Reformation was to last for several centuries and to play an influential role in the history of the Succession. The dynasty's pinnacle came under Elizabeth, with the defeat of the Spanish Armanda, a Protestant religious settlement, and explosion of literary genius.

Henry VII
(August 22, 1485 - April 21, 1509)

HENRY VII, from a 19th century engraving by Thomas Kelly (1830).

BORN: January 28, 1457, at Pembroke Castle in Wales

PARENTS: Edmund Tudor and Margaret Beaufort

CROWNED: October 30, 1485, at Westminster Abbey

CONSORT: Elizabeth of York

DIED: April 21, 1509, at Richmond Palace in Surrey

BURIAL: Westminster Abbey

Whether or not Owen Tudor ever married Catherine of Valois, their sons Edmund and Jasper were still half-brothers of Henry VI, and he liked them, granting them both titles and lands. Edmund married Margaret Beaufort, the great-great-granddaughter of Edward III. She was born on May 31, 1443, at Bletso Castle in Bedfordshire, the daughter of John Beaufort, Duke of Somerset, and Margaret Beauchamp of Bletso. She was first married to John de la Pole, but the marriage was quickly annulled on grounds of consanguinity. Under canon law, Margaret was not bound by the marriage contract anyway, as she entered into it before reaching the age of twelve. Even before the annulment of her first marriage, Henry VI had chosen Margaret as a suitable bride for his half-brother, Edmund Tudor. Margaret was only twelve when she married twenty-four year old Edmund Tudor on November 1, 1455. The Wars of the Roses had just broken out and Edmund was taken prisoner by York forces. While in captivity, he died from plague the following November, and left a thirteen year-old widow who was seven months pregnant. On January 28, 1457, she gave birth to the future Henry VII at Pembroke Castle.

1. LADY MARGARET BEAUFORT, wife of Edmund Tudor and mother of Henry VII, from an engraving by W.H. Mote (1838).

2. TOMB OF EDMUND TUDOR at St. David's Cathedral in Pembrokeshire, Wales.

3. PEMBROKE CASTLE IN WALES, where Henry VII was born on January 28, 1457.

Margaret and her son remained in Pembroke until the Yorkist triumphs of 1461. Young Henry lived with his father's family in Wales and France. By 1485, a series of fortuitous deaths left Henry Tudor, improbably, the lead claimant to the throne of England from the House of Lancaster. Henry landed in Wales, defeated Richard III at Bosworth Field, and was crowned king at Westminster Abbey October 30, 1485. He married Elizabeth of York, the eldest child of Edward IV and Elizabeth Woodville on January 18, 1486. Together they had eight children, one of which was the future Henry VIII. With this marriage the Houses of Lancaster and York were united, cementing Henry's claim to the throne. Although this was a political union, Henry and Elizabeth enjoyed a loving and affectionate relationship.

1. EXTERIOR OF THE LADY CHAPEL at Westminster Abbey.

2. ELIZABETH OF YORK, from an engraving by W. Holl (1838).

3. INTERIOR OF THE LADY CHAPEL at Westminster Abbey, Henry VII and Elizabeth of York's tomb is visible in the background center.

4. TOMB EFFIGY of Henry VII at Westminster Abbey.

It may be that the Wars of the Roses were over, but it was not obvious at the time. Henry had to cope with numerous succession plots, but, by 1506, most people wanted peace. Henry enjoyed the support of parliament and most of his nobles. He was an excellent administrator and used the existing system of taxation and feudal dues to ruthlessly build up his treasury. He spent lavishly on renovations to many of the royal palaces. Through political marriages of his children, he was able to cement his dynasty even further. Catherine of Aragon, daughter of Ferdinand and Isabella of Spain was betrothed to Henry's eldest son, Arthur. Prince Arthur's death at age fifteen, on April 2, 1502 at Ludlow Castle from consumption, diabetes or the mysterious "sweating sickness," was an emotional blow to both parents. Catherine of Aragon was then betrothed to the future Henry VIII. Elizabeth of York became pregnant the following year, and on February 2, 1503, gave birth to a girl, who lived only a few days. The queen developed a post-partum infection and died on February 11, 1503. She was buried at Westminster Abbey within the Lady Chapel, which was rebuilt to house her remains. In the following years, Henry entertained thoughts of remarriage, but nothing serious ever developed. During the last six years of his life, Henry VII suffered from loss of eye sight, gout, and other illnesses. He died on April 21, 1509, from chronic pulmonary tuberculosis at Richmond Palace and was buried next to his wife, Elizabeth of York at Westminster Abbey.

Henry VIII

(April 21, 1509 - January 28, 1547)

HENRY VIII, painted by Hans Holbein the Younger. *Courtesy of the National Portrait Gallery, London.*

BORN: June 28, 1491, at Greenwich Palace

PARENTS: Henry VII and Elizabeth of York

CROWNED: June 24, 1509, at Westminster Abbey

CONSORTS: Catherine of Aragon, Anne Boleyn, Jane Seymour, Anne of Cleves, Catherine Howard, and Catherine Parr

DIED: January 28, 154,7 at Whitehall Palace

BURIAL: St. George's Chapel

"We are, by the sufferance of God, King of England; and the Kings of England in times past never had any superior but God."

- Henry VIII, King of England

Henry VIII was born on June 28, 1491, at Greenwich Palace. He was the second son of Henry VII and Elizabeth of York. In his youth, Henry was not the irascible, overweight tyrant that he became in later life. Henry was athletic, with a strong sense of fun, and was a fine horseman. He never thought he would inherit the throne, but things changed when his older brother Arthur died in 1502. Arthur and Catherine of Aragon had been married only five months when he died.

CATHERINE OF ARAGON, painted by an unkown artist (1701). *Courtesy of the National Portrait Gallery, London.*

At this point, Henry VII faced the challenge of avoiding returning Catherine's dowry to Ferdinand II of Aragon. To sidestep complications, it was agreed she would marry Henry VII's second son. Ostensibly, the marriage was delayed until Henry was old enough (he was only nine at the time).

Henry VII procrastinated so much about Catherine's unpaid dowry that it was doubtful if the marriage would ever take place. In the mean time, Catherine lived as a virtual prisoner at Durham House. While Henry VII and his councilors expected her to be easily manipulated, Catherine went on to prove them wrong. The marriage to young Henry depended on the Pope granting a dispensation. Canon law forbade the marriage of a brother's widow to another brother. Catherine testified that her marriage to Arthur was never consummated and thus invalid. The matter was considered of minor importance at the time, as the Pope had the power to overrule any objections, whether or not they were for religious reasons. Henry ascended to the throne upon the death of his father in April 1509. He and Catherine were wed on June 11, 1509, in a private ceremony at Greenwich Palace. At first, Henry and Catherine got along quite well and she bore him six children. Unfortunately, the only child to survive was a girl, the future Mary I, not the son that Henry and his country thought they needed. Henry was crowned at Westminster Abbey on June 24, 1509.

Early in his reign, Henry was eager to flex his muscles and the Scots were defeated at the Battle of Flodden in 1513, then undertook an invasion of France that came to nothing. In 1520, just outside Calais, Henry staged a wildly expensive but empty spectacle of reconciliation with Francis I of France. Such was the extravagance that it became known as the Field of the Cloth of Gold. Like his father, Henry VIII understood the public relations value of magnificence and he created the palaces of Whitehall and St. James and embellished Hampton Court. He picked able ministers; chief among them was Cardinal Thomas Wolsey, who harbored hopes of one day becoming pope. By the early 1520s, Catherine of Aragon (now in her forties) had still not bore a male heir and Henry found solace in the bed of beautiful Elizabeth Blount, who bore him a bastard son, Henry Fitzroy. Henry now knew he could conceive a male heir and blamed Queen Catherine.

In March 1526, Henry began the courtly pursuit of Anne Boleyn, whose older sister, Mary, had already been a mistress. Anne was born circa 1507 at Hever Castle and was the daughter of Thomas Boleyn, Earl of Wiltshire, and Lady Elizabeth Howard. She spent time at the French Court in her teens and returned to England as one of Queen Catherine's ladies-in-waiting. Although she was not thought of as beautiful at the time, Henry became infatuated, writing her numerous love letters, poems, and sonnets. Anne resisted all his attempts to seduce her, and refused to become his mistress until he divorced Catherine and married her. The annulment of his union to Catherine and subsequent marriage to Anne was Henry's great obsession. When it became clear that Pope Clement VII would not annul the marriage, Henry decided to break with the Catholic Church. Anne began sleeping with Henry in 1532 and soon became pregnant. Henry granted Anne a peerage in her own right as the Marquess of Pembroke and they were secretly married on January 25, 1533. Thomas Cranmer, Archbishop of Canterbury declared Henry and Catherine's marriage null and void on May 23, 1533, and five days later, declared Henry and Anne's marriage to be good and valid. Shortly afterwards, the Pope decreed sentences of excommunication against Henry and Cranmer. Anne was crowned Queen of England on June 1, 1533, and three months later gave birth to Elizabeth. To Henry's displeasure, however, she failed to produce a male heir, but Henry was not totally discouraged, for he said that he loved Elizabeth and that a son would surely follow. However, three miscarriages followed, and by March 1536 Henry was courting Jane Seymour.

The Act of Supremacy of 1534, which declared Henry supreme head of the Church of England, confirmed his profound conviction that his only superior was God. He claimed that by dissolving the monasteries, he was also responding to the demands of the people. Henry asked Parliament not to be influenced by him but rather do what was good for the realm. The monasteries were closed and their treasuries were claimed by the crown. Thomas Cromwell,

(TOP) ANNE BOLEYN, from an engraving by H.T. Ryall (1837).

(BOTTOM) HEVER CASTLE, where Anne Boleyn was born in 1507.

Archbishop Cranmer, and Anne Boleyn were all Reformation-minded, but Henry was not. His religion became a mixture of Catholicism and whatever suited him. He kept a balance between religious conservatives and Reformers. One of his opponents was Thomas More, a one time friend and Lord Chancellor. More was a devout Roman Catholic and opposed Henry's breach with the pope. On April 13, 1534, Thomas More was asked to appear before a commission and swear his allegiance to the Parliamentary Act of Succession but refused to accept Parliament's right to declare Anne Boleyn the legitimate Queen of England. He steadfastly refused to take the oath of supremacy of the Crown in the relationship between the King and the Church in England. Holding fast to the ancient teaching of Papal supremacy, More publicly refused to uphold Henry's annulment from Catherine. Thomas More was charged with high treason and was imprisoned at the Tower of London. On July 1, 1535, he was tried at Westminster Hall and, relying on the legal precedent of silence presumes consent, refused to make comment. He understood that he could not be convicted, as long as he did not explicitly deny that the king was supreme head of the Church. Witnesses were brought forth to testify that More had, in their presence, denied that the king was the legitimate head of the church, and the court, knowing where its own best interests lay, took only fifteen minutes to find More guilty.

Following the verdict More spoke freely stating "no temporal man may be the head of his own spirituality." He was sentenced to death. Prior to his execution on July 6, 1535, on Tower Hill, More stated that he died "the king's good servant, but God's first." Following his execution, More was buried at the Chapel of St. Peter ad Vincula in an unmarked grave. His head was fixed upon a spike over London Bridge. His daughter Margret Roper rescued it, possibly by bribery, before it could be thrown in the River Thames. The skull is believed to rest in the Roper Vault of St. Dunstan's Church in Canterbury, though

The Shrine of Thomas More at St. Peter ad Vincula Chapel at the Tower of London.

some researchers have claimed it might be within the tomb he erected for himself in Chelsea Old Church.

The king and his new queen now enjoyed a reasonably happy accord with periods of calm and affection. Anne Boleyn's sharp intelligence, political acumen, and forward manners, although desirable in a mistress, were unacceptable in a wife. After another miscarriage in late 1534, Henry began discussing the possibility of divorcing Anne. Nothing came of the issue as the royal couple reconciled, and by October, Anne was again pregnant. Many blamed Anne for the tyranny of her husband's government. Public opinion turned further against Anne following yet another miscarriage and sank even lower after the executions of her enemies, Thomas More and Bishop John Fisher.

On January 7, 1536, Catherine of Aragon died at Kimbolton Castle. The next day news of her death reached Henry and Anne. They were both overjoyed and celebrated her death with a banquet. Catherine was buried in Petersborough Cathedral with a ceremony befitting a Dowager Princess of Wales, not a queen. Henry did not attend the funeral and also refused to allow their daughter, Mary, to attend.

Anne was well aware of the dangers she faced if she did not produce a male heir. With Catherine dead, Henry would be free to marry without any taint of illegality. Lady Mary continued to rebuff Anne's overtures, perhaps because of rumors circulating that Catherine might have been poisoned by Anne. Later that month, Henry was unhorsed in a tournament and knocked unconscious for two hours. Because of undue stress, Anne miscarried again. Given Henry's desperate desire for a son, the sequence of Anne's pregnancies has attracted much interest. As Anne recovered from her latest miscarriage, Henry lost patience and declared that he had been seduced into marrying Anne through deception and spells. His new mistress, Jane Seymour, was quickly moved into royal quarters.

According to numerous historians Anne's fall from grace was instigated by Thomas Cromwell. Anne argued with Cromwell over the redistribution of Church revenues and foreign policy. Anne Boleyn had become a major threat to Cromwell, but many believe he only became involved in the marital drama when Henry ordered him onto the case.

Towards the end of April, a musician in Anne's service named Mark Smeaton was arrested, and, perhaps under torture confessed that he and another courtier, Henry Norris,

were Queen Anne's lovers. Norris denied his guilt and swore that Anne was innocent. Others were arrested on grounds of adultery with the queen, Francis Weston, William Brereton (a Groom of the King's Privy Chamber), as well as Thomas Wyatt (a poet and friend of the Boleyn's who was allegedly infatuated with her before her marriage to the king). Wyatt was imprisoned but later released, most likely due to his friendship with Cromwell. Anne's brother, George Boleyn was arrested, and charged with incest with the queen.

On May 2, 1536, Anne was arrested and taken to the Tower of London. On May 12, 1536, Norris, Brereton, Weston, and Smeaton were put on trial for adultery and high treason. All professed their innocence but were quickly found guilty and sentenced to death. Three days later, Anne and George Boleyn were tried separately at the Tower of London, where they were accused of adultery, incest, and high treason. By the Treason Act, adultery on the part of a queen was considered treason (presumably because of the implications for the succession to the throne) for which the penalty was burning at the stake. The accusations, and especially those of incestuous adultery, were designed to impugn Anne's moral character. Although the evidence against them was unconvincing, the accused were found guilty and condemned to death. George Boleyn and the other four were executed on May 17, 1536, on Tower Hill. In the days following her conviction, Anne seemed ready to die. Henry commuted Anne's sentence from burning to beheading and employed an expert swordsman from France to perform the execution.

Shortly before dawn on May 19, 1536, Anne requested the Holy Sacraments and swore on the eternal salvation of her soul, that she had never been unfaithful to the king. She ritually repeated this oath both immediately before and after receiving communion. She was then taken to Tower Green for her execution. She wore a red petticoat under a loose, dark grey gown trimmed in fur. She was accompanied by two female attendants; upon the scaffold, she made a short speech to the gathered crowd:

> *"Good Christian people, I am come hither to die, for according to the law and by the law I am judged to die, and therefore I will speak nothing against it. I am come hither to accuse no man, nor to speak anything of that whereof I am accused and condemned to die, but I pray God save the king and send him long to reign over you, for a gentler nor a more merciful prince was there never: and to me he was ever a good, a gentle and sovereign lord. And if any person will meddle of my cause, I require them to judge the best. And thus I take my leave of the world and of you all and I heartily desire you all to pray for me. O Lord have mercy on me, to God I commend my soul."*

1. KIMBOLTON CASTLE, where Catherine of Aragon died on January 7, 1536.

2. PETERSBOROUGH CATHEDRAL, where Catherine of Aragon is buried.

3. TOMB OF CATHERINE OF ARAGON at Petersborough Cathedral.

4. TOWER GREEN with the Royal Chapel of St. Peter ad Vicula in background, Queen Anne Boleyn was executed here on May 19, 1536.

It is thought that she avoided criticizing Henry to save Elizabeth and her family from further consequences, but even under such extreme pressure Anne did not confess guilt. She then knelt upright, in the French style of executions. Her final prayer consisted of her repeating, "to Jesus Christ I commend my soul; Lord Jesus receive my soul." Her attendants removed her headdress and necklaces, and then tied a blindfold over her eyes. She was executed by Jean Rombaud and according to chroniclers, he was so taken by Anne, that he was shaken and found it difficult to proceed with the execution. In order to have her head correctly positioned, he may have shouted, "Where is my sword?" to distract her prior to wielding the sword.

Archbishop Cranmer, a good friend of Anne's was reported to have broken down in tears after the execution, stating, "she who has been the Queen of England on earth will today become a Queen in heaven." When the charges were first brought against Anne, Cranmer had expressed his belief that she was not culpable. Still, Cranmer felt vulnerable because of his closeness to the queen and on the night before the execution, declared Henry's marriage to Anne void. He made no serious attempt to save her life. Henry failed to provide a proper coffin for Anne's burial and her body lay on the scaffold for an hour before an empty arrow chest was found to house her remains. Anne was then buried in an unmarked grave in the Chapel of St. Peter ad Vincula. During renovations of the chapel in the reign of Queen Victoria, Anne's remains were identified. Today, her grave is marked with a floor tile in the chapel.

On May 30, 1536, just eleven days after Anne's execution, Henry married Jane Seymour at Whitehall Palace. She was born circa 1508 at Wulfhall in Wiltshire and was the daughter of Sir John Seymour and Margery Wentworth. She became a lady-in-waiting to Queen Catherine in 1532, and also served Queen Anne Boleyn. Henry first became interested in Jane Seymour in early 1536. She was proclaimed queen consort on June 4, 1536, but was never officially crowned. Seymour as queen was said to have been strict and formal. The lavish extravagance of the Queen's household, which had reached its peak during the time of Anne Boleyn, was replaced by stringent enforcement of decorum. She was a Roman Catholic and it is believed, because of this and her loyalty to her former mistress, Catherine of Aragon, Jane put forth much effort to restore Henry's first child, Lady Mary to favor. While Jane was unable to restore Lady Mary to the line of succession, she was able to reconcile her with Henry.

1. FLOOR MARKER which designates the location of Anne Boleyn's grave at St. Peter ad Vicula.

2. Jane Seymour, from an engraving by H. Robinson (1838).

3. Hampton Court Palace.

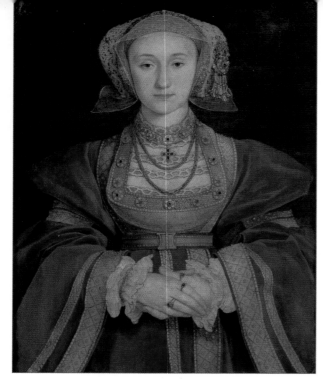

In early 1537, Jane became pregnant and was ordered into confinement to await what was hoped to be a male heir. On October 12, 1537, she gave birth to the future Edward VI at Hampton Court. Seymour's labor had been difficult, lasting over two days, and she developed an infection from a retained placenta. According to some sources, Seymour's death might have been caused by puerperal fever due to a bacterial infection contracted during the birth or a tear in her perineum which became infected. She died on October 24, 1537, at Hampton Court and was buried at St. George's Chapel at Windsor Castle. She was the only wife of Henry to receive a Queen's funeral. In 1540, at Thomas Cromwell's urging, Henry married a foreign Protestant princess, Anne of Cleves. She was born on September 22, 1515, in Dusseldorf and was the daughter of John III of La Marck and Maria of Julich-Berg. Cromwell oversaw negotiations, and a marriage treaty was signed on October 4, 1539.

Anne was described as tall and slim, and of average beauty, with dark hair, with a rather swarthy complexion and appeared older than her actual age. Henry was impatient to see his future bride and went to meet her at Rochester. According to sworn testimony of his companions, he was very disappointed with her appearance. Most historians believe that he later used her bad appearance and incapability in bed as excuses to annul the marriage. He urged Cromwell to find a legal way to avoid the marriage but, by this point, doing so was impossible without endangering the vital alliance with the Germans. Despite Henry's very vocal misgivings, the two were married on January 6, 1540, at the Royal Palace in Greenwich. Anne was commanded to leave the court on June 24th, and, on July 6th, was informed of Henry's decision to reconsider the marriage. Witness statements were taken from a number of courtiers and two physicians which registered the king's disappointment at her appearance. Henry had also commented that he did not believe she was a virgin. Shortly afterwards, Anne was asked for her consent to an annulment, to which she agreed. The annulment was finalized on July 9, 1540, on the grounds of non-consummation. Because of Thomas Cromwell's association with promoting this failed marriage, his enemies at court swiftly moved against him. At a Council meeting on June 10, 1540, Cromwell was arrested and imprisoned at the Tower of London. A long list of indictments including treason, heresy, and corruption were introduced into the House of Lords and was passed on June 29, 1540. Henry deferred the execution until his marriage to Anne of Cleves was officially annulled on July 9, 1540. Cromwell was beheaded on Tower Hill on July 28, 1540. Henry later came to regret his execution.

Following the annulment of their marriage, Anne of Cleves received a generous settlement that included Hever Castle (the former home of the Boleyns). Henry and Anne became good friends and she was referred to as "the King's beloved sister." When Anne's health began

(TOP) ANNE OF CLEVES, painted by Hans Holbein the Younger (1539).

(TOP) CATHERINE HOWARD, from a 17th century sketch by Wenzel Hollar.

to fail in 1557, Queen Mary I allowed her to live at Chelsea Old Manor. She died from cancer on July 16, 1557, and was buried at Westminster Abbey. Her tomb is located to the right of Edward the Confessor's Shrine in a somewhat out of the way niche, slightly above eye level. She is the only wife of Henry VIII to be buried at the abbey. Anne also has the distinction of being the longest living of Henry VIII's wives (she outlived Catherine Parr by nine years).

Henry, now forty-eight, met and quickly married nineteen year-old Catherine Howard. She was born circa 1521 in Wingate and was the daughter of Lord Edmund Howard and Joyce Culpepper. Catherine's uncle, the Duke of Norfolk, found her a place at Court in the household of the Henry's fourth wife, Anne of Cleves. As a young and attractive lady-in-waiting, Catherine quickly caught Henry's eye. As the King's interest in Catherine grew, so did Norfolk's influence. Even before Henry's marriage to Anne of Cleves was annulled, rumors swirled that Catherine was pregnant. Henry and Catherine Howard were married on July 28, 1540, the same day as Cromwell's execution. The king showered his young bride with jewels and other expensive gifts. Early in 1541, Catherine began to lose interest in Henry, who was now extremely obese and foul smelling. She entered into a secret romance with Thomas Culpeper, who was one of Henry's favorite male courtiers, and had known Catherine prior to her coming to court. Their clandestine meetings were arranged by Lady Jane Rochford, the widow of George Boleyn, but as hard as they tried to keep their tryst a secret, word leaked out and Catherine was besieged with people seeking favors to remain silent. Most disastrously, Catherine appointed Francis Dereham, with whom she had been previously betrothed (but failed to divulge prior to marrying Henry), as her personal secretary. This miscalculation would led to charges of treason and adultery.

By late 1541, Catherine's indiscretions had become known to John Lascelles, a Protestant reformer, whose sister, Mary Hall, had been a witness to Catherine's sexual liaisons. Lascelles presented the information to Archbishop Cranmer, who was aware that such conduct would invalidate Catherine's marriage to the king. Armed with this information, Cranmer wrote a letter to the king detailing the queen's indiscretions and a pre-contracted marriage arrangement. On November 1, 1541, he gave the letter to Henry, while attending church services at Hampton Court. At first, Henry did not believe the allegations, but he instructed Cranmer to investigate further. Within a few days, corroborative proof was found, including a love letter from Catherine to Culpeper. Both Dereham and Culpeper confessed (under extreme torture) to having sexual relations with the queen.

Catherine was subsequently charged with adultery and high treason. She never admitted to infidelity, but did admit that she was most unworthy to be called Henry's wife. After being ordered to keep to her rooms at Hampton Court, Catherine, in a desperate attempt to explain herself, escaped and attempted to speak with Henry who was attending Mass in the chapel. According to legend, she ran screaming down the halls and banged hysterically on the doors of the chapel, Henry ignored her pleas and she was quickly subdued and taken back to her quarters. However, there is considerable doubt as to the story's authenticity, since Catherine was not fully aware of the charges against her until Cranmer and a delegation of councilors were sent to question her on November 7, 1541. Even the staunch Cranmer found Catherine's frantic, incoherent state pitiable, and ordered guards to remove any objects that she might use to harm herself. Allegedly, Catherine's ghost still haunts the hallway near the chapel and re-enacts this pitiful scene.

While a pre-contract marriage between Catherine and Dereham would have had the effect of terminating Catherine's marriage, it would have given Henry the right to annul the union and banish her from Court. Catherine would have been disgraced and exiled, but would have been spared execution. However, she steadfastly denied any pre-contract existed and maintained that Dereham had raped her. On November 23, 1541, Catherine was stripped of her title as queen and imprisoned at Syon Abbey in Middlesex. Culpeper and Dereham were both executed at Tyburn on December 10, 1541.

Catherine's fate remained in limbo until Parliament passed a law on February 7, 1542, which made it a treasonable offense, punishable by death, if the queen did not disclose her sexual past within twenty days marrying the king or attempted to incite someone to commit adultery while married to the king. Catherine was found guilty, sentenced to death, and taken to the Tower of London to await her fate.

Her execution was set for the morning of February 13, 1542, and it has been alleged that the night before her death, she spent hours practicing laying her head upon the block. The morning of the execution, she remained relatively composed, but required assistance to climb the scaffold on Tower Green. From the scaffold she spoke briefly, describing her punishment as

worthy and asked for mercy for her family and prayers for her soul. According to popular folklore, her final words were, "I die a Queen, but I would rather have died the wife of Culpeper." Catherine was beheaded with a single stroke of the axe and was buried in an unmarked grave within the Chapel Royal of St. Peter ad Vincula. During excavations of the chapel during the reign of Queen Victoria, Catherine's body was not one of those identified.

Henry married his sixth wife, the already twice widowed Catherine Parr, on July 12, 1543, in the Queen's closet of Hampton Court. She was born in 1512 and was the eldest daughter of Sir Thomas Parr and Maud Green (who was a lady-in-waiting to Catherine of Aragon). In the spring of 1543, Henry noticed Parr and expressed his desire to marry her, for which she felt duty bond to accept.

Religiously Catherine supported the Reform movement and this was not popular with many members of Henry's conservative court. It was also well known that she held immense influence over the king, who was suffering from numerous health issues. Enemies of the queen soon began to plot her downfall by claiming heresy, for she was known to keep banned books in her possession, which was considered grounds for arrest and possible execution. To gain evidence against Parr, Anne Askew, a friend and fellow Protestant Reform advocate was arrested and tortured in an attempt to garner information about the queen. Askew under extreme duress, including being racked, refused to recant her faith or give evidence against Catherine. She was deemed a heretic and burnt at the stake on July 16, 1546. Even without Askew's confession, there was perceived to be enough evidence to issue a warrant for Catherine's arrest. Catherine was given advance warning of the pending arrest, when the warrant was accidentally dropped and found by one of the queen's loyalists. After learning of this, she feigned illness to forestall arrest. Henry was concerned for her health and went to visit her. Catherine confessed everything and Henry chastised her for her outspokenness about the reformed religion, forbade her from discussing the matter any further and had the matter dropped.

Catherine was close with all three of her stepchildren and was personally involved in the educational program of Elizabeth and Edward. When Henry died in January 1547, she expected to play some role in the regency for the new nine-year-old king, but this was not to be. Only a few months after Henry's death, she married Thomas Seymour, but the swiftness of the union caused a scandal. She was still able to take guardianship of Lady Elizabeth and the king's cousin, Lady Jane Grey. It was during this time that rumors of a tryst between Elizabeth and Seymour arose and she was quietly sent to another household in the spring of 1548. Catherine became pregnant for the first time in June 1548, and moved to Sudley Castle to await the birth of her child. On August 30, 1548, a daughter was born, but Catherine fell ill with a fever and died September 5, 1548. She was buried in the Chapel of St. Mary on the grounds of Sudley Castle.

In 1544, an Act of Parliament put Henry's daughters, Lady Mary and Elizabeth back in the line of succession after Edward, Prince of Wales, though they were still deemed illegitimate. By this time, Henry was suffering from numerous health issues. An ulcerated leg injury (from a jousting accident in 1536) grew bloated and he had gained an enormous amount of weight. He had to be pushed around in a specially constructed cart. Suspicious and distrustful, he became menacingly paranoid. It must have been a relief to those around him when he died on January 28, 1547, at Whitehall Palace. The theory that he suffered from syphilis has been dismissed by most historians, but a more credible theory suggests that Henry's medical symptoms are characteristic of untreated Type II diabetes. Henry VIII was buried at St. George's Chapel at Windsor Castle, next to Jane Seymour. Their vault in located beneath the choir area of the chapel and it was originally topped with an ornate tomb. It was destroyed during the English Civil War and replaced with a simple black marble tablet.

1. CATHERINE PARR, from an engraving by H.T. Ryall (1840).

2. CHAPEL AT SUDELEY CASTLE, where Catherine Parr is buried.

3. TOMB OF CATHERINE PARR at Sudeley Castle.

4. HENRY VIII AND JANE SEYMOUR are interred beneath the choir of St. George's Chapel, there tombs are marked by a black marble marker.

Edward VI

(January 28, 1547 - July 6, 1553)

Edward VI, from an engraving by R.T. Ryall (1840).

BORN: October 12, 1537, at Hampton Court Palace

PARENTS: Henry VIII and Jane Seymour

CROWNED: February 20, 1547, at Westminster Abbey

CONSORT: Unmarried

DIED: July 6, 1553, at Greenwich Palace

BURIAL: Westminster Abbe

Edward VI was born on October 12, 1537, at Hampton Court. Henry VIII at long last had a male heir. Because Henry was paranoid about securing the succession to the throne, he ordered strict rules of hygiene and food preparation for the young child. However, the finicky care lavished upon him could not control the fact that the prince had a weak constitution. Though he succeeded his father, and showed signs that he might prove to be a strong and assertive monarch, he did not live to reach adulthood.

Upon Henry VIII's death on January 28, 1547, a council of regency assembled. Edward Seymour was appointed Protector of the Realm and given the title of Duke of Somerset. He was Edward's uncle and leader of the reform faction, supported by Archbishop Cranmer. Edward VI was crowned on February 20, 1547, at Westminster Abbey and his coronation oath was altered to commit the young king to Reformation.

Early in his reign, with the urging of Somerset, numerous reforms were made to the church. These were found to be so threatening to the established church that in 1549, Somerset was overthrown and arrested. He was found guilty of treason and executed on Tower Hill January 22, 1552. John Dudley was now in charge, given the title of Duke of Northumberland; he ran the government efficiently and gained Edward's trust. Soon the young king began to display some of his father's determination and asserted his royal power.

In January 1553, Edward developed a fever and cough that gradually worsened. On June 15, 1553, at the urging of Northumberland and others, Edward composed a document called "My Devise for the Succession," which was meant to alter the Third Succession Act of 1543. It forbade a Catholic and/or any illegitimate female from ascending the throne. Thus eliminating both of his half-sisters, Mary and Elizabeth from the succession. It also specifically named Lady Jane Grey (Edward's first cousin, once removed) as heir to the crown. Edward made all of his councilors swear allegiance to follow these instructions. Edward died at Greenwich Palace on July 6, 1553, and was buried in the vault of the Lady Chapel at Westminster Abbey. The exact reason for Edward's death is not known but most historians agree that tuberculosis was the likely the cause. The young king was known to have had a weakened immune system, possibly caused by an earlier bout with measles and small pox.

Lady Jane Grey

(July 10, 1553 - July 19, 1553)

Lady Jane Grey, from an engraving by H.T. Ryall (1838).

BORN: October, 1537, at Bradgate Park
in Leicestershire

PARENTS: Henry Grey and Lady Frances Brandon

CROWNED: Uncrowned

CONSORT: Lord Guilford Dudley

DIED: February 12, 1554, at the Tower of London

BURIAL: The Chapel of St. Peter ad Vincula

Lady Jane Grey was born circa 1537 in Leicestershire and was the eldest daughter of Henry Grey and Lady Frances Brandon. Lady Frances was the daughter of Mary Tudor and Charles Brandon, Duke of Suffolk. In early February 1547 Jane was sent to live in the household of Thomas Seymour, the husband of Catherine Parr, Henry VIII's widow. Lady Jane lived with the couple until the death of Catherine in September 1548. She married Lord Guilford Dudley on May 21, 1553, at Durham House.

The Third Succession Act of 1544 had restored Henry VIII's daughters Mary and Elizabeth to the line of succession. This act authorized Henry VIII and his successor to alter the succession at any time. Henry's will reinforced the succession of his three children, and then declared that, should none of them leave heirs, the throne would pass to heirs of his younger sister, Mary Tudor, who included Lady Jane Grey. Henry's will excluded his elder sister Margaret Tudor's descendants, owing in part to Henry's desire to keep the English crown out of the hands of the Scottish monarchs.

When Edward VI lay dying in the early summer of 1553, his Catholic half-sister Mary was still the presumptive heir to the throne. However, Edward, in a drafted document witnessed by his councilors restricted the succession to non-Catholic, legitimate heirs, and specifically named his Protestant cousin Jane Grey successor. Edward VI personally supervised the copying of his will which was finally issued on June 21st and signed by the entire Privy Council and other notables. Edward also announced his intention to have this passed in Parliament. Even with this written document, Lady Jane's claim to the throne remained weak.

Edward VI died July 6, 1553, and three days later, Lady Jane was informed that she was now queen. On July 10, 1553, she accepted the crown (with reluctance) and took secure residence at the Tower of London, in preparation of her coronation. Northumberland faced a number of key tasks before consolidating his power after Edward VI's death. Most importantly, he had to isolate and, ideally, capture Lady Mary to prevent her from gathering support. But a wise, Mary, after confirming the death of Edward, set out for the safety of East Anglia and began to rally her supporters. On July 14th, Northumberland with a small brigade of troops, set off in search of Mary. In his absence, the Privy Council switched their allegiance from Lady Jane to Mary, and proclaimed the latter queen on July 19, 1533. Lady Jane and her husband remained in the Tower, but were now prisoners. On August 3, 1533, Mary entered London in a triumphal procession. Northumberland was arrested and convicted of high treason. He was executed on August 22, 1553, at Tower Hill. In September, Parliament declared Mary the rightful queen, denounced Edward VI's "Devise for the Succession" and declared Lady Jane a usurper.

Lady Jane, her husband Lord Guilford Dudley, former Archbishop Thomas Cranmer, and several others were charged with high treason. Their trial, by a special commission, took place on November 13, 1553, at the Guildhall and, as expected, all were found guilty and sentenced to death. The failed Protestant rebellion of Thomas Wyatt the Younger, in late January 1554, sealed Jane's fate, although she had nothing to do with it directly. Wyatt's rebellion started as a popular revolt, precipitated by the proposed marriage of Mary to Philip II of Spain. Jane's father (the Duke of Suffolk) and other nobles joined the rebellion. The Holy Roman Emperor, Charles V, and his ambassadors, pressed Queen Mary to execute Lady Jane and put to rest any future succession controversy. Wyatt's Rebellion fizzled out in early March, and its leaders, including Thomas Wyatt and the Duke of Suffolk were arrested, tried, and executed.

On the morning of February 12, 1554, Guilford Dudley was executed. Lady Jane was then taken to Tower Green and beheaded. With few exceptions, only royalty were offered the privilege of a private execution. Lady Jane's beheading was conducted in private on the orders of Queen Mary, as a gesture of respect for her cousin. According to legend, Lady Jane gave the following speech upon ascending the scaffold:

> *"Good people, I am come hither to die, and by a law I am condemned to the same. The fact, indeed, against the Queen's highness was unlawful, and the consenting thereunto by me: but touching the procurement and desire thereof by me or on my behalf, I do wash my hands thereof in innocence, before God, and the face of you, good Christian people, this day."*

She then recited Psalm 51 (Have mercy upon me, O God) and handed her gloves to an attendant. The executioner asked her forgiveness, and she gave it and she pleaded to be dispatched quickly. She blindfolded herself and was resolved to go to her death with dignity, but once blindfolded, failing to find the block with her hands, began to panic and cried, "What shall I do? Where is it?" An unknown hand helped her find her way to the block. Her last word's were "Lord, into thy hands I commend my spirit," and with one sweep of the axe was beheaded. Both she and her husband were buried in the Chapel of St. Peter ad Vincula at the Tower.

(TOP) EXECUTION OF LADY JANE GREY, painted by Paul Delaroche (1833).

(BOTTOM) GRAVE MARKER of Lady Jane Grey and Guilford Dudley at St. Peter ad Vincula.

Mary I

(July 19, 1553 - November 17, 1558)

Mary I, from an engraving by H.T. Ryall (1838).

BORN: February 18, 1516, at Palace of Placentia in Greenwich

PARENTS: Henry VIII and Catherine of Aragon

CROWNED: October 1, 1553, at Westminster Abbey

CONSORT: Philip II of Spain

DIED: November 17, 1558, at St. James Palace

BURIAL: Westminster Abbey

"In thee, O lord, is my trust, let me never be confounded: if God be for us, who can be against us?"

- Mary I, Queen of England (1516-1558)

Edward VI's death bed prayers went unanswered, for his successor ushered England back to Catholicism. Lady Mary was seventeen when her mother's (Catherine of Aragon) marriage to Henry VIII was annulled. She was declared illegitimate, demoted from Princess, and sent to care for her half-sister, the baby Elizabeth (her father's daughter by Anne Boleyn). Convinced that Anne had bewitched her father, Mary vainly plotted to escape abroad. A staunch Catholic like her mother, she refused to accept the Protestant Reformation despite considerable pressure.

PALACE OF PLACENTIA AT GREENWICH, where Henry VIII (1491), Mary I (1516), and Elizabeth I (1533) were born. Henry VIII also married Anne of Cleves there in 1540. From 1873 - 1998, the Royal Naval College occupied the site and today is used by the University of Greenwich

Mary was born on February 18, 1516, at the Palace of Placentia in Greenwich. She was the only surviving child of Henry VIII and Catherine of Aragon and had a pleasant childhood. As the years progressed, no little brothers followed, and Henry VIII began to look into other marital alternatives. Her father was married six times: Catherine of Aragon was annulled, Anne Boleyn was beheaded, Jane Seymour died after giving birth to Edward VI, Anne of Cleves was annulled, Catherine Howard was beheaded, and Catherine Parr survived him. She was good friends with Jane Seymour, Anne of Cleves, and Catherine Parr, but fought bitterly with her father's other wives. At various times, Mary was both a favorite of her father's and an outcast. Prior to his death in 1547, she was in good favor.

When Henry VIII's health began to fail, he pushed through Parliament the Third Act of Succession (1543) in which Edward was declared heir to throne. Lady Mary was reinstated to the succession but only if Edward died childless, and Henry VIII and Catherine Parr had no children. Lady Elizabeth was also included and would succeed Mary. Queen

Catherine Parr is given credit for helping restore both Mary and Elizabeth to the line of succession. Henry VIII died January 28, 1547, leaving his nine year-old son, king. Edward was a supporter of the Protestant faith, although Mary seems to have hoped at one point he would see the error of his ways and return England to Catholicism. Mary defied Edward's Act of Uniformity and openly celebrated Mass, which had been abolished. Edward and Mary struggled with this issue through the rest of his short reign. Sometime in 1552, Edward began to show signs of the illness that would eventually claim his life.

As Edward lay dying in the summer of 1553, he knew according to the Third Act of Succession that Lady Mary was going to be queen, and feared that she would return the country to the Catholic faith. He drafted "My Devise for the Succession," which amended the Third Act of Succession. It barred any Catholic or illegitimate female from ascending the throne and named Lady Jane Grey as his heir. When Edward died on July 6, 1553, Mary fled London for the safety of East Anglia and began to rally supporters. She knew that fleeing the country entirely would most likely forfeit all chances of becoming Queen, thus she chose to remain and make a stand for her crown. Supporters of the new queen Lady Jane Grey, including the Duke of Northumberland set off to capture Mary.

Once Lady Mary received confirming news that her half-brother was indeed dead, she promptly sent proclamations throughout the country announcing her accession to the throne. By this time, the Privy Council in London realized their error in going along with Northumberland's plot and switched sides, declaring Mary the true Queen of England. Of the conspirators who tried to place Jane on the throne, only a few were initially executed, including Dudley and Grey. Jane and her husband were found guilty of treason, but Mary at first refused to have them executed. When Mary made her formal entry into London on the September 30, 1553, Elizabeth and the surviving wife of Henry VIII, Anne of Cleves, rode in a coach behind the Queen's in the great procession. On the morning of October 1, 1553, Mary was crowned queen at Westminster Abbey.

When Parliament met four days later, it proclaimed Henry VIII's marriage to Catherine of Aragon valid. Mary also attempted to repel all religious laws passed in the reign of her brother and father. She then began a search for a suitable husband. One of the possibilities was Edward Courtenay, who was one of the last descendants of the House of York and most obvious choices for a husband. One of Courtenay's greatest attractions in the view of the people was that he was an Englishman, not a foreign Prince. However, the Holy Roman Emperor Charles V (Mary's cousin), who was an instrumental advisor to the Queen, had other ideas and suggested his son, Prince Philip of Spain. After much thought, Mary accepted Philip's proposal, which was not popular.

In the early days of Mary's reign were filled with numerous plots to depose her. One involved Thomas Wyatt the Younger (son of the poet Thomas Wyatt, a courtly suitor of Anne Boleyn) and Henry Grey, Duke of Suffolk (father of Lady Jane Grey). Wyatt's Rebellion reached London in February 1554, but quickly fizzled out. All of the leading conspirators were arrested and executed. Queen Mary realized the mistake of leniency and decided that both Lady Jane Grey and her husband would have to be executed or she would face more revolts. Elizabeth had been summoned to London for questioning and was eventually imprisoned in the Tower as well, although she was later released.

On July 23, 1554, Philip of Spain arrived at Winchester and met Mary for the first time. It is not known exactly what language they used to converse (quite possibly Latin), but Philip and Mary talked into the evening and by all appearances seemed to get along quite well. Their marriage took place on July 25, 1554, at Winchester Cathedral and, in September, it was announced that Mary was pregnant.

Mary then began to act on her intention to restoring the Catholic faith in England. The nobility was allowed to keep the lands gained in the dissolution of the monasteries, but the Queen encouraged returning personal Church property. The medieval heresy laws were restored by Parliament, which meant that heretics (Protestants) could be executed, and their property and holdings given over to the Crown. In January 1555, heresy arrests and trials began with John Hooper (former Bishop of Gloucester), John Rogers, and John Cardmaster (who all refused to cease Protestant activities). All three men were condemned and burnt at the stake. Instead of deterring Protestant Reformers, these burnings only served as fodder for increased hatred of the Queen. In all about 275 people were executed for heresy and because of this the queen earned the nickname of "Bloody Mary."

As Mary's pregnancy progressed; plans were made for succession in the event the queen was to die in childbirth. Mary wanted to exclude Lady Elizabeth from the throne, which meant that the crown would be left to the Catholic, Mary Queen of Scots. She, howeve, was set to marry the son of the King of France and this was unacceptable for Spanish interests. Philip suggested that Lady Elizabeth marry a Catholic (and ally of the Holy Roman Emperor): the Duke of Savoy. Mary then retreated into privacy to await the birth of her child but her due date came and went. Physicians were baffled because the queen showed all the signs of being pregnant but never gave birth. It is thought that she suffered what is called a "phantom pregnancy," arising from the great emotional need to have a child. She might have been pregnant at some point, but miscarried along the way and the fetus was not expelled. Whatever the case, it became quite clear that Mary was not going to give birth and the subject was not brought up in the Queen's presence.

In late summer 1557, at age forty-seven, Queen Mary was sure she was again pregnant. She entered seclusion at St. James Palace in late February 1558, to await the birth. Those around her seemed to have doubts about the validity of the pregnancy after the earlier incident. By April, no child had come and Mary knew that she was once again mistaken. Her health gradually declined, most likely from stomach cancer. In late October 1558, she added a codicil to her will but did not expressly name Elizabeth as her heir. The next few weeks saw Mary drifted in and out of consciousness, but at one point was lucid enough to agree to pass the crown to her half sister, if she agreed to maintain the Catholic faith in England. On November 17, 1558, Mary died at St. James Palace and was interred at Westminster Abbey. Her tomb is located in the north aisle of Henry VII's Lady Chapel and during the reign of Elizabeth, Mary's tomb became buried under piles of stones from broken altars. When Elizabeth died in 1603, James I built a magnificent tomb that both sisters would share. Today, because of the weight of Elizabeth's sarcophagus, there is great danger of collapse into Mary's tomb.

ST. JAMES PALACE, where Mary I died on November 17, 1558.

Elizabeth I
(November 17, 1558 – March 24, 1603)

ELIZABETH I, painted by George Gower. *Courtesy of the National Portrait Gallery, London.*

BORN: September 7, 1533, at the Palace of Placentia in Greenwich

PARENTS: Henry VIII and Anne Boleyn

CROWNED: January 15, 1559, at Westminster Abbey

CONSORT: Unmarried

DIED: March 24, 1603, at Richmond Palace

BURIAL: Westminster Abbey

"I am no lover of pompous title, but only desire that my name may be recorded in a line or two, which shall briefly express my name, my virginity, the years of my reign, the reformation of religion under it, and my preservation of peace."

-Queen Elizabeth I (1533 – 1603)

Elizabeth was a fascinating figure in her own time and she has remained one since. More books have been written about her than any other British monarch. During her forty-four year reign, England would emerge as a world power, and she would give her name to an era that would be remembered as a golden age. And yet the baby Elizabeth was a disappointment to her parents, as they wanted a son. She was born on September 7, 1533, at the Palace of Placentia in Greenwich, the daughter of Henry VIII and Anne Boleyn. She was named after her paternal grandmother, Elizabeth of York. Though she grew up virtually motherless and was declared illegitimate, she overcame these obstacles to go down in history as one of Britain's greatest monarchs.

It was Catherine Parr, Henry VIII's sixth and final wife, who would have the greatest impact upon Elizabeth's life. A kind woman who believed passionately in education and religious reform, Parr was a devoted stepmother. Understandably, she had far more of an impact with the young Edward and Elizabeth than with Mary, who was just four years her junior. Catherine arranged for ten year-old Elizabeth to have the most distinguished tutors in England. As a result, Elizabeth was educated as well as any legitimate prince, and she displayed a genuine love and aptitude for her studies.

As a young girl, Elizabeth displayed the pragmatic character that would make her future reign as queen very successful. She studied theology and supported the Protestant cause, but was never openly passionate about religion, recognizing its divisive role in English politics. Elizabeth was thirteen years old when Henry VIII died in 1547. They were never particularly close, athough he did treat her with affection on her few visits to court. Under the Second Act of Succession, which declared both Elizabeth and Mary illegitimate, Parliament gave Henry the ability to change the status as he deemed it necessary. Henry allowed both his daughters to live like princesses and gave them precedence over everyone at court except his current wife. But they had been stripped of the title of Princess and were known simply as Lady. Henry's Third Act of Succession did recognize his daughter's crucial place in the succession to the throne, but only if Edward died without heirs. In this case Mary would inherit the throne, and if she died without children, Elizabeth would then become queen.

After Henry's death, Elizabeth had good cause to wish him alive again. Her ten year old half-brother, Edward was king in name only. The rule of England was actually in the hands of his uncle, the Lord Protector Edward Seymour, soon titled Duke of Somerset. Elizabeth was now separated from her brother's household, moving to Catharine Parr's home, which was perhaps the happiest time of her adolescence. But Catharine soon married Thomas Seymour, the younger brother of Lord Protector Somerset. He was handsome, charming, and very ambitious. He had, however terrible political instincts. Seymour was not content to be husband of the Dowager Queen of England. He was jealous of his brother's position and desperate to upstage him. He inadvertently played into the hands of the equally ambitious John Dudley, Earl of Warwick, who wished to destroy the Seymour protector-ship and seize power for himself.

For Elizabeth, the main problem with Seymour was his inappropriate and very flirtatious behavior. As a teenage girl with little experience of men, Elizabeth was flattered by his attention and also a bit frightened. Certainly it placed great strain on Catharine Parr, who had become pregnant soon after her marriage. The queen originally participated in Seymour's early morning raids into Elizabeth's room, where he would tickle and wrestle with the girl in her nightdress. But while Catharine considered this simple fun, her husband was more serious. In the spring of 1548, Edward VI's council heard rumors of these romps and investigated. Elizabeth proved

herself circumspect and clever, managing to admit nothing which would offend but soon left the Seymour home for Hatfield House, ostensibly because of Catherine Parr's failing health. After Catherine Parr's death, Thomas Seymour's position became more dangerous. It was rumored that he wished to marry Lady Elizabeth and thus secure the throne of England in case Edward died. He had already gained the wardship of Lady Jane Grey, a Tudor cousin, who was designated by Edward as heir to the throne. Seymour had plans of uniting Lady Jane and Edward in marriage, thus securing primary influence with his nephew. By the end of 1548, Thomas's grandiose plans had dissolved into a crazy plot to kidnap the king. On the night of January 16, 1549, Thomas broke into the King's apartments at Hampton Court and was arrested. The Privy Council accused him of high treason, was found guilty and executed on March 20, 1549. During the rest of Edward's reign Elizabeth kept out of politics and lived quietly at the Old Palace of Hatfield.

On July 6, 1553, Edward VI died and Lady Jane Grey was proclaimed queen. Grey's reign was short-lived, for a week later Mary ascended the throne. The new queen always disliked Elizabeth, and sensed an innate shiftiness in her character; she was not to be trusted. Mary also believed that Elizabeth's mother, Anne Boleyn, had bewitched her father and alienated his affection toward her mother. After Anne Boleyn's execution, Mary found other reasons to hate Elizabeth, especially her religious position. Like her mother, Mary was a devout Catholic and she recognized Elizabeth's lack of religious zeal. When Sir Thomas Wyatt the Younger led a rebellion in January 1554, matters came to an unpleasant impasse. Wyatt had written to Elizabeth that he intended to overthrow Mary, but his letter was intercepted. It implied that Lady Elizabeth knew of the revolt in advance. The government was able to suppress the rebellion before it spread very far. Wyatt was arrested and executed. Elizabeth denied any involvement in the rebellion and asked to speak with the queen. On March 17, 1554, she was taken from her rooms at Westminster Palace to the Tower of London. As Elizabeth waited under a canopy, her barge began to slow and she saw that they were entering the Tower, beneath Traitor's Gate, which was the traditional entrance for prisoners. The sight terrified her and she begged to be allowed entry by any other gate, her request was denied. She was offered a cloak to protect her from the rain but she pushed it aside angrily and as she stepped upon the landing stated;

"Here landeth as true a subject, being prisoner, as ever landed at these stairs. Before Thee, O God, do I speak it, having no other friend but Thee alone. Oh Lord, I never thought to have come in here as a prisoner, and I pray you all bear me witness that I come in as no traitor but as true a woman to the Queen's Majesty as any as is now living."

1. Old Palace of Hatfield.

2. TRAITOR'S GATE at the Tower of London.

3. TOMB OF MARY, QUEEN OF SCOTS, at Westminster Abbey.

MARY, QUEEN OF SCOTS, from a 19th century engraving.

This was the beginning of one of the most trying times of her life. Elizabeth spent only two months in the Tower of London, but she truly believed harm would come to her. She knew Mary hated her, as did many of the queen's councilors, who encouraged extended imprisonment or execution. However, Elizabeth was popular among the people and Mary refused to sign her death warrant. She was occasionally interrogated by members of Mary's council, but she held firm to her innocence. The stress took a toll on her physical health. Eventually, Elizabeth was released and was reconciled with the queen.

Mary died on November 17, 1558, and Elizabeth became queen. She immediately appointed her trusty friend and advisor William Cecil as chief minster (a post he would keep for the next 40 years). She was crowned on January 15, 1559, at Westminster Abbey. One of her first acts as queen was to approve a return to Protestantism. Next she turned to the issue of marriage and for many years had numerous suitors, but chose never to marry. Putting a positive spin on her marital status, Elizabeth insisted she was married to her kingdom and subjects.

Early in her reign, Elizabeth feared the French were planning an invasion to put Mary, Queen of Scots, on the throne. The Scottish queen was considered by many to be the true heir to the English throne. Elizabeth was persuaded to send troops to Scotland to aid the Protestant rebels, and though the campaign was inept, the resulting Treaty of Edinburgh (1560) removed the French threat in the north and established the Protestant church and a council of Protestant nobles. Mary refused to accept the treaty and in 1565 married Henry Stuart (who carried his own claim to the English throne). Stuart was unpopular in Scotland and, in February 1567, was murdered. Mary was implicated in her husband's death, imprisoned at Loch Leven Castle, and forced to abdicate in favor of her son James. Mary escaped in 1568 and fled across the border into England, where she had been assured of support. Elizabeth's first instinct was to restore her fellow monarch

monarch to the throne, but rather than risk making further enemies she had Mary imprisoned.

Mary Stuart soon became the focal point for rebellion. In 1569 there was a major Catholic uprising in the north, the goal of which was to free Mary and put her on the English throne. The revolt was quickly defeated and hundreds of nobles were executed. In the belief that the revolt had been successful, Pope Pius V excommunicated Elizabeth and released all her subjects from any allegiance. The Papal decree provoked legislative initiatives against Catholics. English Catholics now looked to Mary Stuart as the true sovereign of England. At first, Elizabeth resisted all calls for Mary's death, but by late 1586, she was persuaded that it was necessary to eliminate her rival.

Mary Queen of Scots was executed on February 8, 1587, at Fotheringhay Castle. She spent the last hours of her life in prayer and writing letters. A scaffold was erected in the Great Hall, draped in black with only a disrobing stool, a block, a cushion for her to kneel on, and a bloody butcher's axe that had been previously used on animals. According to contemporary accounts of the execution, Mary's attendants helped remove her red petticoat and satin bodice and as she disrobed, smiling faintly to the executioner, said, "Never have I had such assistants to disrobe me, and never have I put off my clothes before such a company." She was blindfolded and knelt in front of the block. She positioned her head on the block, stretched her arms out behind her and stated "my faith is the ancient Catholic faith. It is for this faith that I give up my life. In thee I trust, O Lord; into thy hands I commend my spirit."

The first blow of the axe missed her neck and struck the back of her head, at which point the Queen's lips moved (witnesses reported they thought she had whispered the words, "Sweet Jesus"). The second blow severed the neck, except for a small bit of skin which the executioner quickly removed. The executioner held Mary's severed head aloft and shouted, "God save the Queen." At that moment, the hair came apart and the head fell to the ground, revealing that Mary was wearing a wig. It was thought that she had tried to disguise the graying of her hair by wearing an auburn wig, the natural color of her hair before her years of imprisonment began. She was twenty-four when first imprisoned in Scotland and forty-four at the time of her execution. Another well-known execution story concerns a small dog owned by the queen, which is said to have been hiding among her skirts, unseen by the spectators. Following the execution, the dog refused to leave Mary's side and was covered in blood. Mary Queen of Scots was originally interred at Petersborough Cathedral, near Fotheringhay but moved to Westminster Abbey by her son, James I. Mary's tomb is located within the south aisle of Henry VII's Lady Chapel.

During Elizabeth's reign, foreign policy was largely defensive. Only through the activities of her navy did Elizabeth pursue an aggressive policy, which paid off in the war against Spain. She knighted Francis Drake after his circumnavigation of the globe from 1577 to 1580, and he won fame for his raids on Spanish ports and fleets. King Philip II of Spain (Elizabeth's brother-in-law) had seen enough and declared war with England. On July 12, 1588, the Spanish Armada set sail for England, hoping to ferry Spanish invasion forces under the leadership of the Duke of Parma to the southeast coast England.

A combination of miscalculation, bad weather, and a well timed attack by the English navy left the great Armada destroyed. Unaware of the Armada's fate, English militias mustered to defend the country under the Earl of Leicester's command. He invited Elizabeth to inspect her troops at Tilbury. Wearing a silver breastplate over a white velvet dress, she addressed the troops in one of her most famous speeches:

> *"My loving people, we have been persuaded by some that are careful of our safety, to take heed how we commit ourself to armed multitudes for fear of treachery; but I assure you, I do not desire to live to distrust my faithful and loving people ... I know I have the body but of a weak and feeble woman, but I have the heart and stomach of a king, and of a King of England too, and think foul scorn that Parma or Spain, or any Prince of Europe should dare to invade the borders of my realm."*

Following the defeat of the Spanish Armada, new difficulties arose for Elizabeth with Spain and Ireland. The costs of waging these wars were costly. The English economy faltered as prices rose and the standard of living fell. During this time, repression of Catholics intensified, and to maintain the illusion of peace and prosperity, Elizabeth increasingly relied on internal spies and propaganda. In her last years, this, along with mounting

criticism, reflected a decline in the public's affection for her. This same period of economic and political uncertainty, however, produced an unsurpassed literary flowering in England. The first signs of a new literary movement had appeared at the end of the second decade of Elizabeth's reign. During the 1590s, some of the great names of English literature entered their maturity, including William Shakespeare and Christopher Marlowe.

As Elizabeth aged her image gradually changed. Her painted portraits became less realistic and more a set of enigmatic icons that made her look much younger than she was. In fact, her skin had been scarred by smallpox in 1562, leaving her half bald and dependent on wigs and cosmetics. However, the more Elizabeth's beauty faded, the more her courtiers praised it. In 1598, Elizabeth's long-time advisor William Cecil died and his political mantle passed to his son, who soon became the leader of the government. One task he addressed was to prepare the way for a smooth succession. Since Elizabeth would never name her successor, Cecil was obliged to proceed in secret. He therefore entered into a coded negotiation with Mary Stuart's son, James VI of Scotland, who had a strong claim to the throne. Cecil coached the impatient James to humor Elizabeth.

Elizabeth's health remained fairly good until the autumn of 1602, when a series of deaths among her friends plunged her into a severe depression. In her last illness, Elizabeth refused to eat or see a physician, and for days lay propped up on cushions. She died from pneumonia in the early morning hours of March 24, 1603, at Richmond Palace. Later that same day the high council set their plan in motion, proclaiming James VI of Scotland, King James I of England. With Elizabeth's death the 118-year Tudor Dynasty came to an end and gave rise the turbulent 111-year reign of the House of Stuart. Elizabeth's coffin

was carried from Richmond Palace down river to Whitehall where she lay-in-state; she was then interred within the north aisle of the Lady Chapel at Westminster Abbey. Elizabeth shares a tomb with her half-sister, Mary. The Latin inscription upon the tomb reads; "Regno consortes & urna, hic obdormimus Elizabetha et Maria sorores, in spe resurrectionis," translated; "Partners both in throne and grave, here rest we two sisters, Elizabeth and Mary, in the hope of one resurrection.

1. DEATH OF QUEEN ELIZABETH I, from an 1800s engraving.

2. TOMB OF QUEEN MARY I AND ELIZABETH I at Westminster Abbey.

3. CLOSE-UP of Elizabeth I's tomb effigy.

Chapter Six

The House of Stuart and the Commonwealth (1603-1714)

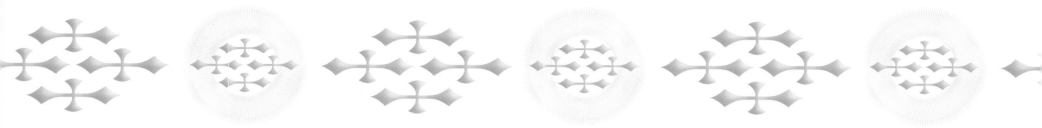

he House of Stuart was the royal house of Scotland from 1371 and of England from 1603. It was interrupted in 1649 by the establishment of the Commonwealth, but was restored in 1660. It ended in 1714, when the British crown passed to the House of Hanover. The royal Stewarts had an unlucky history, dogged by sudden death. Seven succeeded to the throne as minors. The direct male line terminated with the death of James V of Scotland in 1542. The Stuart's were the first monarchs to rule over the entire island of Britain. Under the Tudors the English Parliament had grown strong, under the Stuarts it grew stronger still. James I and Charles I clashed with their Parliaments because of their belief in royal absolutism and the divine right of kings. James was too prudent to endanger his throne, but Charles fought a civil war that cost him both his crown and head. This was followed by the Commonwealth and Puritanism. The crown, in the person of Charles II, was welcomed back in 1660. Cynical and shrewd, he kept his throne for twenty-five years before passing it to his younger brother, James II, a Catholic throwback to Stuart autocracy, who was soon driven out of the country.

The Glorious Revolution replaced him with his daughter Mary and her husband William of Orange. It decisively limited the power of the monarchy. The reign of the last Stuart ruler, Queen Anne, saw Britain triumphant in war on the continent and the development of modern party politics. The crown then passed to Sophia of Hanover, a granddaughter of James I; Sophia's son George became the first English monarch of the House of Hanover. The last of the male Stuarts, James Edward (the Old Pretender), and his son Charles Edward (the Young Pretender, known as Bonnie Prince Charlie), died without any legitimate children.

James I
(March 24, 1603 – March 27, 1625)

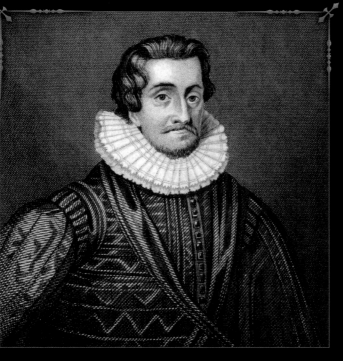

BORN: June 19, 1566, at Edinburgh Castle in Scotland

PARENTS: Mary Queen of Scots and Henry Stuart

CROWNED: July 25, 1603, at Westminster Abbey

CONSORT: Anne of Denmark

DIED: March 27, 1625, at Theobalds Palace

"The state of monarchy is the supreme thing upon earth: for kings are not only God's Lieutenants upon earth, and sit upon God's throne, but even by God himself they are called Gods."

-James I of England

James was the only son of Mary, Queen of Scots, and Henry Stuart. His mother was the granddaughter of Margaret Tudor, the older sister of Henry VIII. Her rule over Scotland was insecure, for both she and her husband were Catholics and faced rebellion by Protestant noblemen. James was born on June 19, 1566, at Edinburgh Castle. His father was murdered on February 10, 1567, by an unexplained explosion at Kirk o' Field in Edinburgh and Mary was widely suspected of plotting the murder. In June 1567, Protestant rebels arrested Mary and imprisoned her in Loch Leven Castle; she never saw her son again. She was forced to abdicate the Scottish throne on July 24, 1567, in favor of the infant James and appoint her illegitimate half-brother, James Stewart, Earl of Moray as regent. One year-old James was crowned King of Scotland on July 29, 1567 at Stirling Castle. Mary was imprisoned for twenty years before being executed in 1587.

Like Elizabeth, James had to grow up without a mother, but also without a father. This left him fearful of violence. He was baptized a

(TOP) EDINBURGH CASTLE, Scotland, where James I was born June 1566.

(BOTTOM) ANNE OF DENMARK, painted by John de Critz the Elder (1605).

Roman Catholic, but raised a Protestant. Three of the four Protestant regents who ruled Scotland during his youth died violent deaths. Because of this, James learned to rule by steering a middle course between Protestants and Catholics. He refrained from religious persecutions and managed to keep Protestant clerics at bay, all the while collecting a substantial annual allowance from Elizabeth I, as he impatiently awaited her death.

James was praised for his chastity and showed little interest in women, preferring male company. A suitable marriage, however, was necessary to reinforce his succession, and the choice fell on the fourteen-year-old Anne of Denmark, the daughter of Frederick II of Denmark. In August 1589, Anne sailed for Scotland but was forced by storms to the coast of Norway. Upon hearing that the crossing had been abandoned, James (being uncharacteristically romantic), sailed to fetch Anne personally. They were married at the Bishop's Palace in Oslo on November 23, 1589. By all accounts, James was at first infatuated with Anne, and in the early years of their marriage always showed patience and affection. Their marriage produced three children, one of which was the future Charles I. On March 2, 1619, Anne died at Hampton Court from edema (an abnormal accumulation of fluid under the skin that produces swelling, formerly known as dropsy).

On March 24, 1603, Queen Elizabeth I died. Within hours of her death a horseman was dispatched to Scotland to inform James of the news. The new king immediately made his way south to accept the throne, and was crowned King of England on July 25, 1603 at Westminster Abbey. One of his first acts as king was to preside over a conference of Anglicans and Puritans at Hampton Court, which came down mainly on the Anglican side and commissioned a new Bible, known today as the King James Version. He found the Church of England, with its moderate stance much to his liking.

James was a shrewd ruler but lacked the charm and glamour of Elizabeth. He has been portrayed as being undignified and lacking refinement. His thick Scottish accent was sometimes incomprehensible. He often neglected the business of government for leisure pastimes and lacked the Tudor's understanding of the English way. Despite this, he managed religious and political tensions skillfully and successfully. His later dependence on young male favorites caused scandal that undermined the respected image of the monarchy. Under his reign North America was colonized, which would lead to a contentious 150-year battle for continental supremacy between England, Spain, and France. He was a staunch believer in the divine right of kings and had a strong dislike for Parliament. Unfortunately, he handed down this belief to his son, Charles.

The later years of James's life were filled with numerous health issues that left him an increasingly peripheral figure, and rarely visited London. In early 1625, he was plagued by severe attacks of arthritis, gout, and fainting fits, and, in March, suffered a stroke. He died after a violent attack of dysentery on March 27, 1625, at Theobalds House in Hertfordshire and was buried at Westminster Abbey. The exact location of his tomb was lost until 1869, when his coffin was found in the same vault as Henry VII and Elizabeth of York. For all his flaws, James had never completely lost the affection of his people, who had enjoyed uninterrupted peace and comparatively low taxation. His death was widely mourned.

Charles I

(March 27, 1625 – January 30, 1649)

CHARLES I, painted by Sir Anthony Van Dyke. *Courtesy of the National Portrait Gallery, London.*

BORN: **November 19, 1600, at Dunfermline Palace in Scotland**

PARENTS: **James I of England and Anne of Denmark**

CROWNED: **February 2, 1626, at Westminster Abbey**

CONSORT: **Henrietta Maria of France**

DIED: **Executed January 30, 1649, in London**

BURIAL: **St. George's Chapel**

"I go from a corruptible to an incorruptible crown, where no disturbance can be, no disturbance in the world."

-Charles I of England (1600-1649)
spoken from the scaffold before his execution on January 30, 1649

Charles I's portraits by Anthony Van Dyke make him look kingly, but he lacked his father's political skillfulness though he inherited the belief in the divine right of kings. This attitude was probably made steadfast by his own lack of self-confidence. He was born on November 19, 1600, at Dunfermline Palace in Scotland, the second son of James I of England and Anne of Denmark. A sickly little boy, Charles grew up with a stammer and in the shadow of his elder brother Henry, the heir to the throne who was six years his senior. Henry was much admired, and Charles idolized him. Sadly, Henry died from typhoid fever on November 6, 1612. The death of Prince Henry was widely regarded as a tragedy for the nation.

HENRIETTA MARIA of France, painted by Sir Peter Lily (1660).

Charles immediately fell ill after his brother's death but fulfilled his duty as chief mourner at the funeral, which James I (who detested funerals) refused to attend. All of Henry's titles were passed to Charles, who was left with the impossible task of living up to his brother's image.

Charles married an attractive French Catholic Princess, Henrietta Maria, the fifteen year-old daughter of Henry IV of France and Marie de Medici. Henrietta was born on November 25, 1609, at the Louvre Palace in Paris. She and Charles were married on June 13, 1625, at St. Augustine's Church in Canterbury. Three years of coldness and indifference ensued, but they eventually became devoted to each other. The marriage to the devoutly Catholic princess further incensed the increasingly Puritan nobility. She was meddlesome and put the wants of her friends above the needs of the realm. She and Charles would have eight children; two sons would be future kings of England, Charles II and James II.

Charles ascended the throne upon the death of his father in 1625, and was crowned on February 2, 1626, at Westminster Abbey. The early years of his reign were dogged by financial problems created by his father and Parliament's refusal to grant relief to a monarch that would not address grievances of the nobility. Between 1625 and 1629, Charles convened and dissolved three Parliaments and went the next eleven years without being summoning any at all.

A problem in Scotland brought an abrupt end to Charles's eleven years of personal rule, which unleashed the forces of civil war upon England. Charles attempted to force a new prayer book on the Scots which resulted in rebellion. Charles lacked the funds to wage war and reluctantly convened Parliament. A stalemate developed where neither the king nor Parliament could reach an agreement. Things came to a boiling point when Charles, on the advice of his wife, foolishly tried to arrest five members of Parliament. This struggle for supremacy between Charles and Parliamentary leaders led to civil war.

Charles raised his standard against Parliamentary forces at Nottingham in 1642. The lines of division were roughly as follows: Charles's (Cavaliers) support came from the peasantry and Episcopalian rooted nobility, while Parliament's (Roundhead) backing came from the emerging middle class and tradesmen of the Puritanical movement. Geographically, the northern and western provinces aided the Cavaliers, with the more financially prosperous and populous southern and eastern counties lending aid to the Roundheads. The bottom line is that the Roundheads, with deeper pockets and more population from which to draw, were destined to win the war. Oliver Cromwell and his New Model Army soundly defeated the Cavaliers on June 14, 1645, at Nasby. Scarcely a year later, Charles surrendered to Scottish forces, who then gave custody of the king to Parliament.

Charles was tried at Westminster Hall in January, 1649, for high crimes against the realm of England. He maintained that no court on earth had the right to try a king, but he was duly charged as a tyrant, traitor, murderer, and public enemy. Over a period of a week, Charles was asked to plead three times and he refused. It was then normal practice to take a refusal plea as an admission of guilt, which meant that the prosecution could not call witnesses. However an exception was made and witnesses were called to testify. On January 27, 1649, by a vote of 67 to 68, the assembled tribunal found the king guilty and his execution was scheduled for January 30, 1649.

Charles Stuart, as his death warrant states, was beheaded on Tuesday, January 30, 1649. Before the execution it was reported that he wore two shirts to prevent the cold weather from causing shivers that would have been mistaken for fear or weakness. The execution took place at Whitehall Palace on a scaffold erected in front of the Banqueting House. The king was separated from the people by large ranks of soldiers, and his final speech reached only those nearest him on the scaffold. In his final remarks, Charles declared that he had desired the liberty and freedom of the people as much as any, stating "I must tell you that their liberty and freedom consists in having government…it is not their having a share in the government; that is nothing appertaining unto them. A subject and a sovereign are clean different things." Charles then put his head on the block after saying a prayer and signaled the executioner he was ready and with one stroke was beheaded. It was noted that after the execution, a great moan was heard from the assembled crowd, some of whom then dipped their handkerchiefs in his blood, thus starting the cult of the Martyr King.

It was common practice for the head of a traitor to be held up and exhibited to the crowd with the words "Behold the head of a traitor!" Although Charles's head was exhibited, the words were not used and, in an unprecedented gesture, Oliver Cromwell, allowed the King's head to be sewn back onto his body so the family could pay its final respects. Charles was buried in private on the night of February 7, 1649, inside the Henry VIII vault at St. George's Chapel, Windsor Castle. After Charles's execution, Queen Henrietta was left destitute and fled to France, where she focused on her faith and her children. Following the restoration of the monarchy in October 1660, she took up residence at Somerset House, and was supported by a generous pension. She had intended to remain in England for the rest of her life, but by 1665 was suffering from bronchitis, which she blamed on the damp British weather. She traveled back to France the same year, taking residence in Paris at the Chateau de Colombres, where she died on September 10, 1669 from an overdose of opiates and was buried at the Basilica of St. Denis.

1. EXECUTION OF CHARLES I, by an unknown artist (1649). *Courtesy of the National Portrait Gallery, London.*

2. BANQUETING HOUSE at Whitehall, where Charles I was executed January 30, 1649.

3. ROYAL BASILICA of St. Denis in Paris, where Henrietta Maria of France, wife of Charles I of England, is buried.

Oliver Cromwell
(1649-1660)

Oliver Cromwell, from an 1800s engraving by E. Scriven.

BORN: April 25, 1599 at Huntingdon

PARENTS: Robert Cromwell & Elizabeth Steward

LORD PROTECTOR: December 1653-September 1658

SPOUSE: Elizabeth Bourchier

DIED: September 3, 1625, at White Hall, London

BURIAL: Westminster Abbey, then Tyburn, London

"No one rises so high as he who knows not whither he is going. Not only strike while the iron is hot, but make it hot by striking. Do not trust the cheering, for those persons would shout as much, if you or I were going to be hanged."

– Oliver Cromwell, Lord Protector (1599-1658)

There was no king in England between the execution of Charles I and the restoration of the monarchy with Charles II, or not in theory. Yet after centuries of monarchy there was no practical possibility of suddenly doing without it. Oliver Cromwell would be king in all but name, with the backing of Parliament's New Model Army. Oliver Cromwell, the First Lord Protector was born on April 25, 1599, at Cromwell House in Huntingdon. He was the son of Robert Cromwell and Elizabeth Steward. He was the Great-Great-Great Grand Nephew of Thomas Cromwell, Henry VIII's chief minister. Oliver was raised a strict Puritan and was educated at Cambridge. He represented the family in Parliament and married Elizabeth Bourchier on August 22, 1620, at St. Giles Cripplesgate in London. She was born in London in 1598 and was the daughter of Sir John Bourchier and Francis Crane. Oliver and Elizabeth had nine children, one of which was Richard (the future Second Lord Protector). Elizabeth died in November 1660 and is buried at Northborough Church.

He quickly made a name for himself by serving in both the Short Parliament (April 1640) and the Long Parliament (August 1640 through April 1660). Charles I, pushing his finances to bankruptcy and trying to force a new prayer book on Scotland, was badly beaten by the Scots, and had no choice but to summon Parliament. The Long Parliament, taking an aggressive stance, steadfastly refused to authorize any funding until Charles was brought to heel. The Triennial Act of 1641 assured that Parliament would be convened at least every three years. This was a formidable challenge to royal authority. A new era of leadership from the House of Commons had commenced and Parliament resented Charles's insincerity.

In 1642, Parliament stripped Charles of the last vestiges of absolute power by abolishing church government and placing the army and navy directly under its supervision. Charles entered the House of Commons (the first king to do so) intent on arresting John Pym, the leader of Parliament, and four others, but the five conspirators had already fled, making the king appear inept. Charles traveled north to recruit an army and raised his standard against the forces of Parliaments (Roundheads) at Nottingham on August 22, 1642. Later that year at the Battle of Edge Hill, the Roundheads were defeated by the superior Royalist (Cavalier) cavalry, prompting Cromwell to develop his own army. Oliver Cromwell proved to a better military leader than expected and, by the Battle of Marston Moor in 1644, his "New Model Army" had routed Cavalier forces. The fighting lasted until June 1645, when Cromwell's forces defeated Charles at the Battle of Naseby and within a year, Charles had surrendered to the Scots, and was turned over to Parliament. By 1646, England was ruled exclusively by Parliament, although Charles was not executed until January, 1649. Following the dissolution of the monarchy, English society splintered into many factions. Levellers (intent on eradicating economic castes), Puritans, Episcopalians, remnants of the Cavaliers, and other religious and political radicals all argued over the fate of the realm. The sole source of authority rested with the army and Oliver Cromwell, who moved quickly to end the debates. In November 1648, the Long Parliament was reduced to a "Rump" Parliament by the forced removal of 110, and 160 refusing to take their seats in opposition to the forced removal. Those that remained were barely enough for a quorum, but embarked on constitutional changes that dismantled the machineries of government that had remained loyal to the king, abolished the monarchy, Privy Council, Courts of Exchequer, the Admiralty, and even the House of Lords. England was now ruled by an executive Council of State with Parliament dealing with day-to-day affairs. With Parliament in firm control, attention was turned to crushing the remaining rebellions within England and the rest of the realm. Cromwell forced submission from the nobility and defeated the Leveller rebels. Disarming the most radical elements of the opposition remained elusive, and, because of this, the monarchy was eventually restored. Eventually, the Rump Parliament devolved into a petty, self-perpetuating and unbending oligarchy, which lost credibility in the eyes of the army. Cromwell ended the Rump Parliament with great indignity on April 21, 1653, ordering the house cleared at the point of a sword and called for a new Parliament of Puritans, who proved as inept as the Rump. By 1655, Cromwell dissolved this Parliament and chose to rule alone, much like Charles I had done in 1629, but the cost of keeping a standing army of 35,000 proved financially impossible and yet another Parliament was convened. A House of Peers was created that was packed with Cromwell's supporters. It had true veto power, but the House of Commons proved antagonistic.

The monarchy was restored in all but name, when Cromwell was given the title of Lord Protector of the Realm. The title of king was suggested, but wisely rejected by Cromwell when a furor arose in the military

ranks. In August 1658, Cromwell's daughter Elizabeth Claypole died and the shock of her sudden death sent Oliver into a deep depression from which he never emerged. At Whitehall Palace on September 3, 1658, on the day of the anniversary of his military victories at the Battles of Dunbar and Worcester, Cromwell, suffering from renal failure and kidney stones, lapsed into a coma and died. A lavish funeral was held at Somerset House and the public was allowed to view the body. On November 23rd, Cromwell was interred at Westminster Abbey in the Lady Chapel vault, near his daughter Elizabeth and the tomb of King Henry VII. Oliver Cromwell's remains did not rest in peace for long, on January 30, 1661 (symbolically the 12th anniversary of the execution of Charles I), he was unceremoniously exhumed from Westminster Abbey, and subjected to a ritual posthumous execution, as were the remains of other members of the Commonwealth. Cromwell's body was hanged in chains at Tyburn, beheaded and thrown into a nearby pit; his severed head was then displayed on a pole outside of Westminster Hall until 1685. Ironically, the Cromwell vault at Westminster Abbey was subsequently used as a burial place for Charles II's illegitimate descendants. Cromwell's head changed hands several times over the next three hundred years, before eventually being buried in 1960 at Sidney Sussex College in Cambridge.

Oliver Cromwell was succeeded as Lord Protector by his son Richard. Although Richard was not entirely without ability, he had no power base in either Parliament or the army, and was forced to resign in May 1659. This ended the Protectorate and no clear leadership developed as numerous factions jockeyed for power. In 1660, a council of state invited Charles II back from exile, and the monarchy was restored. Richard Cromwell fled to France, and traveled throughout Europe, visiting various royal courts. In 1680, he returned to England and settled in Finchley, Middlesex, living off a meager income from his Hursley estate. He died on July 12, 1712, at the age of eighty-five. Although his reign of power was one of the shortest (only 264 days), he was still one of the longest lived "rulers" in British history, (a title now shared with Queen Elizabeth II). Richard Cromwell is buried at All Saints Churchyard in Hursley, Hampshire.

The failure of Cromwell and the Commonwealth was founded upon attempts to placate the army, the nobility, Puritans, and Parliament. Cromwell was unable to make a clear separation from the ancient constitution and traditional customs of loyalty and obedience to monarchy. Parliament could no more exist without the crown than the crown without Parliament. The ancient constitution had never been King "and" Parliament but King "in" Parliament; when one element of that mystical union was destroyed, the other ultimately perished.

FLOOR MARKER within the Lady Chapel at Westminster Abbey, denoting the original burial location of Oliver Cromwell.

ALL SAINTS CHURCH in Hursley, Hampshire, where Richard Cromwell, the 2nd Lord Protector of England, is buried.

Charles II

(May 29, 1660 – February 6, 1685)

Charles II, from an 1800's engraving by W. Finden.

BORN: May 29, 1630, at St. James Palace

PARENTS: Charles I and Henrietta Maria of France

CROWNED: April 23, 1661, at Westminster Abbey

CONSORT: Catherine of Braganza

DIED: February 6, 1685, at Whitehall Palace

BURIAL: Westminster Abbey

"You had better have one King than five hundred."
– Charles II, King of England

Charles II was born on May 29, 1630, at St. James Palace. As Charles I had been unlike his father, so Charles II was unlike his. Worldly and easy going, Charles II was charming, humorous, likeable, and had a very high sex drive. He would not let principles cost him his head like his father. During his reign, Charles II's throne was never seriously threatened. He grew up in Richmond under the tutelage of the Earl of Newcastle, was an expert horseman, not too religious, and cared very little for studies. He spent the first years of the English Civil War with his father, witnessing the horrors of war. At age fourteen, he was sent to the West Country to keep him out of Parliament's hands after the defeat of the Cavaliers at Naseby in 1645. He then fled with his mother to France.

BARBARA VILLIERS, Charles II's most notorious mistress, painted by Peter Lely (1618-1680).

Life in France was comfortable for Charles; he was considered a penniless outsider, who spoke no French. He and other royalist exiles amused themselves with the pursuit of women and he acquired his first mistress, the bold and beautiful Lucy Walter, who bore him a dearly loved son, James (the future Duke of Monmouth) in 1649. Throughout his life Charles would have numerous mistresses, but the most notorious was Barbara Villiers. She was tall, voluptuous, and was considered to be one of the most beautiful of the English Royalist women in France. By 1662, Villiers had more influence at court than Charles' wife, Catherine of Braganza. In point of fact, Barbara chose to give birth to their second child at Hampton Court while Charles and the Queen were honeymooning. In the summer of 1662 she was appointed Lady of the Bedchamber despite opposition from Queen Catherine, with whom she feuded constantly.

Charles was eighteen when his father was executed and he succeeded to the throne, theoretically at least. He was invited to Scotland, where he found the Presbyterians detestable, but by accepting the Scottish crown he gained a coronation at Scone (January 1, 1651) and an army to invade England. He was defeated at Worcester on September 3, 1651, and escaped to the Netherlands. When Oliver Cromwell died on September 3, 1658, the situation changed and secret negotiations began with General George Monck, the commander of the parliamentary army in Scotland. Within the year, Monck marched his men south to London, summoned remnants of Charles I's Long Parliament and, to general approval and relief, secured the restoration of Charles II to the English throne. Parliament sent a fleet to the Netherlands to fetch the new king. He arrived in London on May 29, 1659 (his 30th birthday), to a tumultuous welcome and was crowned on April 23, 1661, at Westminster Abbey.

His first act as king was to have Oliver Cromwell's corpse disinterred, hung on a gallows at Tyburn, and beheaded. The surviving judges, who had condemned his father to death, were either executed or imprisoned, but otherwise the past was not pursued. Many Commonwealth officials remained at their posts and the New Model Army was disbanded. On May 21, 1662, Charles married Catherine of Braganza at the Royal Garrison Church in Portsmouth; she was the daughter John of Portugal and Luisa of Medina-Sidonia. Although not considered a beauty, she had an immense dowry that included Tangier and Bombay. Catherine was not a particularly popular choice of queen, being Roman Catholic; her religion prevented her from being crowned queen. She initially faced hardships due to the language barrier, and suffered silently through Charles's many infidelities. Over time, her quiet decorum, loyalty and genuine affection for Charles changed the public's perception. Catherine had several pregnancies which miscarried. Her position remained tenuous, as Charles continued to have children by his many mistresses (a total of 16 children). Though Catherine was unable to conceive, Charles firmly dismissed the idea of divorce, even when Parliament exerted pressure to declare a Protestant successor.

During his reign, Charles's court was known for its extravagance and wickedness. He had such a bevy of mistresses that he was nicknamed Old Rowley after one of the royal stallions. Besides Villiers, his best known were actress Nell Gwynne, Moll Davies, Lousie de Keroualle, and Frances Stewart. His rule also witnessed a renewed interest in art, literature, and theater, and science flourished. Christopher Wren was appointed to rebuild St. Paul's and many others which were destroyed during the Great London Fire of 1666.

CATHERINE OF BRAGANZA, painted by Dirk Stoop (1660). *Courtesy of the National Portrait Gallery, London.*

PANTHEON OF THE ROYAL HOUSE of Braganza at the monastery of Sao Vincente de Fora. Catherine of Braganza's crypt is located second from the left on the top row.

With Charles unable to produce a legitimate heir, his brother James, Duke of York was next in line of succession but was a known Catholic. Parliament passed the Test Act of 1673, which excluded Catholics from all public offices, although it stopped short of barring James from succession. In 1678, anti-Catholic feelings rose to a frenzy, when Queen Catherine was accused of instigating the "Popish Plot," a conspiracy to poison the king. Although the plot was later discovered to be fabricated, the House of Commons voted (unsuccessfully) to have the Queen and her household banished from Whitehall. Charles, not believing the accusations, stood behind his wife, and kept his nerve, dissolving three parliaments in support of his brother against the Exclusion Bill.

On February 2, 1685, Charles in a fit of rage suffered a minor stroke and for the next few days lingered in a confused state. Physicians recommended that the king be bled and removed over 16 ounces of blood, further complicating the situation. On February 6, 1685, Charles died at Whitehall Palace and the symptoms of his final illness are similar to kidney failure. He was buried in a plain vault in the south aisle of the Henry VII Chapel at Westminster Abbey. During restorations in 1867, the vault was opened and Charles's coffin was noted to be in terrible condition, with the remains visible. In 1977, the vault was again opened and the remains were still visible. Following Charles's death, Queen Catherine showed anxiety and exhibited great grief. She remained in England, living at Somerset House for many years. In 1692, she returned to Portugal. On December 31, 1705, she died at Bemposta Palace in Lisbon and was buried at Jeronimos Monastery. In 1914, her remains where removed and reinterred within the Pantheon of the Royal House of Braganza at the Monastery of Sao Vincente de Fora.

James II

(February 6, 1685 – December 11, 1688)

BORN: October 14, 1633, at St. James Palace

PARENTS: Charles I and Henrietta Maria of France

CROWNED: April 23, 1685, at Westminster Abbey

CONSORT: Anne Hyde and Mary of Modena

DIED: September 16, 1701, at the Chateau Saint Germain-en-laye

BURIAL: The Church of the English Benedictines in Paris

James II was born on October 14, 1633, at St. James Palace, the second son of Charles I and Henrietta Maria of France. He was the last Stuart monarch in the direct male line. In 1646, during the English Civil War, he was captured at Oxford and held prisoner at St. James Palace. In April 1648, he escaped to the Netherlands, then went on to France. The following year, he joined the French army, serving in four military campaigns under French General Turenne, who commended his courage and ability. When his brother Charles II concluded an alliance with Spain against France in 1656 he reluctantly changed sides, and commanded the right wing of the Spanish army at the Battle of the Dunes in June 1658.

After the restoration of his brother Charles II to the English throne in 1660, James was appointed Lord High Admiral of the Navy. He also showed considerable interest in colonial ventures and it was on his initiative that New Amsterdam was seized from the Dutch in 1664 and renamed New York in his honor. He commanded the fleet in the opening campaigns of the Second and Third Dutch Wars.

In politics, James was a strong supporter of the Edward Hyde, Earl of Clarendon. He married Edward's daughter Anne on September 3, 1660, in a private ceremony at Worcester House. She was not considered beautiful, but had tremendous courage, cleverness, and energy. Like his brother, James was a well known womanizer. Anne and James had two daughters, Mary and Anne (both were destined to be Queens of England). Anne Hyde died

on April 10, 1671, from breast cancer only seven weeks after giving birth to Anne, and was buried at Westminster Abbey. In 1668, James secretly converted to Catholicism, but his brother the king, insisted that his daughters, Mary and Anne, be raised in the Protestant faith. His religious conversion had little effect on his political views, which were already formed by his reverence for his dead father. James, in fact, was always more favorable to the Protestant Church than was his brother. He consented to the marriage of his elder daughter, Mary, to the Protestant William of Orange in 1677. For most of his life James was a spokesman for the conservative Protestant courtiers, who believed that his the succession. During this time, he spent long periods in Brussels and Scotland, but, owing largely to tenacious defense of his rights, the exclusionist faction was defeated. In 1682 James returned to England and resumed leadership of the Tories, whose power in local government was reestablished and increased by the remodeling of the borough corporations and the government of the counties in their favor. Charles II died in February 1685; James ascended to the throne and was crowned on April 23, 1685, at Westminster Abbey. His influence on state policy was paramount and, when he finally came to power, there was limited opposition. It seemed on the surface that strong support of the Tories would make him one of the most powerful monarchs of the seventeenth century.

James, Duke of Monmouth, was the illegitimate son of Charles II and his mistress Lucy Walter. He was a Protestant, and the Commander-in-Chief of the English Army under his father. An attempt was made in 1681 to pass the Exclusion Bill that would have bypassed James II in the succession and put Monmouth on the throne, but Charles outmaneuvered his opponents and dissolved Parliament before it could be passed. After a failed attempt to assassinate both Charles and James, Monmouth exiled himself to Holland and gathered supporters. So long as Charles II remained on the throne, Monmouth was content to live a life of pleasure in Holland, while still hoping to accede peaceably to the throne. The accession of James II put an end to these hopes.

In May 1685, Monmouth set sail for South West England with about 400 men and landed near Lyme Regis. On June 14th, he clashed with royalist militia. Afterwards, many of the militiamen defected. On June 20, 1685, Monmouth declared himself king at Taunton and continued north. The Royal Navy captured Monmouth's ships and ended any hope of escape back to the continent. Monmouth was counting on a rebellion in Scotland that never materialized. The morale of Monmouth's forces started to collapse at news of the setback. Monmouth's forces were pushed back and finally defeated by John Churchill (later Duke of Marlborough) at the Battle of Sedgemoor on July 6, 1685. This battle is often referred to as the last battle fought on English soil. Monmouth fled the battlefield, but was captured on July 8th in the New Forest. Despite begging for mercy and claiming conversion to Catholicism, Monmouth was executed on July 15, 1685.

Following the failed Monmouth rebellion, James II took the initiative to consolidate power and asked Parliament to repeal the Test Act and used his dispensing power to appoint Catholics to senior posts. This provoked a quarrel between the king, his Tory allies, and the rest of Parliament. Throughout the next year, the division between the king and his former allies deepened. After judges of King's Bench found in favor of the king's power to excuse individuals from the Test Oath, Catholics were admitted to the Privy Council and other high offices of state. A commission for ecclesiastical causes was established to

MARY OF MODENA, painted by William Wissing (1685). *Courtesy of the National Portrait Gallery, London.*

views on monarchy and Parliament coincided with theirs, they found his formal and humorless nature more congenial than Charles's insincere friendliness.

James resigned all of his offices in 1673 rather than take an anti-Catholic oath imposed by the so-called Test Act. On September 30, 1673, he married Mary of Modena, a Catholic, and the daughter of Alfonso IV, Duke of Modena, which further infuriated the public. From 1679 to 1681 three successive Parliaments strove to exclude James from administer James's powers as supreme governor of the English Church, and its first act was to suspend Henry Compton, Bishop of London, one of the most outspoken critics of royal policy.

In April 1687, James issued the so-called Declaration of Indulgence, suspending the laws against Catholics and Protestant dissenters alike. In July he again dissolved Parliament. In September he launched an intensive campaign to win over Protestant dissenters. With their aid, he secured a new Parliament that was more amenable to his wishes. James had a true belief in religious toleration, but many still believed the king harbored a secret desire to promote Catholicism.

The unexpected news that the queen was pregnant (November 1687), established the prospect of a Roman Catholic succession. This had a great effect on most Protestant leaders, who ever since the spring of 1687 were in secret negotiations with William of Orange, the husband of Princess Mary and the champion of Protestant Europe. The spark of revolt was touched off by James himself, when he reissued his Declaration of Indulgence on April 27, 1688, and ordered it to be read in the churches. It suspended all penal laws in ecclesiastical matter of not attending the Church of England, permitted people to worship anywhere, and ended the requirement of religious oaths for advancement in civil or military positions. The Archbishop of Canterbury and six of his bishops petitioned James to withdraw the order. Their petition was subsequently published and James made the mistake of arresting its authors for seditious libel. Meanwhile, on June 10, 1688, the queen gave birth to a son, James Francis Edward, Prince of Wales (known to history as the Old Pretender).

On June 30, 1687, the seven bishops were acquitted, and that same day William of Orange was invited to lead an army to England and claim the throne. By September William's intentions were obvious, and James was confident in the ability of his forces to repel invasion. William landed in England in November 1688 and in the subsequent campaign, known as the Glorious Revolution, James's army deserted in such large numbers that the king was unable to commit to a pitched battle. This, along with his daughter Anne's defection, shattered his nerves. James attempted to flee to France but was intercepted in Kent; twelve days later, he was allowed to escape. On February 12, 1689, Parliament declared that because James had fled the country, he had abdicated the throne. The next day the crown was offered to William and Mary as co-monarchs.

In March 1689, James attempted to reclaim the throne and landed in Ireland with French supporters. On July 1, 1690, his army was defeated by William at the Battle of the Boyne and James fled back to France. In the brief Irish campaign, James showed none of his former military ability, and, now aging rapidly, he was falling increasingly under the influence of his wife. He became obsessed with religious devotions and even his most ardent supporters soon saw him as a liability. The Treaty of Ryswick between England and France (1697) removed his last hopes of restoration to the throne. During his last years, James lived a quiet and pious life. He died of a brain hemorrhage on September 16, 1701, at Chateau de Saint-Germain-en-Laye. He was buried within the Chapel of Saint Edmund in the Church of the English Benedictines in Paris. During the French Revolution, his tomb was desecrated and the remains were destroyed. Mary of Modena spent the remainder of her life championing the rights of her son, James Francis Edward, and died in virtual poverty from cancer on May 7, 1718. She is buried at the Convent of the Visitation in Chaillot.

Upon the death of his father in 1701, James Francis Edward (Old Pretender), declared himself King of England, which was recognized by France, Spain, the Papal States, and Modena. All of which had refused to recognize William, Mary, or Anne as legitimate rulers. As a result of his claiming his father's throne, James was arrested for treason on March 2, 1702. All his titles were forfeited and he was exiled to France. Six years later, he attempted an invasion of England, landing at the Firth of Forth on March 23, 1708, but his ships were driven back by the Royal Navy. Had he renounced his Catholic faith, he might have strengthened his support from pro-Restoration Tory factions, but his refusal, resulted in a German Protestant being named king.

JAMES FRANCIS EDWARD STUART (The Old Pretender), painted by Antonio David (1720).

In 1713, the War of Spanish Succession ended indecisively and Louis XIV of France was forced to accept peace with Britain and her allies. He signed the Treaty of Utrecht that required him to expel the Old Pretender from France. The following year, there was an attempt in Scotland to put him on the throne but this quickly fizzled. Pope Clement XI offered him sanctuary in Rome and he accepted. On September 3, 1719, James Francis Edward Stuart married Maria Sobieska, granddaughter of John III of Poland. They had two sons, Charles Edward (nicknamed Bonnie Prince Charlie) and Henry. Attention now turned to his son Charles (the Young Pretender), who's rebellion of 1745 came close to success but ultimately failed. With this, all hopes of a Stuart regaining the throne were effectively lost.

James Francis Edward (the Old Pretender) died in Rome on January 1, 1766, and was buried in the crypt of St. Peter's Basilica at the Vatican. His burial is marked by the Monument to the Royal Stuarts. His 64 years, 3 months, and 16 days as the pretender to the thrones of England, Scotland, and Ireland lasted longer than the reigns of almost all monarchs of Britain. To date, the longest serving British monarch is Queen Victoria, who reigned for 63 years, 7 months and 2 days. In order to surpass the record set by the titular James Francis Edward, Queen Elizabeth II would need to remain on the throne until at least May 23, 2016. Charles Edward Stuart (Bonnie Prince Charlie) died in Rome on January 31, 1788, and was first buried in the Cathedral of Frascati. Upon the death of his brother, Henry Benedict Stuart, in 1807, both were interred next to their father in the crypt of St. Peter's Basilica. When the body of Charles Stuart was transferred, his heart was left at Frascati Cathedral and placed below the funerary monument.

(TOP) CHATEAU-SAINT GERMAIN-EN-LAYE, where James II died September 16, 1701.

(BOTTOM) TOMB OF THE ROYAL STUARTS at St. Peter's Basilica in Rome, which contain the remains of James Francis Edward Stuart, his wife, and their two sons, Charles and Henry.

William III and Mary II

(1689 – 1702)

WILLIAM III of Orange, from an 1850s engraving.

BORN: **November 4, 1650, at the Hague in Holland**

PARENTS: **William II of Orange and Princess Mary Stuart**

CROWNED: **April 11, 1689, at Westminster Abbey**

CONSORT: **Mary II of England**

DIED: **March 8, 1702, at Kensington Palace**

BURIAL: **Westminster Abbey**

MARY II, from an engraving by Lundin (1804).

BORN: **April 30, 1662, at St. James Palace**

PARENTS: **James II of England and Anne Hyde**

CROWNED: **April 11, 1689**

CONSORT: **William III**

DIED: **December 28, 1694, at Kensington Palace**

BURIAL: **Westminster Abbey**

William was born on November 4, 1650 at The Hague in Holland, the only child of William II, Prince of Orange, and Mary, Princess Royal (daughter of Charles I of England). He was the grandson of Charles I, nephew of Charles II and James II. Eight days before his birth, William's father died from smallpox. William's mother, Princess Mary, showed little personal interest in her son, sometimes being absent for years, and always kept herself apart from Dutch society. He was well educated, given daily instruction in the Reformed Calvinist religion, and was taught that he was predestined to become an instrument of Divine Providence, fulfilling the historical destiny of the House of Orange. He grew up among family and political power struggles, but emerged as a forceful and determined figure, respected but not well liked. He was reserved, silent, haughty, and abrupt. He had few intimates and really never understood the English way.

In 1672, William was appointed Stadtholder (chief magistrate) and captain-general of the Dutch forces. He forced Louis XIV of France to make peace in 1678 and then concentrated on building a European alliance. On November 4, 1677, at St. James Palace, he married Princess Mary of England, the eldest daughter of James II and Anne Hyde. Princess Mary was born on April 30, 1662, at St. James Palace and she was William's first cousin. The marriage was intended to repair relations between England and The Netherlands, following the Anglo-Dutch wars. William was twelve years older than his English wife, who was a reluctant and tearful bride. Mary became pregnant soon after the marriage, but miscarried and because of illness never conceived again.

In 1688, both William and Mary were invited by Parliament to take the throne from James II. William landed in England on November 5, 1688, unopposed and with an army of 14,000 troops advanced on London in what became known as "The Glorious Revolution." In January 1689, William summoned a Convention Parliament, which met to discuss the appropriate course of action following James's flight. William felt insecure about his position; though his wife ranked higher in the line of succession to the throne, he wished to reign as King in his own right, rather than as a mere consort. The only precedent for a joint monarchy in England dated from the sixteenth century, when Queen Mary I married the Spanish Prince Philip, who remained King only during his wife's lifetime. William, on the other hand, demanded that he remain King even after his wife's death. The House of Commons quickly resolved that the throne was vacant and that it was safer if the ruler was Protestant, but William refused to be a regent or to agree to remaining King only in his wife's lifetime. Through negotiations Parliament agreed by a narrow majority that the throne was vacant and made William accept a Bill of Rights, in which it deemed that James, by attempting to flee, had abdicated, thereby leaving the throne vacant. The

Crown was not offered to James's eldest son, James Francis Edward (who would have been the heir-apparent under normal circumstances), but to William and Mary as joint Sovereigns. It was, however, provided that the sole and full exercise of regal power was exercised by the said Prince of Orange in the names of the said Prince and Princess during their joint lives. It prevented a Catholic for succeeding to the throne (ensuring that Mary's sister, Princess Anne, would become the next queen) and stipulated that the monarchy could no longer pass laws nor levy taxes without parliamentary consent. On April 11, 1689, William and Mary were crowned as co-monarchs at Westminster Abbey. There was never any doubt about who was the dominant partner and Queen Mary spent most of her time sewing and gardening. After a difficult start to their married life, William and Mary became quite fond of one another, once it became clear that Mary had no interest in politics.

Early in their reign they defeated two attempts by James II to regain the throne. In Scotland government troops were initially defeated, but won several key battles. James II landed in Ireland with French allied troops and laid siege to Londonderry. William's navy relieved the siege and then defeated James at the Battle of the Boyne (July 1, 1690). James II fled back to France and never again made a serious attempt to regain the throne.

Mary died of smallpox on December 28, 1694, at Kensington Palace and her body lay in state in Banqueting House at Whitehall. She was buried at Westminster Abbey in the Stuart Vault in the south aisle of the Lady Chapel. Her funeral service was the first to be attended by all members of both Houses of Parliament. William mourned his wife's death, but now ruled alone and his popularity as a sole ruler plummeted. As William's life drew towards its conclusion, he felt concern over the question of succession to the throne of Spain, which brought with it vast territories in Italy, the Low Countries and the New World. The King of Spain, Charles II, was an invalid with no prospect of having children; amongst his closest relatives were Louis XIV (the King of France) and Leopold I, Holy Roman Emperor. William sought to prevent the Spanish inheritance from going to either monarch, for he feared that such a calamity would upset the balance of power. William and Louis XIV agreed to the First Partition Treaty, which provided for the division of the Spanish Empire. Duke Joseph Ferdinand of Bavaria would obtain Spain, while France and the Holy Roman Emperor would divide the remaining territories between them. Charles II accepted the nomination of Joseph Ferdinand as his heir, and war appeared to be averted.

When, however, Joseph Ferdinand died of smallpox, the issue re-opened. In 1700, the two rulers agreed to the Second Partition Treaty (also called the Treaty of London), under which the territories in Italy would pass to a son of the King of France, and the other Spanish territories would be inherited by a son of the Holy Roman Emperor. This arrangement infuriated both the Spanish, who still sought to prevent the dissolution of their empire, and the Holy Roman Emperor, to whom the Italian territories were much more useful than the other lands. Unexpectedly, the invalid King of Spain, Charles II, interfered as he lay dying in late 1700. He willed all Spanish territories to Philip, a grandson of Louis XIV and the French conveniently ignored the Second Partition Treaty and claimed the entire Spanish inheritance. Furthermore, Louis XIV alienated William by recognizing James Francis Edward Stuart (The Old Pretender and son of James II) as king of England. The subsequent conflict, known as the War of Spanish Succession, continued until 1713.

The Spanish inheritance was not the only one that concerned William. His marriage to Mary produced no children and he seemed unlikely to remarry. His sister-in-law, Princess Anne, had given birth to numerous children, but all died either at birth or in early childhood. Anne was left as the only person left in the line of succession, established by the Bill of Rights of 1689. As the complete exhaustion of the line of succession would have encouraged a restoration of James II's line, Parliament saw fit to pass the Act of Settlement (1701), which stipulated that the throne would be inherited by a distant relative, Sophia of Hanover (granddaughter of James I), and her Protestant heirs, if Princess Anne died without surviving issue, and if William III failed to have surviving issue by any subsequent marriage.

On March 8, 1702, William died of pneumonia at Kensington Palace, the result of complications from a fall from his horse. It's coincidental that all three of the first English monarchs named William died from accidents associated with horse riding. Because his horse had reputedly stumbled on a mole's burrow, supporters of the deposed James II, toasted "the little gentleman in the black velvet waistcoat." Sir Winston

Churchill wrote in his epic, *History of the English Speaking Peoples*, that this fall had "opened the door to a troop of lurking foes." William was buried at Westminster Abbey beside his wife, Queen Mary, in the royal Stuart vault located near the altar within the south aisle of the Lady Chapel. None of the Stuart monarchs interred within the abbey have monuments but are marked by simple floor plaques.

(TOP) KENSINGTON PALACE, where Mary II died December 28, 1694, and William III died March 8, 1702.

(BOTTOM) GRAVE MARKER OF WILLIAM III AND MARY II at Westminster Abbey.

Anne

QUEEN ANNE, from a 19th century engraving.

BORN: **February 6, 1665, at St. James Palace**

PARENTS: **James II and Anne Hyde**

CROWNED: **April 23, 1702, at Westminster Abbey**

CONSORT: **Prince George of Denmark**

DIED: **August 1, 1714, at Kensington Palace**

BURIAL: **Westminster Abbey**

Like her mother before her, Anne grew exceptionally stout in later life. Like her sister Mary, she had the advantage of being a strong advocate of the Church of England. Cheerful, kindly, and unabashedly English, unlike her Dutch brother-in-law, Anne was popular with her subjects and she tried to link herself to Elizabeth I by dressing like her. She was born on February 6, 1665, at St. James Palace, the daughter of James II and Anne Hyde. Her mother died when she was only six and her father married Mary of Modena, which probably contributed to her lifelong bias against Catholics. She learned to speak fluent French, but she was not an intellectual.

On July 28, 1683, in the Chapel Royal, Anne married Prince George of Denmark, brother of Christian V of Denmark (her second cousin once removed). Though it was an arranged marriage, they were faithful and devoted partners. Within months of the wedding, Anne was pregnant, but the baby was stillborn. In all, she would endure seventeen pregnancies, twelve of which were either miscarriages or still born. Of the five remaining children none lived beyond the age of eleven, and each of their bodies were interred within the vault next to Mary, Queen of Scots, at Westminster Abbey.

In 1688, Anne abandoned her father, James II, and supported William of Orange's claim to the throne. However, she fell out of grace with the new regime, partly over John Churchill, the Duke of Marlborough (who was accused of supporting James II). Anne was told to dismiss Churchill's wife from her service, but Sarah Churchill was much loved and Anne flatly refused. Anne was removed from her quarters at Whitehall Palace and for the remainder of her life never again spoke to her sister Queen Mary. Following Mary's death in 1694, Anne was reconciled with King William but their relationship remained distant.

On March 8, 1702, William III died, and Anne became queen of England. In a speech to the English Parliament, she distanced herself from William saying "As I know my heart to be entirely English, I can very sincerely assure you there is not anything you can expect or desire from me which I shall not be ready to do for the happiness and prosperity of England." Soon after her accession, Anne appointed her husband Lord High Admiral, giving him nominal control of the Royal Navy, and gave control of the army to Lord Marlborough. She was crowned on April 23, 1702, at Westminster Abbey. Once on the throne, Anne steered a politically middle course through conflicts between the Whigs and Tories. Abroad her reign was dominated by the War of Spanish Succession,

which lasted until 1713. John Churchill won victory after victory in command of the British and allied armies and these successes boosted English national pride and the queen's popularity. In 1707, with Anne's encouragement, the Act of Union at last united both England and Scotland into one single nation, named Great Britain. The Scottish and English Parliaments merged following the election of 1708. The Act was intended to secure the Hanoverian succession after Anne. On October 28, 1708, at Kensington Palace, Prince George died from complications of asthma and dropsy. Anne was devastated and fell into deep despair. He was buried at Westminster Abbey within the south aisle of the Lady Chapel.

In April 1713, the War of the Spanish Succession ended with the signing the Treaty of Utrecht, in which Louis XIV of France recognized the Hanoverian succession in Britain and restored the balance of power in Europe. Queen Anne was quite ill from late 1713 through the summer of 1714, suffering from numerous health issues, chief among them obesity, gout, lupus, and kidney failure. On July 30, 1714, the anniversary of her son William's death, she suffered a stroke. Two days later, on August 1, 1714, Queen Anne died at Kensington Palace and was buried in an almost square coffin (because of her size), beside her husband in the south aisle of the Lady Chapel. With Anne's death, the 111 year reign of the House of Stuart came to an end.

Chapter Seven

The House of Hanover (1714-1917)

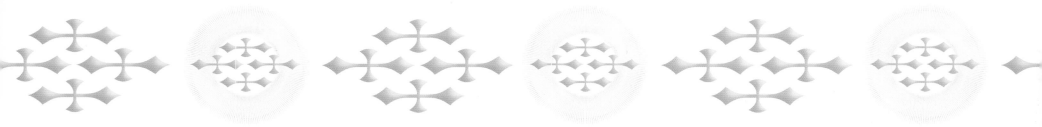

eorge, Duke of Brunswick-Luneberg, is considered the first member of the House of Hanover. In 1635, he inherited the principalities of Calenberg and Gottengen, and moved his residence to Hanover. His son, Duke Ernest Augustus, was elevated to Prince-Elector of the Holy Roman Empire in 1692. Ernest Augustus's wife, Sophia, was declared heir presumptive of the throne of Great Britain by the Act of Settlement, which decreed Roman Catholics, could not accede to the throne. She was the granddaughter of James I of England.

Ernest Augustus and Sophia's son, George, became the first British monarch of the House of Hanover. In succession, George I, II, and III also served as electors and dukes of Brunswick-Luneberg, and Hanover, as well as Kings of Great Britain. In 1837, however, the personal union of the thrones of Britain and Hanover ended. Succession of a Hanoverian was regulated by Salic law, which forbade inheritance by a woman, so that it passed not to Queen Victoria but to her uncle, the Duke of Cumberland. In 1901, when Queen Victoria died, her son and heir Edward VII became the first British Monarch of the House of Saxe-Coburg and Gotha, Edward taking his family name from that of his father, Prince Albert of Saxe-Coburg-Gotha.

British democracy was difficult for any foreign ruler to adjust to. It had no equivalent on the Continent. Even so, the new German dynasty dashed the hopes for a Stuart restoration under James III, "the old pretender," or his son Charles "the young pretender." The Hanoverian dynasty would help Britain grow into the greatest maritime, industrial, and imperial power on earth. Two hundred years later Edward VII was monarch of a fifth of the entire land surface of the globe, this in spite of the loss of the thirteen American colonies. George III's reign lasted an unprecedented 59 years, but Queen Victoria out did him with 63 years on the throne. Both of them set an example of duty, responsibility, and moral decency that many of their subjects valued. At the same time, the Industrial Revolution made Britain the workshop of the world and Victoria presided over a period of tremendous vitality and achievement in science, engineering, literature and the arts, from Faraday and Darwin, to Brunel and Paxton, Dickens and Tennyson. Meanwhile, through successive reigns the power of the monarchy ebbed away, as effective authority passed from kings and their councilors to Prime Ministers and party politics.

George I
(August 1, 1714 – June 11, 1727)

George I of Great Britain, from a 19th century engraving.

BORN: May 28, 1660, at Herrenhausen Palace, Hanover

PARENTS: Ernest Augustus, Elector of Hanover and Sophia of Hanover

CROWNED: October 20, 1714, at Westminster Abbey

CONSORT: Sophia Dorothea of Celle

DIED: June 11, 1727, at the Bishop's Palace at Osnabruck, Hanover

BURIAL: Hanover Mausoleum in Berggarten

The Hanoverian succession did not seem as sure a thing at the time as it looks in retrospect. Queen Anne had not let any of the Hanoverians settle in England and they waited in Germany with their fingers crossed for the news of her death. They were in close contact with leading Whig politicians and when the word came, George Louis made for England to be crowned as George I. A Lutheran and soldier at heart, he had fought in various campaigns in Europe and had been Elector of Hanover since 1698. He spoke several languages, but his command of English was never more than rudimentary, so affairs of state were conducted in either Latin or French.

He was born on May 28, 1660, at Herrenhausen Palace in Hanover, the son of Ernest Augustus, Duke of Brunswick-Luneburg and Sophia of Hanover (the granddaughter of James I of England). For the first year of his life, George was the only heir to the German territories of his father and three childless uncles. In 1661, George's brother, Frederick Augustus, was born and the two boys were brought up together. Their mother was absent for almost a year (1664–1665) during a long convalescent holiday in Italy, but she corresponded regularly with her sons' governess and took a great interest in their upbringing. George was described as a responsible and conscientious child, who set an example for his younger brothers and sisters. His father often took him hunting and riding, and introduced him to military matters. Mindful of his uncertain future, Ernest Augustus took the fifteen year-old George on campaign in the Franco-Dutch War with the deliberate purpose of testing and training his son in battle.

SOPHIA DOROTHEA OF CELLE, by William Faithorne, Jr; published by Edward Cooper (1683). *Courtesy of the National Portrait Gallery, London.*

In 1682, George married his first cousin, Sophia Dorothea of Celle, thereby securing additional incomes that would have been outside Salic laws requiring male inheritance. This political marriage was arranged primarily to ensure a healthy annual income and assisted with the eventual unification of Hanover and Celle. George's mother was at first against the marriage because she looked down upon Sophia Dorothea's mother (who was not of royal birth). However, she was eventually won over by the inherent financial advantages of the marriage. In 1683, Sophia Dorothea bore George a son named, George Augustus (the future George II of England). Following the birth of a daughter in 1687, the couple became estranged, with George preferring the company of his mistress,

Melusine von der Schulenburg, by whom he had two illegitimate daughters. Sophia Dorothea, meanwhile, had her own romance with a Swedish count, which threatened the Hanoverian court. It was urged that they end their romance. In July 1694, the count was murdered, possibly with the collusion of George, and his body thrown into the River Leine weighted with stones. It was alleged that the murder was committed by four of Ernest Augustus's courtiers, one of whom was paid an enormous sum. George's marriage to Sophia Dorothea was dissolved in 1694, not on the grounds that either of them had committed adultery, but on the grounds that Sophia Dorothea had abandoned her husband. With the agreement of her father, George had Sophia Dorothea imprisoned in Ahlden House in her native Celle, where she stayed until she died more than thirty years later. She was denied access to her children and was forbidden to remarry. She was forbidden to leave the castle without supervision. Before dying on November 13, 1726, she wrote a scathing letter to her husband, cursing him from beyond the grave. George would not allow mourning in Hanover or London. Her body was deposited in the castle's cellar and, in May 1727, was quietly moved to Celle and interred beside her parents.

On January 23, 1698, Ernest Augustus died, leaving all of his territories to George. Shortly after George's accession to his paternal dukedom, Prince William, Duke of Gloucester, who was second-in-line to the British thrones died. By the terms of the English Act of Settlement of 1701, George's mother, Sophia was designated as the heir to the throne, if the then reigning monarch William III and his sister-in-law, Princess Anne died without surviving issue. The succession was so designed because Sophia was the closest Protestant relative of the British Royal Family; fifty-six Catholic relations with superior hereditary claims were bypassed. The likelihood of any of them converting to Protestantism for the sake of the succession was remote; some had already refused.

In September 1701, the nearest Catholic claimant to the throne of England, ex-King James II, died and William III died the following March and was succeeded by Anne. Sophia became heir presumptive to the new Queen of England. Sophia was in her seventy-first year, older than Anne by thirty-five years, but she was healthy and invested time and energy in securing the succession either for herself or her son. However, it was George who understood the complexities of English politics and constitutional law, which required further acts in 1705 to naturalize Sophia and her heirs as English subjects, and to detail arrangements for the transfer of power through a Regency Council.

Though both England and Scotland recognized Anne as their Queen, only the English Parliament had settled on Sophia of Hanover, as the heir. The Scottish Parliament had not formally settled the succession question for the Scottish throne. Eventually both Parliaments agreed on an Act of Union of 1707, which united England and Scotland into a single political entity, the Kingdom of Great Britain, and established the rules of succession as laid down by the Act of Settlement of 1701. George's mother, Electress Sophia, died on May 28, 1714. She had collapsed after rushing to shelter from a rain storm. George was now Queen Anne's announced successor, and swiftly revised the Regency Council that would take power after her death, as it was well known that Anne's health was failing. On August 1, 1714, Queen Anne suffered a stroke and died. The list of regents was opened, its members were sworn in, and George was proclaimed King of Great Britain. He did not arrive in his new kingdom until September 18th and was crowned at Westminster Abbey on October 20, 1714.

Four-fifths of his life had passed before he arrived in London to claim the British throne. He was resented as a foreigner and criticized for neglecting England for his native Hanover (where often spent months at a time). Though his reign was peaceful and prosperous, the main focus remained on foreign affairs. In 1715, an uprising by James Francis Edward Stuart ("the old pretender") was defeated. A financial scandal known as the South Sea Bubble of 1721 had negative effect on George's court. In June 1727, on one of his many trips to Hanover, he suffered a stroke and was taken by carriage to the Bishop's Palace at Osnabruck, where he died in the early hours of June 11, 1727. George I was interred near his parents at the Hanover Mausoleum in Berggarten.

BERGGARTEN MAUSOLEUM in Hanover, where King George I of Great Britain is interred.

George II
(June 11, 1727 – October 25, 1760)

GEORGE II OF GREAT BRITAIN, painted by Enoch Seeman (1730).

BORN: November 10, 1683, at Herrenhausen Palace, Hanover

PARENTS: George I and Sophia Dorothea of Celle

CROWNED: October 4, 1727, at Westminster Abbey

CONSORT: Caroline of Ansbach

DIED: October 25, 1760, at Kensington Palace

BURIAL: Westminster Abbey

George II was born on November 10, 1683, at Herrenhausen Palace in Hanover and was the last British monarch to be born outside of Britain. He was the son of George I and Sophia Dorothea of Celle.

CAROLINE OF ANSBACH, queen consort of King George II, from a 19th century engraving.

As a boy he was separated from his mother, when his parents divorced and she was imprisoned. He was raised at the court of his Stuart grandmother, Sophia of Hanover. George's father did not want his son to enter into a loveless arranged marriage as he had, and wanted him to have the opportunity of meeting his bride before any formal arrangements were made. In June 1705, under a false name, George visited the Ansback court to investigate secretly, a potential marriage prospect, Caroline of Ansbach, the ward of his aunt Queen Sophia Charlotte of Hanover. An English envoy to Hanover, reported that George was so smitten with Caroline's beauty and good character that he would not consider anyone else for marriage. They were married on August 22, 1705, at Herrenhausen Palace. An intelligent and attractive woman, Caroline was much sought-after as a bride and George's grandmother, the Electress Sophia called her "the most agreeable Princess in Germany." By May of the following year, Caroline was pregnant, and her first child, Prince Fredrick was born on January 20, 1707. A few months after the birth, in July, Caroline fell seriously ill with smallpox followed by pneumonia. Her baby was kept away from her, but George II devotedly remained by her side, catching and surviving the infection himself. Over their entire marriage, Caroline would give birth to a total of eight children.

George and Caroline had a successful marriage, though he continued to keep mistresses, as was customary for the period. In contrast with her mother-in-law and husband, Caroline was known for her marital fidelity; she never made any embarrassing scenes, nor did she take lovers. She preferred her husband's mistresses to be ladies-in-waiting, as she believed that it was a way she could keep a closer eye on them. On June 11, 1727, George I died and Prince George Augustus was now king. He was crowned on October 4, 1727, at Westminster Abbey. George II's relationship with his son and heir apparent, Fredrick, Prince of Wales, was always tentative but worsened during the 1730s.

Meanwhile, rivalry between George and his brother-in-law, Fredrick William I of Prussia, led to tension along the Prussian–Hanoverian border, which eventually led to mobilization of troops in the border zone. Negotiations for a marriage between the Prince of Wales and Frederick William's daughter Wilhelmine dragged on for years, but neither side would make the concessions demanded of the other and the idea was shelved. Instead, Prince Fredrick married Princess Augusta of Saxe-Gotha in April 1736.

George II had an explosive temper and he and his son, quarreled often and remained at odds for years, which eventually led to the later being banished from court.

At the birth of her eighth and final child in December 1724, Queen Caroline suffered an umbilical hernia which never healed. On the evening of November 9, 1737, she felt an intense pain and after struggling through a formal reception, took to her bed. It was found that her womb had ruptured and over the next few days, she slowly bled to death. The king refused to allow Prince Frederick permission to see his mother, a decision with which she complied; though she sent her son a message of forgiveness through Prime Minster Walpole. She also asked her husband to remarry after her death, which he rejected saying he would take only mistresses. Queen Caroline died on November 20, 1737, at St. James Palace and was buried within the royal vault in the Lady Chapel at Westminster Abbey. Prince Frederick was not invited to the funeral and the king arranged for a pair of matching marble coffins with removable sides, so that when he followed her to the grave (23 years later); they could lie together for eternity. George II was deeply affected by her death and, to the surprise of many, displayed a tenderness of which was thought utterly incapable.

The reign of George II was dogged by numerous wars, most notably, the War of Austrian Succession (174-1748). In June 1743, an allied force of Austrian, British, Dutch, Hanoverian, and Hessian troops engaged the French at the Battle of Dettingen, where George II personally accompanied the army and led them to victory. He was the last British monarch to lead troops into battle. Though his actions in the battle were admired, the war became unpopular with the British public, who felt that the king was subordinating British interests to those of Hanover. During this same period, French opponents encouraged rebellion by supporters of the Roman Catholic claimant to the throne (known as Jacobites). In April 1746, Charles Edward Stuart, known as Bonnie Prince Charlie or the Young Pretender, was soundly defeated at the Battle of Culloden. Following this defeat, there were no further serious attempts at restoring the House of Stuart to the throne. The War of the Austrian Succession continued until 1748, when Maria Theresa was recognized as Archduchess of Austria.

On March 20, 1751, Prince Fredrick died at Leicester House from a burst abscess in his lung. This was probably caused from a cricket accident, as the Prince was an ardent enthusiast and often played. He was buried at Westminster Abbey in the royal vault within the Lady Chapel. Fredrick's eldest son, George William Fredrick was now the heir presumptive to the British throne. In 1754, hostilities between France and Britain escalated, particularly over the colonization of North America, culminated in the Seven Years' War.

A LATE 19TH CENTURY PHOTO OF THE HENRY VII's Lady Chapel at Westminster Abbey from Cassell's The British Isles (1905). In the back ground is the tomb shrine of Henry VII and Elizabeth of York. The royal vault is located beneath the floor in front of Henry VII's tomb. Within in it are interred the remains of King Edward VI, George II, and Queen Caroline of Ansbach.

By October 1760, George II was blind in one eye and hard of hearing. At Kensington Palace on the morning of October 25, 1760, George II arose as usual at 6:00 am, drank a cup of hot chocolate, and retired to the privy chamber. After a few minutes, his personal valet heard a loud crash and found the king on the floor; he was taken to his bed, where he died. The right ventricle of his heart had ruptured as the result of an incipient aortic aneurysm, possibly caused by syphilis. At the age of nearly seventy-seven, George II had lived longer than any of his predecessors. He was buried on November 11th at Westminster Abbey. In his will, left specific instructions that the sides of his and Caroline's coffins were to be removed, so that their remains could mingle side by side for all eternity. George II was the last British monarchs to be interred at Westminster Abbey.

George III

(October 25, 1760 – January 29, 1820)

GEORGE III, painted by Allan Ramsay. *Courtesy of the National Portrait Gallery, London.*

BORN: **June 4, 1738, at Norfolk House in St. James Square, London**

PARENTS: **Fredrik, Prince of Wales and Princess Augusta of Saxe-Gotha**

CROWNED: **September 22, 1761, at Westminster Abbey**

CONSORT: **Charlotte of Mecklenberg-Strelitz**

DIED: **January 29, 1820, at Windsor Castle**

BURIAL: **St. George's Chapel**

"Once vigorous measures appear to be the only means left of bringing the Americans to a due submission to the mother country, the colonies will submit."

-George III of Great Britain

George William Fredrick had been waiting impatiently for years for his imperious grandfather to die and get out of his way. He had an ideal of kingship and wanted to put it into practice. The first of the Hanoverians to be born and raised entirely in England, George III spoke English as his first language and, although he spoke fluent German, took no interest in Hanover and never went there in his life. He would concentrate his attention on Britain and the wider empire, much to the dismay of politicians who would have preferred he stay out of their business. He was born on June 4, 1738, at Norfolk House at St. James Square, London and was the eldest son of Fredrick, Prince of Wales, and Princess Augusta of Saxe-Gotha.

George III spent his boyhood mainly at Leicester House in London and at Kew, where his father had bought a country retreat. In 1759, Princess Augusta, opened a botanical garden in Kew. George II took little interest in his grandchildren. However, in

1751 the Prince of Wales died unexpectedly and George William Fredrick became heir apparent to the throne. Now more interested in his grandson, the elderly king, offered his thirteen year old grandson a luxurious home at St. James Palace, but young George refused the offer, instead deciding to remain at Kew with his mother.

In 1760, George II died and George William Fredrick succeeded to the throne. He was crowned on September 22, 1761, at Westminster Abbey. Afterwards, the search for a suitable bride intensified and the choice fell on a plain German Lutheran princess, Charlotte of Mecklenburg-Strelitz. She was born on May 19, 1744, at the Palace of Schloss Mirow, the daughter of Charles Louis Fredrick,

CHARLOTTE OF MECKLENBURG-STREITZ, by Thomas Frye (1762). *Courtesy of the Library of Congress, Prints and Photographs Collection, LC-USZ62-115301.*

Duke of Mecklenburg-Strelitz, and Princess Elizabeth of Saxe-Hildburghausen. George and Charlotte were married on September 8, 1761, at the Chapel Royal of St. James Palace; remarkably they had only been introduced to each other six hours before the wedding ceremony. They remained devoted to one another their entire lives and they had 15 children, nine sons and six daughters. In 1762, George purchased Buckingham House (on the site now occupied by Buckingham Palace) for use as a family home. He disliked Kensington Palace, Hampton Court, and St. James's Palace (which he thought lacked privacy) and spent his entire life in southern England.

George's court was quiet, frugal, and eminently respectful, with a focus on piety. He was also contentious, hard working, and punctual. George III embodied the ideal of the "patriot king," who would override party factions and rule in the nation's best interest. He wanted to end the long Whig supremacy and brought the Tories back into favor. Many within Parliament accused him of wanting to restore tyranny. A succession of administrations in the 1760s brought about an end to the Seven Years War, but gained Canada as a dominion and there were signs of unrest in the American colonies. In 1770, George found an efficient Prime Minister, Lord North, and now interfered less in government affairs. Twelve years later, in the wake of the unsuccessful war against the thirteen American colonies, Lord North fell out of favor, and George III seriously considered abdicating.

By 1788, George was entering a time of his great ordeal and was showing severe signs of mental illness. His constant "What? What?" was also a sign of a nervous disorder. He was seen talking to a tree in Windsor Great Park, under the impression it was the King of Prussia, babbling incoherently and frothing at the mouth. These symptoms suggest that he might have been suffering from porphyria, a blood disorder that causes poisoning of the nervous system. However, at the time, the

unfortunate king was treated with a brutality that was considered necessary to affect a cure. He was put in a straight jacket or a restraining chair and his head was blistered to draw out malignant tumors from the brain. Some members in Parliament called for his eldest son (the future George IV), to be made regent but the king eventually recovered.

After the French Revolution, there was heightened suspicion of radicals in England. That the British monarchy was still an important institution, no one doubted, but what powers the sovereign should exact were uncertain and needed to be clarified. During this time, George III worked hard to preserve an effective role for the crown, but the development of party politics and the office of Prime Minister contributed to the slow decline in the monarchy's political power. The Crown was becoming more a symbol of the nation and a rallying point for national pride, than an actual policy maker.

Belying his image and nickname of Farmer George, the king was a keen patron of the arts; he loved music and played the harpsichord. His reign saw the beginnings of the Industrial Revolution. He was generally liked by his subjects. His popularity rested on his image as a devoted family man, but behind the scenes he was a domestic tyrant. He was particularly hard on his eldest son, George Augustus Fredrick, who resented his father's constant preaching and interference. George III was much easier on his daughters, but put every possible difficulty in the way of their marrying, which they also resented.

In 1800, George survived an assassination attempt, while attending a play at the Drury Lane Theater. Trouble in Ireland led to the Act of Union, which united England, Scotland, and Ireland into one nation called the United Kingdom. Prime Minister William Pitt resigned over the king's refusal to grant Catholic emancipation. Soon after, George lapsed into another bout of madness, but quickly recovered. This episode so frightened Queen Charlotte that she never again let her husband enter her bedchamber.

In 1801, Britain began its long military struggle against the tyranny of French Emperor Napoleon. Inspiring victories at sea, including Admiral Horatio Nelson's triumphs at the Nile and Trafalgar, combined with the Duke of Wellington's land successes in Spain, Portugal, and Belgium, eventually led to the defeat of the French dictator at the Battle of Waterloo in 1815. This victory helped boost national pride in king and country. But soon George's madness returned, and he spent his final years shut away within Windsor Castle, slowly going blind and deaf. He would often hold private conversations with Lord North or other long dead people, and inspect imaginary parades. In the end, he could no longer recognize his own family. On November 17, 1818, after being a virtual widow for many years, Queen Charlotte died at Kew Palace and it is highly unlikely that her husband was aware of her passing. She was the second longest-serving consort in British history (after the present Duke of Edinburgh), having served as such for a total of fifty-seven years. She was buried at St. George's Chapel at Windsor Castle.

George III's health continued to deteriorate and he died at Windsor Castle in the early evening of January 29, 1820, six days after the death of his fourth son, Edward, Duke of Kent. George III's health issues resembled porphyria (an inherited disorder of the nervous system) and James I and is mother, Mary Queen of Scots, also appear to have suffered from the disease. Apparently, it was inherited from, Margaret Tudor (sister of Henry VIII) and passed down from the Tudors, to the Stuarts and then onto the Hanovers. George III was buried at St. George's Chapel beside his wife in the royal vault. In 1810, George commissioned the excavation of the vault beneath what is known today as the Albert Memorial Chapel. The chapel was built by Henry VII for his burial place, but abandoned it for Westminster Abbey. His son, Henry VIII bestowed the chapel upon Cardinal Wolsey who built a magnificent tomb, which was never used. For a long time, the chapel was known as Wolsey Chapel or Wolsey's Tomb-House.

1. KEW PALACE, where Queen Charlotte died on November 17, 1818.

2. VIEW OF WINDSOR CASTLE from Great Windsor Park.

3. ALBERT MEMORIAL CHAPEL within St. George's Chapel at Windsor Castle. Beneath this chapel is the Royal Vault which contains the remains of King's George III, George VI, and William IV.

George IV
(January 29, 1820 – June 26, 1830)

George IV, from an engraving by T. Lawrence (1830).

BORN: August 12, 1762, at St. James Palace

PARENTS: George III and Charlotte of Mecklenburg-Streitz

CROWNED: July 18, 1821, at Westminster Abbey

CONSORT: Maria Fitzherbert and Caroline of Brunswick-Wolfenbuttel

DIED: June 26, 1830, at Windsor Castle

BURIAL: St. George's Chapel

(TOP) CAROLINE OF BRUNSWICK, queen consort of George IV, painted by unknown artist.

(BOTTOM) PRINCESS CHARLOTTE AUGUSTA, daughter of George IV and Caroline of Brunswick, from an 1800's engraving by E. Scriven.

George Augustus Fredrick was the eldest son of George III and Charlotte of Mecklenburg-Strelitz. He was born on August, 12, 1762, at St. James Palace. He was a handsome and intelligent, and enjoyed Shakespeare. He was an extravagant patron of the arts and was an avid reader of the novels of Sir Walter Scott and Jane Austen. As a young man, George became a leading figure in fashionable society and was known as the first gentleman of Europe for his polished and refined manners. His overcritical father strongly disapproved of his extravagance, mounting debts, and political associates. Prince George, in turn, loathed his father and the typical Hanoverian grouchiness. In 1785, much to his father's chagrin, the Prince secretly married Maria Fitzherbert (a Catholic widow), of whom he had become obsessively enamored, but who refused to become his mistress. Since it contravened the Royal Marriages Act of 1772, (which forbade royal marriages without the permission of the sovereign), the marriage was deemed illegal.

In 1795, Prince George was forced into an arranged marriage with his first cousin, Caroline of Brunswick. She was the daughter of Princess Augusta Charlotte of Wales and Charles William, Duke of Brunswick-Wolfenbuttel. Caroline was not a particularly attractive woman, was quite ill-mannered, and neglected personal hygiene. On first sight of his future wife, Prince George was thoroughly distressed. The marriage took place on the evening of April 8, 1795, at the Chapel Royal at St. James Palace. The distraught bridegroom spent his wedding night lying on the bedroom floor by the fireplace in a drunken stupor. Although initially repelled by his wife, Prince George eventually did his duty and brought himself to consummate the marriage. On January 7, 1796, Princess Caroline gave birth to a daughter, Princess Charlotte. Prince George quickly abandoned Caroline, who lived abroad, invited scandal by taking lovers, and ran up vast amounts of debt. For the last ten years of his father's reign Prince George was appointed Regent.

On March 2, 1816, Princess Charlotte married Leopold of Saxe-Coburg-Saalfield at Carlton House. In February 1817, after two unfortunate miscarriages, Charlotte was again pregnant with what was hoped to be a son and future heir to the British throne. She went into labor on November 3, 1817, at Claremont House. The labor proved to be difficult, lasting fifty hours. Finally the child (a boy) was born at nine o'clock on November 6th, but

died shortly after birth. Though Charlotte appeared to be recovering, later that evening she complained of severe stomach pains, began to vomit, went into convulsions, and died. Prince George was awakened and informed that Charlotte was dead. Highly emotional by nature, he was extremely distraught. Princess Charlotte and her still born son were interred together at St. George's Chapel, Windsor.

George's recovery from his bereavement was slow; he became reclusive and dwelled excessively on the sad event. Princess Charlotte's physician, Sir Richard Croft was publically blamed for causing her death. Even though Prince George and Leopold publicly exonerated him from blame, the damage to his reputation was already done. Croft, never able to live down the disgrace, committed suicide eighteen months later. Prince George's sorrow was not yet complete; the death his daughter was followed the next year by the passing of his mother Queen Charlotte. These deaths affected him deeply; he had enjoyed a very close relationship with his mother, who was his closest confidante.

Prince George became king, upon his father's death on January 29, 1820. Immediately, Caroline of Brunswick saw herself as Queen of England and to George's consternation, promptly returned from the continent. She was very popular with the people and her return was greatly welcomed. On the day of his coronation (July 19, 1821), Caroline showed up at Westminster Abbey, but was turned away at the doors. She died on August 7, 1821, at Brandenburg House. She was thought to have died from intestinal cancer, but there were rumors of possible poisoning. The exact cause of her death remains a mystery. Afraid that a funeral procession through London would spark public unrest, George IV decided that the Queen's funeral cortege would avoid the city. The crowds accompanying the procession were incensed and blocked the official route with barricades. The scene soon descended into chaos, with honor guards firing on the crowd and killing two people. Eventually, Caroline's body was placed on a ship and sent to Brunswick. She was buried at Brunswick Cathedral, where her coffin is engraved "Caroline of Brunswick, the injured Queen of England."

Early in his reign, George IV embarked on an extensive program of repair and refurbishment at Windsor Castle. His architect swept away the last traces of the medieval fortress, a series of state apartments were created, and the Waterloo Chamber was built. He also employed the architect John Nash to rebuild what was then known as Buckingham House, turning it into the Buckingham Palace. From 1824 onwards, George IV suffered badly from gout and, to relieve the pain, he took ever increasing doses of laudanum. Now obese and aging rapidly, he became highly sensitive to the inquisitive gaze of his subjects and grew ever more reclusive. In 1828, his eyesight began to fail, he suffered from bouts of insomnia and his legs became grotesquely bloated from edema. George IV died on June 26, 1830, at Windsor Castle and was buried at St. George's Chapel. A postmortem examination of his body revealed that he had been suffering from arteriosclerosis for many years with the immediate cause of death being a ruptured blood vessel in the stomach.

1. PRINCESS CHARLOTTE memorial at St. George's Chapel.   3. TOMB OF CAROLINE OF BRUNSWICK at Brunswick Cathedral.

2. BRUNSWICK CATHEDRAL, burial location of Caroline of Brunswick.

William IV

(June 26, 1830 – June 20, 1837)

WILLIAM IV, from a 19th century engraving.

BORN: August 21, 1765, at Buckingham House

PARENTS: George III and Charlotte of Mecklenburg-Streitz

CROWNED: September 8, 1831, at Westminster Abbey

CONSORT: Adelaide of Saxe-Meiningen

DIED: June 20, 1837, at Windsor Castle

BURIAL: St. George's Chapel

(TOP) DOROTHY JORDAN, the longtime companion of William IV, by John Jones (1791).

(BOTTOM) ADELAIDE OF SAXE-MEININGEN, queen consort of William IV by John Jones, (1791)

At sixty-four, William was the oldest person ever to ascend to the British throne. The simplicity of his career before his accession corresponds with that of his original mind and disposition. He met with no adventures on a grand scale, displayed no gross or memorable attributes. He was the third son of George III and Queen Charlotte, born on August 21, 1765, at Buckingham House. William's youth was spent in the royal family's unofficial boarding school at Kew Palace. As George III's third son, he was not expected to take the throne, so it was not seen worthwhile to continue his education for long. At thirteen years of age he was sent off to serve in the Royal Navy, where he lived as his shipmates did. Being a prince, however, he was rapidly promoted. By 1786, he was a captain and became good friends with Horatio Nelson. At this stage of his career William still seemed to have an old conception of monarchy, which gave him divine right to govern. This put him at odds with naval authority, which since the seventeenth century had been relatively meritocratic.

William, it seems, was not suited to being a successful naval officer, in spite of the relatively high rank he reached. He wanted to be a duke like his brothers, and pressed his father for a title. When King George refused, William threatened to become a member of Parliament. The prospect of having a disgruntled son in Parliament making life difficult had the desired effect, and William was made Duke of Clarence. Leaving the navy in 1790, William settled down to a long period of domesticity. All marriages entered into by princes had to be cleared by George III, and, fearing a negative judgment, William chose to simply live with the woman of his choice, Dorothea Bland, better known as Mrs. Jordan. She was not considered princess material, being born in Ireland and making her living as an actress. William and Mrs. Jordan lived together for twenty years and had ten children. This large family was housed at Bushy House in southwest London. The pressure of money eventually drove William to seek a richer and more respectable wife. In 1811, Mrs. Jordan was paid off and fled abroad where she died in poverty.

Meanwhile William's search for a suitable consort led him, in 1818, to twenty-five year-old Princess Adelaide of Saxe-Meiningen. They were married on July 11, 1818, at Kew Palace. The marriage, which lasted almost twenty years until William's death, was a happy one. William is not known to have had any mistresses during their marriage. They had no surviving children. Adelaide was beloved by the British people for her piety, modesty, and charity. A large portion of her household income was given to charitable causes. She also treated her step-children and the young Princess Victoria of Kent (William's heir presumptive) with kindness, despite her own inability to produce an heir and the open hostility between William and Victoria's mother, the Duchess of Kent. She never spoke about politics in public; she was, however, a strong Tory.

By now it was clear that George IV would have no surviving children to inherit his throne, which meant there was a possibility that William might actually become king. Then, with the death of George III's second son Frederick in 1727, William moved into first place as heir to the throne. George IV died on June 26, 1830, and William became king. Immediately, William IV was aware of his difficult position in a society that no longer had an automatic respect for social precedence. The awkward and arrogant young man who had served in the navy seemed to have mellowed. William did not want to have a coronation ceremony, fearing it would be a focus for protests. Prime Minster Earl Grey would not accept this, and the compromise solution was a cut-price coronation, taking place on September 8, 1831, at Westminster Abbey.

William was only king for seven years, but these were years of momentous change. His reign coincided with the five-year voyage of HMS Beagle 1831 to 1836, on which Charles Darwin gathered information that would eventually lead to the theory of evolution. This was also the age of the Industrial Revolution. During most of his reign he kept a low profile and had little involvement in politics, but he was not a completely

T.R.H. THE DUCHESS OF KENT AND THE PRINCESS VICTORIA
From the miniature by H. Bone, after Sir W. Beechey, at Windsor Castle
To face p. 8, Vol. I.

VICTORIA, Duchess of Kent with her daughter, Princess Victoria, from The Letters of Queen Victoria, (1908).

passive figure. He was the last king to remove a prime minister against the wishes of Parliament, removing Lord Melbourne in November 1834 and replacing him for a short time with Robert Peel. Most significantly perhaps, the Reform Act, whereby the electoral processes of Parliament became more democratic, was passed during William IV's reign. He had to assist in this process by creating new peers who helped the Reform Bill through the House of Lords.

William also stood up to the scheming Duchess of Kent, who was maneuvering to maintain her influence over her daughter and heir to the throne, Victoria. Both the King and Queen were fond of their niece, Princess Victoria. Their attempts to forge a close relationship with the girl were frustrated by the conflict between the King and the Duchess of Kent, the young princess's mother. The King, angered at what he took to be disrespect from the Duchess to his wife, took the opportunity at what proved to be his final birthday banquet, in August 1836, to settle the score. Speaking to those assembled at the banquet, which included the Duchess and Princess Victoria, William expressed his hope that he would survive until Princess Victoria was 18 so that the Duchess of Kent would never be Regent. He said;

"I trust to God that my life may be spared for nine months longer...I should then have the satisfaction of leaving the exercise of the Royal authority to the personal authority of that young lady, heiress presumptive to the Crown, and not in the hands of a person now near me, who is surrounded by evil advisers and is herself incompetent to act with propriety in the situation in which she would be placed."

The speech was so shocking that Victoria burst into tears, while her mother sat in silence. William's outburst undoubtedly contributed to Victoria's tempered view of him as "a good old man, though eccentric." William did survive, and saw Princess Victoria reach adulthood. He died from heart failure caused by pneumonia in the early morning hours of June 20, 1837, at Windsor Castle, and was buried at St. George's Chapel in the royal vault created by his father George III. As he had no living legitimate issue, the Crown of the United Kingdom passed to Princess Victoria. Queen Adelaide outlived her husband by twelve years, dying from natural causes on December 2, 1849, at Bentley Priory in Middlesex. She was buried at St. George's Chapel with little fanfare as she had requested.

Victoria

YOUNG VICTORIA, from an engraving by P Jackson (1835).

BORN: May 24, 1819, at Kensington Palace

PARENTS: Edward, Duke of Kent and Victoria of Saxe-Coburg-Saalfeld

CROWNED: June 28, 1838, at Westminster Abbey

CONSORT: Albert of Saxe-Coburg and Gotha

DIED: January 22, 1901, at Osbourne House on the Isle of Wight

BURIAL: Royal Mausoleum at Frogmore in Windsor Great Park

"Great events make me quiet and calm; it is only trifles that irritate my nerves."

– Queen Victoria (1819-1901)

Queen Victoria's 63-year reign was the longest in British history. When she died, most of her subjects could not remember a time when she had not been on the throne. Her time coincided with an unprecedented period of scientific invention and innovation, immense social, political and economic change, a huge expansion of British power around the world, and the transformation of the monarchy into the constitutional model that is recognized today. Alexandrina Victoria was the only child of Edward, Duke of Kent and Victoria Maria Louisa of Saxe-Coburg and was born on May 24, 1819, at Kensington Palace.

In 1820, when she was only eight months old, Victoria's father died. Her mother then developed a close relationship with Sir John Conroy. He would have a major influence and come to be despised by Victoria. Her uncle William IV had no surviving legitimate children and she became heir to the throne. When the kings health began to fail, there was fear that Conroy would become the power behind the throne if Victoria became queen before her eighteenth birthday. William IV lived long enough to see her reach the age of majority, dying on June 20, 1837, just 27 days after Victoria's birthday. She was crowned at Westminster Abbey on June 28, 1838. One of her first acts as queen was to banish Conroy from the Royal Court.

PRINCESS VICTORIA receiving the news of her accession to the throne, June 20, 1837, from a 19th century engraving by H.T. Wells.

Lord Melbourne was Prime Minister when Victoria became queen and Victoria grew fond of him and dependent upon his political advice. Melbourne was leader of the Whig party and, although radical in his youth, his views were now extremely conservative. An apartment was made available for Melbourne at Windsor Castle and it was estimated that he spent six hours a day with the queen. Some people objected to their close relationship. At the start of her reign, Victoria was very popular, but numerous scandals, political infighting and bad press soon eroded public sentiment. In 1839, Melbourne resigned after a defeat

H.R.H. THE PRINCE CONSORT, 1840
From the portrait by John Partridge at Buckingham Palace

To face p. 176, Vol. I.

in the House of Commons, and Sir Robert Peel, the Tory leader, became Prime Minister. It was customary for the Queen's ladies of the bedchamber to be of the same political party as the ruling government and Peel asked Victoria to replace Whig ladies with Tories. In what became known as the bedchamber crisis, Victoria, objected to their removal, Peel then refused to govern under such restrictions and resigned. Melbourne was then returned to office.

Victoria's cousin, Prince Albert of Saxe-Coburg-Gotha, visited London in 1839. She thought he was extremely good looking and immediately fell in love. Although Albert had initial doubts about the relationship, he also fell in love. Protocol stated that as sovereign, Victoria had to propose marriage to Albert, which he accepted. They were wed on February 10, 1840, at the Chapel Royal at St. James Palace. Albert became an important political adviser as well as the Queen's companion, replacing Lord Melbourne as the dominant influential figure in the first half of her life. They had frequent arguments, which were blazing on her side and coldly reserved on his, but their marriage was a strong and loving one. Albert was serious-minded and hard working. He was always by her side, never as a king but as her consort. He gave her realistic advice and described himself as "the private secretary of the sovereign and her permanent minister." He ran the royal household and oversaw their nine children's upbringing. Lord Melbourne resigned as Prime Minister in 1841 and the queen had a good relationship with the next two prime ministers, but disliked Lord Henry Palmerston. Shortly afterward there was a failed assassination attempt, while Victoria was riding in a carriage. This was followed by six other attempts in 1842 (twice), 1849, 1850, 1872, and 1882.

In March 1861, Victoria's mother died, with Victoria at her side. Through reading her mother's papers, Victoria discovered that her mother had loved her deeply; she was heart-broken, and blamed Conroy for "wickedly" estranging her from her mother. To relieve his wife during her intense and deep grief, Albert took on most of her duties, despite being ill himself with chronic stomach trouble. By the beginning of December, Albert's health began to fail and he was diagnosed with typhoid fever. He died on December 14, 1861, at Windsor Castle. The contemporary diagnosis of typhoid fever was quite common for the period, but modern historians have pointed out that Albert was ill for at least two years prior to his death, which may indicate that a chronic disease, such as renal failure or cancer was the ultimate cause. Following Albert's death, a devastated Victoria entered a state of mourning and wore black for the remainder of her life. She avoided public appearances and rarely set foot in London in the following years. Her seclusion earned her the nickname "the Widow of Windsor."

(TOP) PRINCE ALBERT of Saxe-Coburg and Gotha, from a 19th century engraving by John Partridge.

(BOTTOM) QUEEN VICTORIA and Prince Albert, circa 1854.

1. QUEEN VICTORIA and John Brown at Balmoral Castle, circa 1863.

2. QUEEN VICTORIA, circa 1887. *Courtesy of the National Portrait Gallery, London.*

3. OSBORNE HOUSE on the Isle of Wight, where Queen Victoria died January 22, 1901.

4. ROYAL MAUSOLEUM at Frogmore, Great Windsor Park, where Queen Victoria and Prince Albert are interred.

The queen's self-imposed isolation from the public diminished the popularity of the monarchy, and encouraged the growth of the republican movement. Although she did undertake her official government duties, she chose to remain secluded at her royal residences at Windsor Castle, Osborne House, and Balmoral Castle in Scotland. While in Scotland, Victoria became very close to a servant named John Brown, and her friendship with him caused some concern. Rumors began to circulate that they had secretly married (but this was never proven). Hostility within the government increased with some Radical members of Parliament favoring abolishing the monarchy.

On September 23, 1896, Victoria surpassed George III as the longest-reigning monarch in British history, but she requested that any special celebrations be delayed until 1897, to coincide with her Diamond Jubilee. The Queen's Diamond Jubilee procession through London included troops from all over the empire. The celebration was marked by great outpourings of affection for the Queen. In 1900, following a custom she maintained throughout her widowhood, Victoria spent the Christmas holidays at Osborne House on the Isle of Wight. Her health was an issue, with rheumatism in her legs rendering her basically lame, and her eyesight was clouded by cataracts. Through early January, her health worsened and by mid-month, it became apparent that she was dying. On January 22, 1901, at 6:30 in the evening with her son, Edward VII, and her eldest grandson, Kaiser Wilhelm II of Germany, at her bedside, the aged queen died.

In her will, Victoria left specific instructions for her funeral. It was to be military in nature, befitting a soldier's daughter, and mourners were to wear white instead of black. She was buried in a white dress with her wedding veil. An array of mementos commemorating her extended family, friends, and servants were laid in the coffin with her, which included one of Albert's dressing gowns, and a plaster cast of the prince's hand. A lock of John Brown's hair, along with a picture of him, were placed in her left hand concealed from the view of the family by a carefully positioned bunch of flowers. Her funeral was held on Saturday February 2nd at St. George's Chapel, Windsor Castle, and after two days of lying-in-state, she was interred beside Prince Albert in the Royal Mausoleum at Frogmore, Windsor Great Park. As she was laid to rest, snow began to fall.

Edward VII

(January 22, 1901 – May 6, 1910)

Edward VII, circa 1902.

BORN: November 9, 1841, at Buckingham Palace

PARENTS: Victoria and Albert of Saxe-Coburg and Gotha

CROWNED: August 9, 1902, at Westminster Abbey

CONSORT: Alexandra of Denmark

DIED: May 6, 1910, at Buckingham Palace

BURIAL: St. George's Chapel

Edward had been Prince of Wales from the age of one month until he was fifty-nine. For most of that time he had been dismissed by his parents as lazy and irresponsible, his behavior recalling that of his shameless Hanoverian Great-Uncles. But when he finally acceded to the throne, he proved to a far abler monarch than might have been expected. Though he reigned for less than ten years, the new king would leave his name to the period, an age of opulent comfort and self-indulgence. He was born on November 9, 1841, at Buckingham Palace, the eldest son of Queen Victoria and Prince Albert. He was nicknamed "Bertie" by the family, and he had the typical Hanoverian pattern of an unfulfilled relationship with his parents, who were profoundly disappointed, considering him light-minded and prone to listlessness. They were seriously worried about his backwardness and not surprisingly, he stammered (much like his grandson, the future George VI).

At age seventeen, he was given his own household at White Lodge in Richmond Park, and two years later was sent to military training. While in Ireland, he became romantically linked to an Irish actress named Nellie Clifden. When word of the affair leaked out, a huge scandal erupted in the press and the episode caused his parents tremendous stress and strain. Queen Victoria went so far as to blame the incident for causing Prince Albert's death. Throughout his life, Edward was a known womanizer and it is alleged that he had at least 55 mistresses, best known among them were Lillie Langtry (American actress), Sarah Bernhardt (French actress), Frances "Daisy" Greville, Countess of Warwick, Lady Jeanette Churchill (mother of Winston), Susan Pelham-Clinton, Hortense Schneider (opera singer), Agnes Keyser, and Alice Keppel.

Queen Victoria was concerned with finding her son a suitable wife and enlisted the aid of her daughter, Princess Victoria of Prussia, in seeking a suitable candidate. On September 24, 1861, she introduced her brother to Princess Alexandra of Denmark (the daughter of King Christian IX of Denmark), but it was not until almost a year later, in 1862, that he proposed marriage. They were wed on March 10, 1863, at St. George's Chapel. They had very similar tastes and both spent money like water. They entertained lavishly at Marlborough House and she overlooked his many infidelities. Alexandra bore six children, one of which was the future King George V.

Beginning in the 1870s, Queen Victoria allowed Edward to make public appearances on her behalf. He traveled to Canada and then India, which set an example for future grand royal travels. Wise investments made him extremely rich. On January 22, 1901, Queen Victoria died, and Edward was king. He was crowned at Westminster Abbey on August 9, 1902. He disliked the Liberal government and often intervened to help pass

1. FRANCES "DAISY" GREVILLE, Countess of Warwick, one of Edward VII's many mistresses, circa 1899.

2. ALEXANDRA OF DENMARK, queen consort of Edward VII of Great Britain. This was one of the last photographs of Queen Alexandra, taken in 1921 at Sandringham House. *Courtesy of the National Portrait Gallery, London.*

3. FUNERAL CORTEGE OF EDWARD VII on May 10, 1910. *Courtesy of the Library of Congress, Prints and Photographs, George G. Bain Collection, LC-DIG-ggbain-08210.*

4. BUCKINGHAM PALACE, where Edward VII was born November 9, 1841, and died May 6, 1910.

important legislation. He had a keen eye for foreign affairs, especially military and naval matters. The royal court, unlike his mother's, was the center of smart society and fashion. Above all else, he enjoyed being king and his delight was infectious.

Edward smoked twenty cigarettes a day and towards the end of his life suffered from bronchitis. In March 1910, he suffered a heart attack in Biarritz, France, while vacationing with his mistress Alice Keppel. He remained in France until April 27th, when he returned to Buckingham Palace. The next day he suffered another heart attack, but refused to go to bed saying, "No, I shall not give in; I shall go on; I shall work to the end." For a week he drifted in and out of consciousness, and died in the late evening of May 6, 1910.

His funeral took place on Friday, May 20, 1910, and it was one of the largest gatherings of European royalty. Nine sovereigns, including George V and Kaiser Wilhelm I of Germany, marched behind the funeral cortege. Huge crowds watched the procession as it made its way from Buckingham Palace to Westminster Hall, then on to Paddington Station, from where a train would convey the body to Windsor and burial within St. George's Chapel. Edward VII's elaborate tomb is found just outside of the choir area in the south aisle. Following Edward's death, Queen Alexandra moved to Marlborough House. She continued the public side of her life, devoting time to her charitable causes. In 1917, her nephew, Czar Nicholas II of Russia, was overthrown and he, his wife, and children were killed by revolutionaries. Her sister Maria, the Dowager Empress was rescued from Russia in 1919 and brought to England, where she lived for some time with Alexandra. The Dowager Queen suffered increasing ill-health and, towards the end of her life, memory and speech became impaired. On November 20, 1925, she died at Sandringham House after suffering a heart attack. She was interred next to her husband at St George's Chapel.

Chapter Eight

The House of Windsor (1910-Present)

he British royal family changed its official name to the House of Windsor in 1917, to avoid any backlash from anti-German feelings during the First World War. It was one of many changes and challenges that the monarchy had to survive, including two world wars, the end of the British Empire and its replacement by the Commonwealth, the onward march of socialism, the coming of the mass media, the gradual melting away of old class distinction, and the replacement of Britain by the United States as the world's strongest power. George V overcame his shyness to become a popular and effective monarch, but Edward VIII seemed to have no serious interest in politics and George VI, who had never expected the throne, lacked the self-confidence to use his political influence in the way earlier monarchs had done. He repaired some of the damage caused by his brother's abdication and he and his family were a rallying point during World War II, but constitutional monarchy now came to mean carrying out a traditional ceremonial role and acting as a symbol of the nation rather than wielding political power.

George V
(May 6, 1910 – January 20, 1936)

George V, circa 1923. Courtesy of the Library of Congress, Prints and Photographs, George G. Bain Collection, LC-DIG- ggbain-35407.

Born: June 3, 1865, at Marlborough House

Parents: Edward VII and Alexandra of Denmark

Crowned: June 22, 1911, at Westminster Abbey

Consort: Mary of Teck

Died: January 20, 1936, at Sandringham House in Norfolk

Burial: St. George's Chapel

"My father was frightened of his mother. I was frightened of my father and I am damned well going to see to it that my children are frightened of me."

-George V (1865 – 1936)

George brought to the monarchy a renewed air of solid responsibility, was faithful to his wife, straightforward, and took his duty as king seriously. He was a man of simple tastes, and unlike his father disliked fashionable society and took only a limited interest in foreign affairs. He was meticulous about detail and was obsessed with punctuality. George was born on June 3, 1865, at Marlborough House in London. He was the second son of Edward VII and Alexandra of Denmark. He never expected be king. When his older brother Albert Victor died from double pneumonia on January 14, 1892, George was propelled into the position of heir to the throne.

Mary of Teck, queen consort of George V. Courtesy of the Library of Congress, Prints and Photographs, George G. Bain Collection, LC-DIG-ggbain-31282.

Mary of Teck was descendant from a poor German royal family; she was born on May 26, 1867, at Kensington Palace, in the same room as Queen Victoria. Her parents were Francis, Duke of Teck, and Princess Mary Adelaide of Cambridge (who was a granddaughter of George III). In December 1891, she was engaged to Prince Albert Victor, Duke of Clarence. The choice of Mary as bride for the Duke owed much to Queen Victoria's fondness for her, as well as to her strong character and sense of duty. However, the Duke of Clarence died six weeks later. Prince George, now second in line to the throne, became close friends with Mary during their shared period of mourning. Queen Victoria still viewed Mary as a suitable candidate to marry a future king. In May 1893, the queen pushed George to propose to Mary and they soon fell in love. Unlike his father, George was completely devoted to his wife and never took a mistress. They were married on July 6, 1893, at the Chapel Royal in St. James Palace. Their first son, Edward Albert was born within a year and a second, Albert Fredrick, followed the next year. Though Mary complained of his lack of emotion, she and George remained together for more than 40 years in what turned out to be one of the longest lasting royal marriages on record. They lived mainly at York Cottage in Norfolk, where George enjoyed the life of a country gentleman, and spent countless hours each week stamp collecting.

Upon his father's death in 1910, George ascended to the throne and was crowned at Westminster Abbey on June 22, 1911. Edward VII had attempted to train his son for his future role as king but George lacked his father's charm. He found being king difficult, but he stuck to it with duty and honor. In 1914 Europe was plunged into the cataclysmic catastrophe of the First World War. The royal family was embarrassed by its German ancestry (George V and Kaiser Wilhelm were grandsons of Queen Victoria). The war gave the king a lasting distaste for Germans and, in 1917, on government advice, he decided to adopt the House of Windsor as the official family name. For fear of stimulating revolutionary ideas in Britain, he refused to let his cousin, Czar Nicholas II take refuge in England. He and his family were murdered in 1918, but George never regretted his decision.

Although, he was a constitutional monarch, this did not stop George from trying to influence politics during his reign. At Christmas 1932, the king made a radio address to his people. It was written by Rudyard Kipling. It was the first time any monarch had been able to speak directly to the masses in this way. It went well and cemented the king's popularity. In 1935, at his silver jubilee, he was astonished by the out pouring of affection from his subjects. The king's health had begun to deteriorate. He developed breathing problems, exacerbated by years of heavy smoking, and it was clear that he was dying. On the evening of January 15, 1936, George V took to his bedroom at Sandringham House complaining of a cold; he would never again leave the room alive. He became gradually weaker, drifting in and out of consciousness. His physicians issued a bulletin with words that became famous: "The King's life is moving peacefully towards its close." George V died in the late evening hours of January 20, 1936. Years later, when the private diary of Dr. Bertrand Dawson was found, it revealed that the King's last words, a mumbled "God damn you!" were addressed to his nurse when she gave him a sedative, and it was learned that he had hastened the King's end by giving him a lethal injection of cocaine and morphine, both to prevent further strain on the family and so that the King's death at 11:55 pm could be announced in the morning edition of *The Times* newspaper, rather than less appropriate evening journals.

At the procession to George's lying-in-state at Westminster Hall, part of the Imperial State Crown fell from on top of the coffin and landed in the gutter. The new king, Edward VIII, saw it fall and wondered whether it was a bad omen for his new reign. Edward would abdicate before the year was out, leaving his younger brother, Albert to ascend the throne (taking the title George VI). As a mark of respect to their father, the late king's four surviving sons, mounted the guard, known as the Vigil of the Princes, at the catafalque on the night before the funeral. The vigil was not repeated until the death of George's daughter-in-law, Queen Elizabeth, the Queen Mother in 2002. George V was interred at St. George's Chapel, Windsor, on January 28, 1936, and his tomb is found in the north aisle of the nave, near the Urswick Chantry.

Following George's death, Queen Mary took an interest in the upbringing of her granddaughters, Princesses Elizabeth and Margaret. She was an avid collector of objects and pictures with royal connection. In 1952, when her son George VI died, Princess Elizabeth, ascended the throne as Queen Elizabeth II. On March 24, 1953, Queen Mary died from lung cancer at Marlborough House, only ten weeks before her granddaughter Elizabeth's coronation. The aged Dowager Queen made it known that, in the event of her death, the coronation was not to be postponed. Her remains lay in state at Westminster Hall, where large numbers of mourners filed past her coffin. She was buried beside her husband at St. George's Chapel.

1. SANDRINGHAM HOUSE, Norfolk, where George V died January 20,1936.

2. MARLBOROUGH HOUSE, London, where George V was born June 3, 1865 and where Mary of Teck died March 24, 1953.

3. TOMB OF GEORGE V and MARY OF TECK at St. George's Chapel.

Edward VIII

(January 20 – December 11, 1936)

BORN: **June 23, 1894, at White Lodge in Richmond**

PARENTS: **George V and Mary of Teck**

CROWNED: **Uncrowned**

CONSORT: **Wallis Warfield Simpson**

DIED: **May 28, 1972, in Paris**

BURIAL: **Royal Burial Ground at Frogmore**

"I was shocked and angry with the startling suggestion that I should send from my land, my realm, the woman I intended to marry."

– Edward VIII

Edward enjoyed fashionable society and pursued married women who were generally older than himself. He disliked the pomp and ceremony of royalty, which he thought antiquated. He dressed casually, chained smoked, and resented his father's attempts to discipline him. He was born on June 23, 1894, at White Lodge in Richmond. George V and Queen Mary were not unloving parents, but they lacked any understanding of children, were very stern, and did not easily show affection. As small children, Edward (known as David to the family) and his brother Albert (nicknamed, Bertie, the future George VI) were placed in charge of a nursemaid, who doted on Edward but neglected his younger brother. In his teen years, Edward attended the Royal Naval College (which he hated) and Magdalen College in Oxford, where he excelled and was well-liked. During the First World War, he was commissioned in the Grenadier Guards, and pressed hard to serve at the front but was denied. Out of harm's way in London, he fell in love with a married woman named Freda Dudley Ward, who became his substitute mother and mistress much to the embarrassment of his parents. This affair was followed by another with Lady Thelma Furness (whose niece is fashion designer, Gloria Vanderbilt).

Wallis Warfield was born on June 19, 1896, at Square Cottage at Monterey Inn, Blue Summit, Pennsylvania, the only daughter of Henry Warfield and Alice Montague. Her father was a flour merchant in Baltimore, where he ran unsuccessfully for mayor in 1875. She married Earl Spencer in 1916 and they divorced in December 1927. Wallis married for a second time in July 1928 to Englishman Ernest Simpson (a shipping executive), after which the couple settled into the Mayfair section of London. In January 1931, Wallis was introduced to Prince Edward by Lady Furness. It is generally accepted that Edward and Simpson became lovers in 1934, though Edward adamantly insisted to his father that he was not intimate with her. His relationship with Simpson further weakened his poor relationship with his father. Although the King and Queen met Simpson at Buckingham Palace in 1935, they later refused to receive her. Edward's affair with the American divorcee led to such grave concern that the couple was followed by members of the Metropolitan Police, who examined in secret the nature of their relationship. The prospect an American divorcee with a questionable past having such sway over the heir apparent led to great anxiety in the government.

On January 20, 1936, George V died and Edward was king. He was determined to marry Simpson, though she tried to break off the relationship. In the end Edward won her affection. In November 1936, Edward spoke with Prime Minster Stanley Baldwin, who told him that marriage to a twice-divorced woman could not be reconciled with his position as head of the Church of England. Edward stated he must marry Simpson, or abdicate the throne. Although there was much sympathy for Edward in the public, the government and the Church of England were adamantly against the marriage. Simpson again offered to renounce the king, but he would not allow it. He signed abdication documents at Fort Belvedere on December 10, 1936, in the presence of his three surviving brothers. The next night, he broadcast by radio his intention to abdicate the throne, in which he famously said, "I have found it impossible to carry the heavy burden of responsibility and to discharge my duties as king as I would wish to do without the help and support of the woman I love." After the broadcast, Edward departed England for Austria, though he was unable to join Simpson until her divorce became official a few months later. Prince Albert, Duke of York, succeeded to the throne as George VI. On December 12th, at a meeting of the Privy Council, George VI announced he was granting Edward the title of "His Royal Highness, The Duke of Windsor." George's decision to make Edward a royal Duke ensured that he could neither stand for election to the House of Commons nor speak on political subjects in the House of Lords.

On June 3, 1937, Edward married Wallis Simpson at the chateau de Cande in Tours, France. George VI forbade members of the Royal Family to attend and Simpson, although the Duchess of Windsor, was not allowed to be called "Her Royal Highness." Edward and Wallis lived a quiet life in France, until the outbreak of World War II, during which the former king was embroiled in scandal for allegedly leaking top secret information to the Germans (which was never substantiated). Many historians have suggested that Adolph Hitler was prepared to reinstate Edward on the throne in the hope of establishing a fascist Britain. It is widely believed that the Duke and Duchess sympathized with fascism before and during World War II, and were moved to the Bahamas to minimize their opportunities to act on those feelings. The Allies became sufficiently disturbed by the German plots that U.S. President Franklin Roosevelt ordered covert surveillance of the Duke and Duchess when they visited the U.S. in April 1941. After the war, Edward admitted in his memoirs that he admired the Nazi leadership, but stopped short of being pro-Nazi.

The Duke and Duchess returned to France and spent the remainder of their lives essentially in retirement. The City of Paris provided Edward with a house for a nominal rent. They took on the role of minor celebrities and were regarded as part of cafe society in the 1950s and 1960s, hosting parties in Paris and New York. On George VI's death in 1952, Edward returned to England for the funeral, but the Duchess did not attend. In June 1953, instead of attending the coronation of his niece, Queen Elizabeth II, in London, the Duke and Duchess, watched the ceremony on television. The Royal family never fully accepted the Duchess, and Queen Mary refused to receive her formally.

In the 1960s, Edward's health began to deteriorate and in December 1964, he had an operation for an aneurysm of the abdominal aorta. In late 1971, he was diagnosed with lung cancer. He had been a heavy smoker all of his life. On May 28, 1972, Edward died at his home in Paris, less than a month before his 78th birthday. His funeral service was held at St. George's Chapel on June 5th in the presence of Queen Elizabeth II and the entire royal family. He was buried at the Royal Burial Ground behind the Mausoleum of Queen Victoria and Prince Albert at Frogmore. Until 1965, Edward and Wallis planned to be buried at Green Mount Cemetery in Baltimore, where the father of the Duchess was interred.

GRAVES OF EDWARD AND WALLIS, Duke and Duchess of Windsor, the Royal Burial Ground at Frogmore.

After Edward's death, Wallis became increasingly frail and suffered from dementia. She lived the remainder of her life as a recluse, supported by her husband's estate and an allowance from the Queen. In 1980, Wallis lost the power of speech and became bedridden. She died on April 24, 1986, at her home in Paris and was buried next to Edward, where her marker simply reads; "Wallis, Duchess of Windsor."

George VI

(December 11, 1936 – February 6, 1952)

BERTRAM PARK

BORN: December 14, 1895, at York Cottage on the Sandringham Estate

PARENTS: George V and Mary of Teck

CROWNED: May 12, 1937, at Westminster Abbey

CONSORT: Elizabeth Bowes-Lyon

DIED: February 6, 1952, at Sandringham House

BURIAL: St. George's Chapel

"The highest of distinctions is the service to others."
– George VI

George VI was horrified by the prospect of being king. He was shy, painfully self-conscious, and afflicted with a bad stammer that made public appearances a nightmare. In contrast, he had inherited his father's courage and sense of duty. He also had the advantage of having exactly the right wife and the two of them would win the respect and affection of the majority of their subjects. Queen Victoria was still alive when the future king was born on December 14, 1895, at York Cottage on the Sandringham estate (it was the anniversary of Prince Albert death, which greatly upset the Queen). Christened Albert, he was known as "Bertie" in the family. As a child he did poorly in school, misbehaved, was often ill, and suffered frequent rages. At age seven, his father realized he was left handed and forced him to write with his right hand. This could have been one of the contributing causes of the stammer. Later in life, Lionel Logue, an Australian speech therapist was instrumental in helping George overcome this speech defect.

In 1908, Albert was sent to the Royal Naval College, where he did not fare well, but he was intent on a career in the navy. In 1916, he saw action at the Battle of the Jutland and then enrolled in the Royal Air Service (becoming the first member of the royal family to qualify as a pilot). In 1919, he attended Trinity College in Cambridge and studied history and economics. Later that year was given the title of Duke of York.

In a time when royals were expected to marry fellow royals, it was unusual that Albert had a great deal of freedom in choosing a prospective wife. In 1920 he met Lady Elizabeth Bowes-Lyons, the youngest

152

daughter of the Earl of Starthmore. Although Elizabeth was a descendant of King Robert the Bruce of Scotland and King Henry VII of England, she was, according to British law, a commoner. She twice rejected Albert's marriage proposals, because she was reluctant to make the sacrifices necessary to become a member of the royal family, but after a protracted courtship she finally agreed to marry him. Albert and Elizabeth were married on April 26, 1923, in Westminster Abbey. Albert's marriage to a commoner was considered a modernizing gesture. Their union would produce two daughters, Elizabeth (the future queen) and Margaret.

Because of his stammer, Albert dreaded public speaking. After his closing speech at the British Empire Exhibition at Wembley in October 1925 (one which was an ordeal for both him and the listeners), he began to see Lionel Logue, an Australian-born speech therapist. The Duke and Logue practiced breathing exercises, and the Duchess rehearsed with him patiently. Subsequently, he was able to speak with less hesitation and his delivery improved. Upon the death of his father King George V in 1936, Albert's brother Edward ascended to the throne, but controversy followed within the year, when the new king chose to abdicate the throne to marry his mistress, Wallis Simpson. On December 13, 1936, Edward abdicated and Albert became king, assuming the name "George VI" to emphasize continuity with his father and restore confidence in the monarchy. Due to the controversy surrounding the abdication of Edward VIII, popular opinion of the throne was at its lowest point since the latter half of Victoria's reign.

The abdication, however, was soon overshadowed by continental developments, as Europe inched closer to yet another World War. After several years of pursuing "appeasement" policies with Germany, Great Britain and France declared war on Germany on September 3, 1939. George VI followed in his father's footsteps, visited troops, munitions factories, supply docks, and bomb-damaged areas to support the war effort. The royal family remained at Buckingham Palace and George went so far as to practice firing his revolver, vowing that he would defend Buckingham to the death. Fortunately, such defense was never necessary. The actions of the King and Queen during the war years greatly added to the prestige of the monarchy.

George predicted that hardships would follow the end of the war. The Bank of England, as well as most facets of industry, transportation, energy production, and health care were brought to some degree of public ownership. The beginnings of the Welfare State and the change from Empire to multiracial Commonwealth troubled the high-strung king. The stress of the war, post-war political turmoil, and economic hardships left George physically and emotionally drained. His health began to deteriorate and was exacerbated by his heavy smoking. Princess Elizabeth took on more royal duties as her father's health declined. On September 23, 1951, George's left lung was removed following the discovery of a malignant tumor. On February 6, 1953, George VI died at Sandringham House in Norfolk from a coronary thrombosis in his sleep; he was interred at St. George's Chapel in the Royal Vault until transferred to the King George VI Memorial Chapel inside St. George's on March 26, 1969.

Following George's death, Elizabeth simply became known as the Queen Mother or the Queen Mum. She was devastated by George's death and retired to Scotland. However, after a meeting with Winston Churchill, she resumed her public duties. She was known for her personal charm and was by far the most popular member of the royal family. In December 2001, the Queen Mother had a fall in which she fractured her pelvis, yet insisted on standing for the National Anthem during the memorial service for her husband on February 6, 2002. Just three days later, her second daughter Princess Margaret died. On the afternoon of March 30, 2002, Elizabeth Bowes-Lyon, the Queen Mother, died in her sleep at the Royal Lodge at Windsor with her surviving daughter, Queen Elizabeth II, at her bedside. She had been suffering from a cold and died from natural causes at the age of 101. Her body was taken to Westminster Hall, where more than 200,000 people filed past her coffin. At one point, the Queen Mother's four grandsons, Princes Charles, Andrew, and Edward and David Armstrong-Jones, Viscount of Linley (Princess Margaret's son), stood guard as a mark of respect known as the Vigil of the Princes, a very high honor only bestowed once before, at King George V's funeral. On the day of the Queen Mother's funeral more than a million people filled the area outside Westminster Abbey and along

the 23-mile route from central London to her final resting place beside her husband and younger daughter at St. George's Chapel.

In the context of royal history, George VI was one of only five monarchs who succeeded the throne in the lifetime of his predecessor; Henry IV, Edward IV, Richard III, and William III were the other four. George, upon his ascension, wrote to Prime Minister Stanley Baldwin concerning the state of the monarchy: "I am new to the job but I hope that time will be allowed to me to make amends for what has happened." His brother Edward continued to advise George on matters of the day, but such advice was a hindrance, as it was contradictory to policies pursued by George's ministers. The "slim, quiet man with tired eyes" (as described by Logue) had a troubled reign, but he did much to leave the monarchy in better condition than he found it.

TOMB OF KING GEORGE VI AND QUEEN ELIZABETH at St. George's Chapel, Windsor.

Elizabeth II
(February 6, 1953 – Present)

Queen Elizabeth II, from a May 2008 photograph taken on a visit to the NASA Goddard Space Flight Center in Greenbelt, Maryland.

BORN: April 21, 1926, in London

PARENTS: George VI and Elizabeth Bowes-Lyon

CROWNED: June 2, 1953, at Westminster Abbey

CONSORT: Prince Philip, Duke of Edinburgh

Born on April 21, 1926, Queen Elizabeth II was just 25 years old when she ascended to the British throne on the death of her father, George VI, in 1952. Throughout her long reign, Elizabeth II has sought to discharge her role with an enormous sense of duty. Her reign has experienced profound social and economic change. Within the royal family there have been numerous difficult experiences, but despite all difficulties and testing times she has retained the respect of the nation. The 1950s could be seen as the "golden age" for the Queen. It was an era of greater deference to royalty; in particular, press intrusion was far less. Elizabeth was young and beautiful, and the world looked upon her as a fairytale princess. She was crowned Queen Elizabeth II on June 2, 1953, at Westminster Abbey.

The 1960s saw remarkable social change. The advent of TV gave the public a greater insight into the life of the Royal family. With increased exposure, the distance between the royal family and the public diminished. It created a real appetite for greater knowledge and information about royalty. This frenzy of media interest would later create real problems for the Royal family.

In the 1970s the queen celebrated her Silver Jubilee to widespread public interest and support. In the 1980s the focus of the royal family switched to Charles and Diana. In particular the media became increasingly fascinated with Princess Diana. The 1990s saw a catalog of problems for the queen. In one Christmas message she referred memorably to an "annus horribilis," but in reality it would have been an appropriate description for many years. In particular the acrimonious break up of Princess Diana and Prince Charles divided the Royal family, with reports saying the queen was less than sympathetic to Princess Diana. The death of Princess Diana on August 31, 1997, was a critical moment in the reign of Queen Elizabeth. The unprecedented outpouring of grief around the world left the queen looking rather aloof. Amidst intense pressure, the Queen relented and, after three days, instructed the flag to be raised at half mast over Windsor.

Over the ensuing years these dark days have been put aside. Elizabeth's Diamond Jubilee in 2012 marks sixty years as queen, with celebrations throughout her realm, the wider Commonwealth, and beyond. In a message released on Accession Day, the Queen stated: "In this special year, as I dedicate myself anew to your service, I hope we will all be reminded of the power of togetherness and the convening strength of family, friendship and good neighborliness...I hope also that this Jubilee year will be a time to give thanks for the great advances that have been made since 1952 and to look forward to the future with clear head and warm heart." Elizabeth is the longest lived and second longest reigning monarch of the United Kingdom.

Conclusion

Why is the British Monarchy still significant after 1500 years? Despite the essentially ceremonial role of the British monarch, the royal family of Great Britain remains enormously popular throughout the world. The monarchy evolved from absolute ruler to ceremonial head of state and symbolically provides stability and continuity. It is a fundamental link from the past to the present. For the ancient rulers of Britain, the rural, land-owning elite, the king and queen were the symbols of an ancient and, therefore, hallowed constitution; the merging of power, religion, and history. Thus power is preserved and sanctified to those who understand the symbolism, not the reality of political power.

For centuries, the British monarchy has been an essential part of the nation's culture and history. As England's oldest secular institution, it is intertwined with the nation's identity and political culture. When functioning properly, the monarchy embodies the best of English society. In a modern democracy, many have questioned the legitimacy of the monarchy. Such a concern is logical, but the institution performs many important roles for the nation. Twentieth century monarchs occupy a position in which they fulfill two primary tasks. One is to represent the unity of the nation and the other is to carry out certain political functions on the advice of ministers. The Crown occupies a hereditary post as England's head of state. It is a symbolic position, delicately balanced between governmental representation and participation. As with all symbols, however, the significant meaning of this position exemplifies the government at its best. The monarchy acts as a unifying agent, with all government performed in its name. The monarchy and all it represents triggers an emotional, but not sentimental, bond to a truly English institution, inspiring loyalty among the people. Thus, in this capacity, the monarchy functions as an effective barrier against nondemocratic government.

Objections have been raised against the legitimacy of the monarchy's political roles, and it is largely misunderstood that the monarchy's political duties, such as dissolving parliament and appointing ministers, are governed by convention. These duties present no threat to England's political structure because they are tempered by a council of ministers that reduce any authority to token responsibilities. This condition is necessary because the Crown must maintain a nonpartisan and tempered stance to insure its survival; any participation in governmental affairs could render the Crown vulnerable to political attacks from Parliament. Ultimately, the Crown must appear to transcend all political activity or it will not survive. The monarchy may be enshrouded in debate, but it still retains its basic reputation and integrity. In an era of rapid political change, the monarchy has adjusted, rather than bend to the winds of revolution. It matters little that the House of Windsor has produced few effective monarchs. The monarchy has acted as a buffer against real (i.e., significant) political change. With all its pomp and circumstance, it's all a marvelous show, but perhaps, a deeply cynical one.

The Kings and Queens of England have been bequeathed by history, not by reason; they emerged from cataclysm not from debate. For better or worse, Britain has a monarchy. Unless the House of Windsor chooses to dismiss itself, the monarchy will remain. It is an integral part of Britain's past and present. Many of us are nostalgic for the past, and the monarchy has become a sort of religion. Less and less people are attending church, but people still go and cheer outside Buckingham Palace and, of course, there is the sheer pageantry of it all. The cynics say that Britain should get rid of the Monarchy because it's outdated and costs too much to maintain, while others argue that it's Britain's number one tourist trade. People still visit the royal palaces in France, but they're not as much fun without real royal people living in them. The idea of looking at Buckingham Palace and wondering, is the queen there, which is her window, is she looking out at me? That's all part of the strange mystique of the monarchy.

Why then are the lives, deaths, and gravesites of these crowned heads so fascinating to us? Is it that their joys, loves, triumphs, defeats, and last moments, all encompass a life we do not have? In other words, are these people more than the granite, the marble, and the ornate edifices that mark their tombs? I think the answer is simply yes, they are more.

In the end, I believe it is very simple, the reason we search out these final resting places is because we all wish to be remembered. We all have a story to tell, and the kings and queens of England all lived and died, like the rest of us (except with a lot more pageantry and drama). Although their stories have been told and retold over the past 1,500 years, we're still captivated by the sheer majesty of it all. In the end, the cult of celebrity in which many people propel themselves has become a new form of religion. The searching out and visitation of the graves of the famous, infamous, and noteworthy, has become a growing pasttime for a large number of fans. Whatever the reason for visiting the graves of these people, the main enjoyment is being as close to history as possible. Our presence in these cemeteries, mausoleums, churches, and cathedrals, announces that there is an unbroken chain that stretches back to the roots of Western civilization and this by extension links us to the future. How a society venerates its dead is a direct reflection of the morals and ethics upon which a society is to be judged by future generations.

Bibliography

Ashley, Mike. *The Mammoth Book of British Kings and Queens.* London: Robinson, 1998.

Barber, Richard. *The Devil's Crown: A History of Henry II and His Sons.* Conshohocken, PA: Richard W. Barber, 1996.

Barlow, Frank. *William Rufus.* Berkeley, CA: University of California, 1983.

Barnes, Margaret Campbell. *The Tudor Rose.* Napereville, Illinois: Source Books, 2009.

Bartlett, Robert. *England Under The Norman and Angevin Kings 1075–1225.* Oxford: OUP Oxford, 2002.

Best, Nicholas. *The Kings and Queens of England.* London: Weidenfeld & Nicolson, 1995.

Bland, Olivia. *The Royal Way of Death.* London: Constable, 1986.

Bradbury, Jim. *Stephen and Matilda: The Civil War of 1139-53.* Stroud, UK: The History Press, 2009.

Brewer, Clifford. *The Death of Kings.* London: Abson Books, 2010.

Buckle, Henry Thomas. *History of Civilization in England.* New York: Vanguard Press, 1926.

Campbell, John. *The Anglo-Saxons.* London: Penguin, 1991.

Croft, Pauline. *King James.* New York: Palgrave Macmillan, 2003.

Cunningham, Sean. *Henry VII.* New York: Routledge, 2007.

Dales, Douglas J. *Dunstan: Saint and Statesman.* Cambridge: Lutterworth Press, 1988.

Dodd, Gwilym, ed. *The Reign of Richard II.* Stroud: Tempus, 2000.

Douglas, David C. *William the Conqueror; the Norman impact upon England.* London : Yale University Press, 1999.

Duckett, Eleanor Shipley. *Alfred the Great.* Chicago: The University of Chicago Press, 1956.

Dunn, Jane. *Elizabeth & Mary: Cousins, Rivals, Queens.* New York: Alfred A. Knopf, 2003.

Earle, Peter. *The Life and Times of Henry V.* London: Trafalgar Square, 1993.

Erickson, Carolly. *Mistress Anne.* New York: St. Martins Griffin, 1984.

Farmer, D.H. ed. *Bede's Ecclesiastical History of the English People.* Trans. Leo Sherley-Price, revised R.E. Latham. London: Penguin, 1990.

Fields, Bertram. *Royal Blood: Richard III and the Mystery of the Princes.* New York: Harper Collins, 1998.

Fletcher, Richard. *Who's Who in Roman Britain and Anglo-Saxon England.* London: Shepheard-Walwyn, 1989.

Fraser, Antonia. *The Lives of the Kings and Queen of England.* London: Weidenfeld and Nicolson, 1975.

Gillingham, John. *Richard the Lionheart.* New York: Times Books, 1979.

Green, John Richard. *History of the English People.* 4 vols., New York: Belford, Clarke & Company, 1887.

Green, Judith A. *Henry I, King of England and Duke of Normandy.* Cambridge University Press, 2008.

Grinnell-Milne, Duncan. *The Killing of William Rufus: An Investigation in The New Forest.* Newton Abbot: David & Charles, 1968.

Haines, Roy Martin. *King Edward II: Edward of Caernarfon, His Life, His Reign, and Its Aftermath, 1284–1330.* Montreal, London: McGill-Queens University Press, 2003.

Hatton, Ragnhild. *George I: Elector and King.* London: Thames and Hudson, 1978.

Herman, Eleanor. *Sex with the Queen.* New York: Harper Perennial, 2006.

Higham, Nick. *The Death of Anglo-Saxon England.* Stroud: Sutton, 1997.

Hilton, Lisa. *Queen's Consort.* New York: Pegasus, 2010.

Hough, Richard. *Edward & Alexandra: Their Private and Public Lives.* London: Hodder & Stoughton, 1972.

Howarth, David. *1066 The Year of the Conquest.* London : Collins, 1977.

Hunter Blair, Peter. *An Introduction to Anglo-Saxon England.* Cambridge University Press, 1960.

Hunter Blair, Peter. *Roman Britain and Early England: 55 B.C. – A.D. 871.* New York: W.W. Norton & Company, 1966.

Hutton, Ronald. *Charles II: King of England, Scotland, and Ireland.* Oxford: Clarendon Press, 1989.

Kenyon, J.P. *Stuart England.* Harmondsworth: Penguin Books, 1978.

Kirby, D. P. *The Earliest English Kings.* London: Routledge, 1992.

Kuhn, William M. *Democratic Royalism: The Transformation of the British Monarchy, 1861–1914.* Basingstoke, England: Macmillan, 1996

Lapidge, Michael. *The Blackwell Encyclopedia of Anglo-Saxon England.* Oxford: Blackwell Publishing, 1999.

Marwick, Arthur. *A History of the Modern British Isles, 1914-1999.* Malden, MA: Blackwell, 2000.

Miller, Sean. *The Blackwell Encyclopedia of Anglo-Saxon England.* Oxford: Blackwell, 1999.

Mortimer, Ian. *The Perfect King: The Life of Edward III, Father of the English Nation.* London: Jonathan Cape, 2006.

Mortimer, Richard ed. *Edward the Confessor: The Man and the Legend.* Woodbridge: The Boydell Press, 2009.

Myers, A.R. *England in the Middle Ages.* 8th ed., New York: Penguin, 1988.

Ormrod, W.M. *The Kings & Queens of England.* Stroud: Tempus, 2004.

Ross, Charles. *Richard III.* New York: Methuen, 1981.

Saul, Nigel, ed. *The Oxford Illustrated History of Medieval England.* Oxford: Oxford University Press, 1997.

Schor, Esther. *Bearing the Dead: The British Culture of Mourning from the Enlightenment to Victoria.* Princeton, NJ: Princeton University Press, 1994.

Sinclair, David. *Two Georges: The Making of the Modern Monarchy.* London: Hodder and Stoughton, 1988.

Starkey, David. *Six Wives: The Queens of Henry VIII.* New York: Harper Collins, 2003.

Stenton, Frank. *Anglo-Saxon England.* 3rd ed., Oxford: Oxford University Press, 1971.

Strachey, Lytton. *Queen Victoria: The Definitive Biography of England's Famous Ruler.* New York: Harcourt, Brace & Company, 1921.

Swanton, Michael. *The Anglo-Saxon Chronicle.* New York: Routledge, 1996.

Waller, Maureen. *Ungrateful Daughters: The Stuart Princesses Who Stole Their Father's Crown.* London: Hodder & Stoughton, 2002.

Watson, Fiona J. *Under the Hammer: Edward I and the Throne of Scotland, 1286–1307.* East Linton: Tuckwell Press, 1998.

Weir, Alison. *Eleanor of Aquitaine.* New York: Ballantine, 1999.

Weir, Alison. *Henry VIII the King and His Court.* New York: Ballantine, 2002.

Weir, Alison. *Innocent Traitor.* New York: Ballantine, 2007.

Weir, Alison. *The Children of Henry VIII.* New York: Ballantine, 1996.

Weir, Alison. *The Lady Elizabeth.* New York: Ballantine Books, 2008.

Weir, Alison. *The Six Wives of Henry VIII.* New York: Grove Press, 1991.

Williams, Ann. *Æthelred the Unready: The Ill-Counselled King.* London: Hambeldon & London, 2003.

Yorke, Barbara. *Kings and Kingdoms of Early Anglo-Saxon England.* London: Seaby, 1990.

Yorke, Barbara. *Wessex in the Early Middle Ages.* London: Leicester University Press, 1995.

Ziegler, Philip. *King Edward VIII: The Official Biography.* New York: Alfred A. Knopf, 1991.

Photo/ Illustration Credits

All photographs are either the personal property of the author, public domain, the property of yaymicro.com, the National Portrait Gallery (London), the Library of Congress or have been cited otherwise.

Index